A Pragmatic Guide to Business Process Modelling

The British Computer Society

The British Computer Society is the leading professional body for the IT industry. With members in over 100 countries, the BCS is the professional and learned Society in the field of computers and information systems.

The BCS is responsible for setting standards for the IT profession. It is also leading the change in public perception and appreciation of the economic and social importance of professionally managed IT projects and programmes. In this capacity, the Society advises, informs and persuades industry and government on successful IT implementation.

IT is affecting every part of our lives and that is why the BCS is determined to promote IT as *the* profession of the 21st century.

Joining the BCS

BCS qualifications, products and services are designed with your career plans in mind. We not only provide essential recognition through professional qualifications but also offer many other useful benefits to our members at every level.

Membership of the BCS demonstrates your commitment to professional development. It helps to set you apart from other IT practitioners and provides industry recognition of your skills and experience. Employers and customers increasingly require proof of professional qualifications and competence. Professional membership confirms your competence and integrity and sets an independent standard that people can trust.

www.bcs.org/membership

Further Information

Further information about BCS can be obtained from: The British Computer Society, First Floor, Block D, North Star House, North Star Avenue, Swindon, SN2 1FA, UK.

Telephone: 0845 300 4417 (UK only) or +44 (0)1793 417 424 (overseas)

Email: customerservice@hq.bcs.org.uk

Web: www.bcs.org

A Pragmatic Guide to Business Process Modelling

Jon Holt

Published by British Informatics Society Limited (BISL), a wholly owned subsidiary of BCS, First Floor, Block D, North Star House, North Star Avenue, Swindon, SN2 1FA, UK.
www.bcs.org

ISBN 978-1-906124-12-0

British Cataloguing in Publication Data.
A CIP catalogue record for this book is available at the British Library.

Typeset by Lapiz Digital Services, Chennai, India.
Printed at CPI Antony Rowe Ltd., Chippenham, UK.

This book is dedicated to my beautiful wife, Rebecca

Contents

List of figures and tables   xi

Author   xvii

Foreword Paul MacNeillis   xix

Acknowledgements   xxi

Abbreviations   xxiii

Glossary   xxv

Useful websites   xxix

Preface   xxxi

1 Introduction   1
    The magic of processes   1
    Background   3
    Some basic definitions   4
    Risk   5
    The process   8
    Conclusions   15

2 The UML Diagrams   16
    Introduction   16
    Modelling   16
    The UML   18
    The class diagram   19
    The activity diagram   30
    The sequence diagram   33
    The use case diagram   35
    Consistency between the diagrams   41
    Conclusions   41

3 Requirements for Process Modelling   42
    Introduction   42
    Specific process modelling requirements   42
    Meeting the requirements through modelling   45

Tailoring processes   47
The process meta-model   50
Conclusions   52

4   The Process Meta-model Expanded   53
Introduction   53
Process concept view   53
Process realization view   57
The seven views of the meta-model   59
Consistency between views   77
Using the meta-model   79
Extending the process meta-model   86
Conclusions   90

5   Process Mapping and Metrics   91
Introduction   91
A process for process mapping   93
Process mapping metrics   100
Application of metrics   104
Interpreting the results   113
Conclusions   114

6   Case Study   115
Introduction   115
Background   115
The approach   117
Interpreting the process model   118
The case study process model   119
Process mapping   143
Conclusions   146
Exercises   146

7   The Bigger Picture – Enterprise Architecture   148
Introduction   148
Enterprise architecture   149
Enterprise architecture structure   150
Requirements for enterprise architecture   151
Existing sources   153
Modelling an enterprise architecture   154
Conclusions   159

8   Presentation   160
Introduction   160
Presentation issues   160
Example mappings to different notations   161
Conclusions   172

9 Teaching Guide   173

    Introduction   173

    Professional training   175

    Teaching as part of an undergraduate or postgraduate course   176

    Conclusions   183

10 Tools and Automation   184

    Introduction   184

    General capabilities of a tool   184

    Specific capabilities of a tool   185

    Business considerations   188

    Automation tools   189

    Conclusions   190

11 Answers to Exercises   191

    Appendix A: Summary of the Process Modelling Meta-model   201

    Appendix B: Summary of UML Notation   203

    References   205

    Further reading   207

    Index   209

List of figures and tables

Figure 2.1   Graphical notation for class diagrams   20
Figure 2.2   Graphical notation of a class   20
Figure 2.3   Graphical notation of an association
              relationship   21
Figure 2.4   Naming an association   21
Figure 2.5   Showing direction on an association   21
Figure 2.6   Showing numbers on classes   22
Figure 2.7   Examples of attributes for the class 'Cat'   23
Figure 2.8   Example of operations for the class 'Cat'   24
Figure 2.9   Example of the aggregation relationship   25
Figure 2.10   Overlapping aggregations to tidy up a diagram   26
Figure 2.11   Example of the specialization relationship   26
Figure 2.12   Example of inheritance   27
Figure 2.13   Example of dependencies   29
Figure 2.14   Graphical notation for activity diagrams   30
Figure 2.15   Example of an activity diagram   32
Figure 2.16   Graphical notation for sequence diagrams   34
Figure 2.17   Example of a sequence diagram   35
Figure 2.18   Graphical notation for use case diagrams   36
Figure 2.19   Example of a use case diagram showing
              a context   38
Figure 2.20   Example of a use case diagram showing a
              decomposition of a higher-level requirement   39
Figure 2.21   The <<constrain>> relationship   40
Figure 3.1   The complexity of relationships   44
Figure 3.2   Simple definition of a process   46
Figure 3.3   Compact definition of a process   47
Figure 3.4   Example process: 'System design'   49
Figure 3.5   Tailored processes   50
Figure 3.6   Process meta-model: Process concept view   51
Figure 3.7   Process realization view   52
Figure 4.1   Process meta-model: Process concept view   54
Figure 4.2   Process concept view with groupings   57
Figure 4.3   Process realization view   58
Figure 4.4   Example requirements view for an
              invoicing process   61

Figure 4.5	Simple process structure view	63
Figure 4.6	More detailed process structure view, highlighting types of 'Process group'	63
Figure 4.7	More detailed process structure view, highlighting life cycle concepts	64
Figure 4.8	Process structure view for the Welsh National Curriculum	65
Figure 4.9	Example of a potentially dangerous process structure view	66
Figure 4.10	Example of a dangerous process structure view	67
Figure 4.11	Process content view: Example process	68
Figure 4.12	Process content view: Warning signs	69
Figure 4.13	Process behaviour view for the 'Meeting logistics' process	72
Figure 4.14	Example information view showing relationships between artefacts	74
Figure 4.15	Generic stakeholder view	75
Figure 4.16	Process instance view	77
Figure 4.17	Example scenario: Analysing existing processes	81
Figure 4.18	Process instance view for creating a process model from scratch	82
Figure 4.19	Process instance for abstracting tacit process knowledge for a new system	84
Figure 4.20	Process instance for abstracting tacit process knowledge for an existing system	84
Figure 4.21	Process instance for process improvement	85
Figure 4.22	Typical generic Gantt chart	87
Figure 4.23	Extension to meta-model conceptual view	88
Figure 4.24	Extension to meta-model realization view	89
Figure 5.1	Simple requirements view	94
Figure 5.2	Stakeholder view	95
Figure 5.3	Process content view	96
Figure 5.4	Extended process content view	97
Figure 5.5	Process instance view for the mapping exercise	97
Figure 5.6	Process behaviour view for the 'Process identification' process	98
Figure 5.7	Process behaviour view for the 'PM set-up' process	98
Figure 5.8	Process behaviour view for the 'Process analysis' process	99
Figure 5.9	Information view for process mapping	100
Figure 5.10	New process for the process content view	101

Figure 5.11	Extended information view	102
Figure 5.12	Process behaviour view for the 'Metric application' process.	103
Figure 5.13	Process quagmire	105
Figure 5.14	Process structure views for ISO 15288 and 15504	106
Figure 5.15	Process structure views, with an emphasis on the grouping level, for the standards	107
Figure 5.16	Process content views for the standards	108
Figure 6.1	Process structure view	120
Figure 6.2	Further breakdown of the 'Project' process group	121
Figure 6.3	Process content view for the 'Enterprise' process group	122
Figure 6.4	Process content view for 'Enterprise' with an emphasis on 'Personnel'	123
Figure 6.5	Process content view for the 'Technical' process group, with an emphasis on the 'Training' processes	124
Figure 6.6	Process content view for the 'Technical' process group, with an emphasis on 'Product development'	125
Figure 6.7	Process content view for the 'Technical' process group, with an emphasis on 'Maintenance' processes	126
Figure 6.8	Process content view for the 'Project' process group, with an emphasis on 'Management'	127
Figure 6.9	Process content view for the 'Project' process group, with an emphasis on 'Support'	128
Figure 6.10	Process content view for the 'Agreement' process group	130
Figure 6.11	Stakeholder view with an emphasis on 'Customer'	131
Figure 6.12	Stakeholder view with an emphasis on 'External'	132
Figure 6.13	Stakeholder view with an emphasis on 'Supplier'	132
Figure 6.14	Enhancing stakeholders with additional relationships	133
Figure 6.15	Defining skills and responsibilities for stakeholders	134
Figure 6.16	Simple context for training-related processes	135
Figure 6.17	Breakdown of the 'organize course' requirement	136
Figure 6.18	Requirements view for invoice-related processes	137

Figure 6.19	Information view for the 'Course set-up' process artefacts	138
Figure 6.20	Information view for the 'Customer invoice' process artefacts	138
Figure 6.21	Information view relating artefacts	139
Figure 6.22	Process instance view for the 'Ensure payment' requirement for a normal project scenario	140
Figure 6.23	Process instance view for the 'Ensure payment' requirement for the scenario of running a course	140
Figure 6.24	Process instance view including stakeholder instance	141
Figure 6.25	Process behaviour view for the 'Customer invoice' process	142
Figure 6.26	Process behaviour view for the 'Course set-up' process	142
Figure 6.27	Process behaviour view for the 'Meeting logistics' process	143
Figure 6.28	Process structure view for Prince II	144
Figure 6.29	Process structure view for ISO 15288	145
Figure 6.30	Process structure view for Prince II, with an emphasis on 'Component'	146
Figure 6.31	Process structure view for ISO 15288, with an emphasis on 'Process group'	146
Figure 7.1	Enterprise architecture meta-model	149
Figure 7.2	Generic requirements view for enterprise architecture	152
Figure 7.3	Example ontology	156
Figure 7.4	Ontology with area of interest for a competency view shown	157
Figure 7.5	Simple requirements view for a competency view	158
Figure 7.6	Example viewpoint definition showing an expansion of the 'Competency scope' element from the ontology	158
Figure 8.1	Process structure view for the BPMN language	162
Figure 8.2	Graphical representation of core modelling elements in BPMN	163
Figure 8.3	BPMN notation showing a process behaviour view	165
Figure 8.4	BPMN notation showing a process instance view	166
Figure 8.5	Process meta-model realization view with BPMN notation shown as stereotypes	167
Figure 8.6	Process structure view for the flowchart notation	168

Figure 8.7	Symbol legend for the flowchart notation	168
Figure 8.8	Flowchart notation showing a process behaviour view	170
Figure 8.9	Process meta-model realization view with flowchart notation stereotypes	171
Figure 9.1	Generic teaching or training context	174
Figure 9.2	Generic course structure for a university-type course	178
Figure 9.3	Example project description	182
Figure 11.1	Extended process structure view	191
Figure 11.2	A more populated requirements view	193
Figure 11.3	Possible stakeholder view	194
Figure 11.4	Another possible stakeholder view	194
Figure 11.5	Increased number of artefacts in an information view	195
Figure 11.6	A detailed breakdown of a single artefact	195
Figure 11.7	A populated process shown as a class	195
Figure 11.8	Increased number of processes on a process content view	196
Figure 11.9	A more populated process instance view	196
Figure 11.10	A new scenario shown as a process instance view for a single requirement	197
Figure 11.11	Expansion to the process meta-model realization view	197
Figure 11.12	Possible process behaviour view for a single process	198
Figure 11.13	Increased quagmire showing additional process models	199
Figure A.1	Process concept view	201
Figure A.2	Process realization view	202
Figure B.1	Graphical notation for class diagrams	203
Figure B.2	Graphical notation for activity diagrams	203
Figure B.3	Graphical notation for sequence diagrams	204
Figure B.4	Graphical notation for use case diagrams	204
Table 4.1	Structural consistency checks	78
Table 4.2	Mechanical consistency checks	79
Table 5.1	Basic terminology mapping	109
Table 5.2	Process grouping terminology mapping	109
Table 5.3	Process terminology mapping	110
Table 5.4	Process feature mapping	110

Table 6.1   Initial mapping between ISO 15288 and
               Prince II   144
Table 7.1   Comparison of terms between process
               modelling and enterprise architecture   155
Table 11.1   Consistency-checking table   193

Author

Jon Holt obtained his PhD from the University of Wales Swansea in 1991 in the field of real-time systems modelling. Since then, Jon has worked extensively in a wide variety of industries applying modelling techniques to many types of systems, including: requirements, process modelling, enterprise architecture, competencies and education systems.

Jon is the founder-Director of Brass Bullet Ltd, a consultancy and training company based in Swansea in South Wales. Jon is a popular public speaker and has won several awards, at both national and international levels, for his public speaking and writing. He also holds posts at several universities.

Jon currently lives in Swansea with his wife, three children and two cats. When not working, his interests include writing, martial arts and performing magic.

Foreword

Organizational design is one of the biggest challenges facing business in the 21st century. In the knowledge economy, the ability of the human intellect to solve problems and add value is the key source of competitive advantage. But most of the organizational structures in existence today were designed to add value through the processing of physical assets by labour. So how do you organize for success when your primary resources are intangible? How do you unleash the potential of knowledge workers to transform ideas into value? With so many mutations of organizational forms into networks, communities and collaborative ventures what will the organizational forms of the future look like? No one can be sure of the answers to these questions. But one thing is certain. Whatever the structures and forms of the organizations of the future, people will come together as stakeholders to apply their minds and efforts to the transformation of assets. In other words, they will take part in business processes.

The organizations of the future will face increasing complexity in the external environment. The speed of change will continue to increase as global markets open up all value propositions to ever faster cycles of innovation and imitation, fuelling fast, effective and aggressive competition. Demands on organization from stakeholders will also build. Sometimes it will be expressed through regulators; sometimes through more direct channels. Faced with this growing external complexity, organizations will require highly evolved internal and inter-organizational processes to cope with managing and balancing these multiple demands in transparent, effective and systemic ways. Achieving this will require a language that is up to the task and a discipline that has proven value.

Until recently the languages available for modelling processes were rather inadequate for this task. Neither was there a systematic discipline or approach that promised much. As a result, business process modelling has, to date, greatly underachieved its potential. The ground was ripe for an innovation. In Jon Holt's first book, *UML for Systems Engineering*, he delivered that innovation by taking a language forged in the rigours of software development and opening our eyes to the potential of this language in a creative yet robust modelling approach. A lot of good work followed this innovation and the modelling approach has since been applied to processes as diverse as fishing, taxation, and the management of biodiversity.

In this new volume, Jon builds on this experienced success and takes us further into a modelling approach that should have broad appeal to those with a stake in business processes. The book is a lesson in good practice on business process modelling with relevance to important areas such as risk management, dealing with complexity and the modelling and application of key business standards. Jon's clear and engaging style makes a potentially difficult subject highly accessible and the reader's progress is helped along by the mixture of good examples, humour and flair for explanation that we have come to expect from this author. A book that demonstrates what can be achieved with business process modelling would have been welcome in itself, but a book like this that teaches, inspires and gives real insight into the field will be a valuable catalyst for modelling businesses in all sectors and geographies.

Paul McNeillis MBA, PhD, MCIM
Head of Professional Services, BSI

Acknowledgements

First of all, thanks to everyone who bought the first edition of the book since it was first published in 2005. There are five new chapters in this new edition which reflect both my experiences since the first edition was published and the feedback and response that I have had from various people over the years. I have tried to keep everybody happy – even the academic world who wanted the answers to the exercises from the first edition!

The list of people who need to be thanked is way too long to include here, so I will mention only a few by name – as ever, apologies if I have missed you out. Thanks to Duncan and his team (Jon, Nicky and Steve) who have provided me with all sorts of feedback on the techniques discussed here. Thanks to everyone from the world of EA who contributed their opinions and a special mention for Nigel. Thanks to Alec (and his people) who has been a long-term supporter, despite his dodgy geography of the hostelries of Plymouth. Mick and Tracey also deserve a mention, who will hopefully spread the word in Oz.

Thanks to everyone involved with the IET Systems Engineering Professional Network and the good folk of INCOSE. A big thank you to everyone at the BCS who have not only been involved with the publishing of the books, but have also allowed me to air my views at various talks, papers and presentations under their Banner. Special mentions for Matthew and Elaine who continue to encourage me in all BCS matters. Also thanks to Sarah and her little pink cloud and Jessica from Sunrise.

Thanks to all at Brass Bullet Ltd who are always happy to give me the support and resources to actually write this book.

No book of mine would be complete without thanking Mike and Sue, who are always there for me. Mike and Sue celebrate 40 years of glorious marriage this year, so a big 'congratulations' and may you both share many more!

Finally, all my love goes to my wife Rebecca and my three children: Jude, Eliza and Roo. Unfortunately, my evil cat has died since the last edition, so a brief mention for Olive and Betty who have big cat-shoes to fill.

Abbreviations

BPMI	Business Process Modelling Initiative
BPML	Business Process Modelling Language
BPMN	Business Process Modelling Notation
BSI	British Standards Institution
CMM	capability maturity model
CMMI	capability maturity model integrated
CORBA	Common Object Request Broker Architecture
eGIF	Electronic Government Interoperability Framework
EMC	electro-magnetic compatibility
EN	European Normative
ESA	European Space Agency
HMRI	Her Majesty's Railway Inspectorate
HSE	Health and Safety Executive
IEC	International Electrotechnical Commission
ISO	International Standardization Organization
PAPS	pen and paper system
PBV	process behaviour view
PCV	process content view
PGI	process group index
PGR	process group ratio
PI	process index
PMI	process model index
PR	process ratio
RACI	responsible, accountable, consulted and informed
UML	Unified Modelling Language
XMI	XML modelling interchange
XML	extensible markup language

Glossary

Activity   The behavioural steps involved in a process that produce and consume artefacts and that are owned by stakeholders.

Artefact   Anything that is produced or consumed by a process or activity.

Assessment   A review of a process that is based on a standard. Assessments may be formal or informal and carried out either internally or externally to the organization.

Audit   A formal review of a process based on a standard. Audits are carried out by independent, third-party auditors.

Business process management   The coordination and management of a business process which will, invariably, involve some sort of business process modelling.

Business process modelling   Any process modelling exercise that is performed in order to enhance the overall operation of a business.

Business process re-engineering   Used specifically when business process modelling is applied to existing processes as part of a process improvement exercise.

Class   Used as template for something and usually a noun. For example, the class 'Person' would represent all people generally, rather than a specific person. Classes are represented graphically by rectangles and can be further described by identifying attributes and operations. Classes form the basic nodes in the class diagram.

Hazard   Anything that occurs that can lead to a risk. The terms 'hazard' and 'risk' are often confused, but there are subtle differences between them. It is possible for many hazards to lead to the same risk. For example, there is a risk in a hospital that a power failure will lead to many problems, perhaps even endangering the lives of some patients. There are, however, many hazards that may lead to this risk manifesting itself, such as: a lightening strike, terrorist action, not paying the utility bill, lack of maintenance, and so on.

Instance   A specific item within a class. A specific person, for example, Fred Smith, would be an instance within the class 'Person'.

Iteration   A self-contained set of process executions within a process. For example, different teams working on the same project will have their own iterations within the same process.

Model   This book uses the classic UML definition of a model, which is 'a simplification of reality'. In this way, a model may be an equation, a diagram, a physical model, a piece of text or any verbal description.

Operation   Usually represented by a verb that signifies something that a class does.

Operations management   Often used in the context of business and management courses and, although it has a wider scope than just process modelling, contains, and relies very heavily upon, process modelling.

Process   An approach to doing something that consists of a number of activities, each of which will produce and/or consume some sort of artefact. Each of these activities is the responsibility of a single stakeholder role.

Process group   A container for processes that is defined based on functionality of processes, rather than phases in a life cycle. Process groups are often abstract.

Process mapping   Refers to relating different processes to one another and forms an integral part of any audit or assessment exercise. Of course, in order to map effectively, all processes must be modelled in some way.

Process meta-model   A meta-model is a model of a model, and the process meta-model is a model of a model that is used for process modelling.

Process re-alignment   Often applied to existing processes that have, over a period of time, gone out of date for some reason – usually because the requirements for the process have changed and the process is no longer fit for its original purpose.

Relationship   Represents the identification of a conceptual relationship between one or more classes. A relationship is represented graphically by variations on a line, depending on the type of relationship. There are four types of relationship used for process modelling: the association, the aggregation, the generalization/specialization and the dependency. Relationships form the basic paths in the class diagram.

Risk   A product of the likelihood, or probability, of the risk occurring and the effect of the hazard. In many scenarios, risk is defined by a simple mathematical formula, where $risk = probability \times severity$, or it is defined in terms of a simple matrix that has one axis defining the likelihood in words and the other axis defining the severity of the outcome.

Role   Part played by a person, place or thing that has an interest in the system or project. The term is often used interchangeably with the term 'stakeholder role'.

Stakeholder   Refers to the *role* played by a person, place or thing that has some sort of interest in the system or project. Stakeholders should not be confused with people, as it is possible for a single person to have more than one stakeholder role and, conversely, it is possible for a single stakeholder role to have a number of individuals' names against it. Stakeholders are often not actually people, but the roles of organizations, the environment, places, things, and so on.

Stereotype   A way of tailoring the UML language for a particular application.

System   Any entity or collection of entities that collaborate in some way to meet a set of requirements. In this way, a system can be a person, a group of people, a family, a computer, a network of computers, mechanics, electronics or just about anything else.

Swim lane   An area on an activity with a defined border, the contents of which are assocated with a stakeholder. The stakeholder is then responsible for all activities within the swim lane.

UML meta-model   A UML model of the UML. This term is fully defined in the UML standard (see www.omg.org).

Validation   Refers to something that meets its original requirements or, to put it another way, that does what it's supposed to do. In order to understand validation, the question 'am I building the correct system?' may be asked. It is possible and, indeed, not uncommon for a system to be built that works but that does not meet the original requirements, which makes the system useless.

Verification   Refers to something that works correctly and without error. For example, this could be a system that has been tested and runs in an error-free fashion. In order to understand verification, the question, 'am I building the system correctly?' may be asked.

Useful Websites

www.bcs.org
The website of the British Computer Society, which provides useful information and from which you can purchase books on subjects related to process modelling.
www.bpmi.org
The website of the Business Process Management Initiative.
www.bsi-global.org
The website for the British Standards Institution, where standards may be purchased and from which there are links to other standards sites.
www.govtalk.gov.uk
The website of the UK Cabinet Office, which provides information on policies and standards for e-government.
www.iso.org/iso/en/ISOOnline.frontpage
The website of the International Organization for Standardization, from which you can order copies of the ISO standards referenced in this book.
www.omg.org
The Object Management Group website, from which you can download the original UML standard.
www.sei.cmu.edu/cmmi
Information about CMMI provided by the Software Engineering Institute.
http://tarpit.rmc.ca/cficse/2000/resources/stsc-framework.pdf
The Systems and Software Consortium software quagmire.

Preface

Processes form the heart of any organization, regardless of its size, type or age. Any organization that actually does anything will, whether it realizes or not, follow processes. These processes may be formal, documented processes or may be informal processes that exist only inside people's heads. Regardless of the nature of the processes, they will all exhibit three features: they will be complex, require a deep level of understanding and will need to be communicated. This is where the modelling fits in.

The process modelling approach adopted in this book is based on the most popular and widely used modelling language in the world – the UML (Unified Modelling Language), which was created as an open standard and is now an ISO standard.

The approach detailed in this book is the result of ten years of definition, refinement and application of such modelling techniques to all aspects of process modelling and to all types of process. This approach has been implemented in many fields, including: defence, government departments, transport, manufacturing, finance, food, IT, communications, education, aerospace and many more.

Process modelling is by no means a simple task and, therefore, to approach such a project requires the use of appropriate and powerful tools. The approach in this book provides a set of 'sharp tools' that may be employed in any process initiative.

Introduction

THE MAGIC OF PROCESSES

Processes are an integral part of everyday life. Every time we, as human beings, perform any kind of action, we are actually carrying out a process. This may vary from the way that we get dressed each morning, the way we cross the street on the way to work, to the way that we cook our food in the evenings. The key word used here is 'way' as, in essence, a process simply describes the way to do something or, to put it another way, an 'approach'. It is possible to identify and relate processes for every single action that we take in life. However, this would clearly be a very large number, if not infinity!

Using processes effectively, however, is often not quite so straightforward. There is a big difference between observing a process and performing a process effectively. Consider the example of a magic trick being performed by a magician who is, quite clearly, following some sort of predefined process. It is easy to watch and follow a magic trick, such as a card trick. The magician shuffles the cards and asks a member of the audience to choose one. The audience member selects the card, memorizes it, shows it to the rest of the audience and then places back into the pack. The deck is then shuffled. After a few clever words and a bit of showmanship, the card reappears underneath a vase, or in a pocket or on the other side of the room. The crowd are impressed and give their applause, much to the pleasure of the magician.

A trick such as this is one that everyone can follow and appreciate, but one that most people cannot actually perform themselves. In fact, it is possible for someone to follow the *exact* steps that were carried out by the magician, but to fail utterly in producing the chosen card. There are a number of possible reasons for this:

- The layman, when trying to perform the trick, simply does not understand what has actually gone on. There is a big difference between what is perceived by an observer and what actually occurs. Invariably, this is deliberate on behalf of the magician but something that can be quite clear to a fellow magician who has the relevant domain knowledge. Such trickery may involve a deck that is arranged into a particular order, the use of false cards or the pre-placing of copies of cards around a room.

- The trick itself is far more complex than it first appears. There are subtleties and nuances of the activities carried out by the magician – false cuts, double lifts, palmed cards and the like. The deception is not just limited to the cards themselves, but may also include sneaking looks at various cards, distracting the attention of the audience by waving the hands or orally catching people's attention. All of these activities are designed to look like natural actions to a casual observer.
- The information conveyed by the magician is not the true reality of what has actually happened. Deliberate distractions and misdirection techniques can be employed to send the wrong information to the audience.

The effective manipulation of processes is very much like the manipulation of playing cards, albeit without the deliberate intention to mislead. To capture a process is very often not as simple as just watching somebody perform a task and then copying the perceived actions. Without a good knowledge of what is actually going on, this task can be very difficult. If the process is not captured effectively and accurately, then it will be impossible to reproduce the results of the process. There are a number of ways to ensure that the process is captured correctly:

- The trick must be looked at from several points of view, rather than purely from the point of view of a casual observer. In fact, with a rigorous and structured approach to observing what is going on from a number of different perspectives, almost any trick can be worked out to some degree.
- The end result must be related back to the initial conditions of the trick and full traceability established. How is it possible to go from one set of conditions to another – if it does not seem possible then there is some key information missing.
- The role of all the participants must be examined, including the audience members and the magician. But it is not good enough to stop there, as there may be several other roles that exist that are not obvious – what about the possibility of the magician having an accomplice either in the audience or on the other end of a phone line or radio link? These are techniques that are regularly employed by magicians.
- Finally, and perhaps most importantly, it is essential to understand what the overall intention of the trick is and what effect it will have on the audience.

The intention of this book is to help you to master the magic of processes. It will increase your understanding of processes, enable you to control complexity and to communicate your ideas effectively. This is achieved by identifying a number of 'views' that are required in order to model a process completely and fully. Seven views are identified and each one is described in detail. This approach has become known as the 'seven views' approach process modelling.

BACKGROUND

It is not just people that follow processes, as every organization in existence, whether it is a single-person company or a multinational organization, will rely on a number of processes to function effectively. Depending on the size of the organization and the complexity of its set up, the number of processes that a company uses can be huge – almost infinite, again.

Process modelling is arguably one of the most important aspects of any organization in terms of the management and control of all of the organizational activities. These activities will range from the high-level business activities, including mission statements, business processes and requirements, right down to very detailed technical processes that may be executed on a daily basis within the organization.

Business process modelling goes under many different names and labels so, in order to keep things simple, the term *process modelling* in this book may be replaced by any of the following terms:

- **Business process modelling:** any process modelling exercise that is performed in order to enhance the overall operation of a business.
- **Business process management:** the coordination and management of a business process which will, invariably, involve some sort of business process modelling.
- **Business process re-engineering:** used specifically when business process modelling is applied to existing processes as part of a process improvement exercise.
- **Operations management:** often used in the context of business and management courses and, although it has a wider scope than just process modelling, it contains and relies very heavily upon process modelling.
- **Process mapping:** refers to relating different processes to one another and forms an integral part of any audit or assessment exercise. Of course, in order to map effectively, all processes must be modelled in some way.
- **Process re-alignment:** often applied to existing processes that have, over a period of time, gone out of date for some reason – usually because the requirements for the process have changed and the process is no longer fit for its original purpose.

This book covers all of the above definitions at various points but, as should be clear from this list, all of these different concepts rely heavily on the fact that processes can be modelled in some way. As the book focuses on business process modelling, the modelling techniques can be applied to any or all of the above areas.

SOME BASIC DEFINITIONS

This section presents some definitions for the basic terminology that is used in this book.

- **Process:** although a term that is very widely used, the term 'process' is also one that, depending on the source, has many different interpretations. The following list contains just a few definitions:
- a series of actions, changes, or functions bringing about a result (*Oxford English Dictionary*, 2002);
- a series of operations performed in the making or treatment of a product (*Oxford English Dictionary*, 2002);
- a set of interrelated activities, which transforms inputs into outputs (ISO/IEC 15504, 2004).

For the purposes of this book, a process is simply *an approach to doing something that consists of a number of activities, each of which will produce and/or consume some sort of artefact. Each of these activities is the responsibility of a single stakeholder role.*

There are many types of process that are defined, such as operational processes, business processes, technical processes, natural processes, biological processes, political processes, financial processes, and so on. For the purposes of this book, the term 'process' may be applied equally to any or all of these types of process.

- **System:** any entity or collection of entities that collaborate in some way to meet a set of requirements. In this way, a system can be a person, a group of people, a family, a computer, a network of computers, mechanics, electronics and just about anything else.
- **Artefact:** defined as anything that is produced or consumed by a process or activity.
- **Stakeholder:** refers to the *role* played by a person, place or thing that has some sort of interest in the system or project. Stakeholders should not be confused with people, as it is possible for a single person to have more than one stakeholder role and, conversely, it is possible for a single stakeholder role to have a number of individuals' names against it. Indeed, stakeholders are often not actually people, but the roles of organizations, the environment, places, things, and so on.

- **Model:** in this book, the definition of 'model' is taken from the classic UML (Unified Modelling Language) definition, which is 'a simplification of reality'. In this way, a model may be an equation, a diagram, a physical model, a piece of text or any verbal description.
- **Verification:** refers to something that works correctly and without error. For example, this could be a system that has been tested and runs in an error-free fashion. In order to understand verification, the question 'am I building the system correctly?' may be asked.
- **Validation:** refers to something that meets its original requirements or, to put it another way, that does what it is supposed to do. In order to understand validation, the question 'am I building the correct system?' may be asked. It is possible and, indeed, not uncommon for a system to be built that works but that does not meet the original requirements, which makes it useless!

Some of these terms will be redefined at other points in this book, as they are so fundamental and important to understanding process modelling, that they can never be defined too often.

RISK

Risk is something that affects every person, every day of their lives. Most activities carried out in life have some sort of inherent risk associated with them, for example, crossing the street, eating or travelling.

Businesses can be threatened in many ways, whether it is through physical means, such as acts of nature, sabotage or terrorism, or by more subtle means, such as financial mismanagement, lack of competence or basically getting everyday project activities 'wrong'. In order to address these threats, there are several possible courses of action:

- **Elimination:** in some cases it is possible to eliminate the risk altogether. For example, if there is a risk involved with dealing with new companies for contracts with a value of over £10,000, then the simple way to eliminate this is, of course, simply not to deal with such organizations. Caution must be exercised, however, as very often one risk may be replaced by another. In the example above, there may then be a risk that it would be difficult to keep up-to-date with key technologies, as only new, dedicated companies, are exploiting them.
- **Replacement:** it is often the case that a risk may be addressed by replacing it in some way. This may be through the use of a different technology; for example, if there is a risk involved with using a specific design notation, due to possible obsolescence or limited expertise available, then replace the technique used with one that is more readily acceptable and accessible (such as the UML) which will address this problem.

- **Control:** in many cases, the risks may not be able to be eliminated nor reduced by replacement, in which case it is necessary to minimize the risk by introducing controls. These controls will vary enormously, depending on the type of risk, for example, wearing appropriate safety clothing, taking regular breaks, using only established technologies, only dealing with preferred suppliers, and so on.

- **Transfer:** transferring the risk onto a third party is considered by many as the easiest way to address risk. Although this seems like a good idea, extreme caution must be exercised, as the risk still exists and, regardless of who takes the rap, the project may fail anyway. For example, when using a financial software package for doing company accounts, there is a risk that the software will not perform the calculations correctly, in which case who takes the blame – the users or the software producers? Even in the scenario where the software producers are guaranteeing that the software will be fit for purpose, does it really help the company stay in business if the accounts system fails?

There are several key terms that must be defined so that risk management can be fully understood, managed and implemented, and these are:

- **Hazard:** anything that occurs that can lead to a risk. The terms 'hazard' and 'risk' are often confused but there are subtle differences between them; it is possible for many hazards to lead to the same risk. For example, there is a risk in a hospital that a power failure will lead to many problems, perhaps even costing the lives of some patients. There are, however, many hazards that may lead to this risk manifesting itself, such as: lightening strike, terrorist action, not paying the utility bill, lack of maintenance, and so on.

- **Risk:** defined as a product of the likelihood, or probability of the risk occurring and the effect of the hazard. In many scenarios, risk is defined either as a simple mathematical formula, $risk = probability \times severity$, or in terms of a simple matrix that has one axis defining the likelihood in words and the other defining the severity of the outcome.

An important aspect of risk is the responsibility associated with it. For example, if you started smoking in the 1920s and later, as a result, developed cancer, the responsibility for the risk, it may be argued, lies with the tobacco companies. This may be argued whether or not the tobacco companies were actually aware of the risks, as everyone has a duty of care to provide safe products. The argument is that when cigarettes were sold to the general public in the 1920s, the health risks were not known and potential smokers did not think it would cause any harm. Today, however, if someone starts to smoke and develops a smoking-related illness, the responsibility is firmly on the shoulders of the smoker, as all cigarette and tobacco products now carry a government health warning that describes the risks involved in smoking.

In the UK, the Health and Safety Executive (HSE) identify five steps that are essential for any sort of risk assessment:

1. **Identification of hazards:** this can never be a complete and exhaustive list of hazards, as there are simply too many in most situations – even the most unlikely and improbable events may lead to problems. Take the smoking example: hazards will include smoking, being with smokers and being in smoky environments.

2. **Identification of who and how:** it is important to identify who or what is at risk and then to ascertain how they will be at risk. For instance, in the smoking example, the smokers will be affected directly, but what about other people who may suffer the effects of indirect passive smoking? Also, what about expectant mothers smoking and affecting their unborn children?

3. **Risk evaluation and control setting:** risk evaluation and control involves asking the question, 'how serious is the risk and is there anything that can be done to minimize it?' Consider the difference between someone walking through a smoky room, where the risk may be relatively small, compared to, say, spending three hours in a train carriage full of smokers with the windows closed. In terms of controls, consider air conditioning, opening windows, not inhaling (not recommended), and so on.

4. **Record findings:** it is important to be able to look at risks and learn from them in some way. In terms of smoking, many public places have now outlawed smoking from the premises (notice that they have not outlawed smokers, just the actual smoking activity), which is often due to customer responses, research suggesting health implications, and so on.

5. **Review:** it is important that all activities are reviewed periodically, as the hazards associated with risk often change along with the nature of the risk itself. As a final consideration of the smoking example, the hazards of smoking have shifted dramatically in the UK since the introduction of the country-wide smoking ban in public places. This means that whereas before the ban it was relatively safe to sit outside a pub in the fresh air leaving the smokers to their fume-filled interiors, the situation is now reversed. Pub gardens are now the places where the smokers are forced to lurk, whereas people with families are now often forced to go inside the pub itself to avoid them, hence, acclimatising their children to going into pubs from an early age and increasing the chance of them drinking heavily. It never rains, yet it pours.

One way to reduce risk is to improve the way that things are done – or the approach. There are many approaches to solving a single problem, some of which will be higher in risk than others. If these different approaches can be captured in some way, then it is possible that they can be compared and reviewed. In fact, the way to minimize or control a risk is very often to define processes on how to avoid the risk in the first place or, when necessary, define processes concerning what to do when the risk manifests itself. Therefore, process modelling is an essential part of any risk management exercise as the solutions are often the processes that are necessary to keep everyone safe and well.

THE PROCESS

Standards, processes, procedures and guidelines

In real life, processes can manifest themselves in many different shapes or forms. When a process is written down in some way, it will often take the form of, for example, a standard, a procedure, a set of guidelines or work instructions. Although there are no absolute, globally accepted definitions for any of these terms, it is important to consider the underlying concepts and to understand them. In fact, the difference in terminology often relates to the level of detail in the process itself. Consider the following:

- Very high-level processes, such as international standards: there are many international standards bodies, such as the International Standards Organization (ISO), International Electrotechnical Commission (IEC) and European Normative (EN). Some national bodies have also obtained recognition globally and sit at the same sort of level, such as the British Standards Institution (BSI).
- High-level processes, such as industry standards: an industry standard is one that is driven by the actual industry and does not have the formal recognition of international and national standards. An industry standard may have international recognition, such as the UML or Common Object Request Broker Architecture (CORBA), or may simply be two organizations agreeing to work in the same way.
- Medium-level processes, such as in-house company standards and processes: many companies, particularly large ones, have very welldefined process models and standards and, in some cases, these may even be published, as in the case of the European Space Agency (ESA) (Mazza *et al.*, 1994).
- Low-level processes, such as in-house procedures: a typical procedure will describe how a process may be implemented. Indeed, it is possible for a single process to be implemented in different ways using different procedures.
- Very low-level processes, such as guidelines and work instructions: these will typically show a preferred or best-practice approach to carrying out a procedure. These may include specific methods and methodologies that may be applied, whether they are in-house, bespoke or commercial approaches.

The preceding list is not intended to be exhaustive, but provides a general idea of the scope of this book. The process modelling approach advocated in this book may be applied to any or all of these different types of processes.

Problems with processes

There are many problems associated with processes, which, unfortunately, often turn people off to the whole world of process modelling. In fact, mentioning processes or standards is often greeted with groans and sighs from people whose only experience has been one (or many) of disappointment. This really just goes to reinforce the fact that the whole world of process modelling is very badly affected by the three 'evils of life', described in detail in Chapter 4: complexity, lack of understanding and poor communications. So why are processes and standards so badly thought of by many people, and is this feeling justified? These two questions will be answered separately. Some of the reasons why people feel this way are discussed below:

- **Too long:** Some process descriptions are very long which, on first appearance, can be very off-putting to any potential users of the process. In fact, the length of the process description can often be misleading, as the number of pages is often not an indicator of the complexity of a process description, and it is the complexity of the process description, rather than the length of it that causes problems. However, this aside, being faced with a process description of several hundred pages is soul-destroying, regardless of how well written it may be. For example, two standards associated with process improvement are ISO 15504 (process assessment) (ISO/IEC, 2004) and CMMI (capability maturity model integrated) (Carnegie Mellon Software Engineering Institute, 2002), both of which stand at several hundred pages in length. The standard for the UML is also several hundred pages long. Although all of these standards are well written, bear in mind that, when printed out as hard copies, they each fill several volumes of folders. It is important, therefore, to be able to have a simplified representation of such a description that can be understood, at a high level, in a single glance. This will be supported by a number of other simple views, each of which can also be easily understood.
- **Too short:** Some process descriptions are very short and stand at only a few pages. Although, at first glance, such process descriptions can appear to be simple, this is often not the case. Take as an example ISO 9001 (ISO, 2000), which applies to quality systems for just about any type of organization that exists. When the standard is reduced to its actual contents (excluding front sheets, and so on) it stands at only 17 pages in length. The very fact that the standard

applies to many applications means that it needs to be generic, which leads to ambiguity, an indicator of the three 'evils of life'.

- **Written by committee:** according to the old adage, you can't keep all of the people happy all of the time, which is the *raison d'être* of committees. One of the basic requirements of a committee is that it represents the viewpoints of different stakeholders. Unfortunately, this has the potential to cause as many problems as it solves and too many different viewpoints, when expressed in an unstructured way, can lead to a fragmented, ambiguous and often inconsistent process description.

- **Too many:** it is very rare indeed to find a single process model that does not relate to, or rely on some other process model. In fact, it is also rare to find a process model that relates to one or two other process models as, in real life, the number of related process models tends to be very high. Consider the situation where a process model is being created for a particular industry. For the sake of the example, let's consider a process model relating to the rail industry, but it should be borne in mind that these same principles apply to any another process model, for example, the healthcare industry. In the case of rail, the process model may have to be compatible with generic international standards, such as ISO 9001 (ISO, 2000). Also, the process model will also have to be compatible with various national and international industry-specific standards. Alongside this, consider any government or country-specific standards, safety or security standards, best practice standards and legal requirements that may have to be met. Also, we have not yet even considered any standards or procedures within the organization itself, such as Her Majesty's Railway Inspectorate (HMRI) in the UK.

- **Unrealistic:** many process descriptions have little connection to reality, which often results in a process description 'gathering dust' on a shelf through lack of use. This may be because the process is asking for too much work to be done on top of the existing working practices, such as excessive documentation, replication of existing information or requiring too much input from too many different people. If the new process differs significantly from the existing process (even if it is an informal, undocumented one), there will be a natural level of resistance to the changes. It is essential that any new process definitions are connected to existing practice wherever possible.

- **Language:** the language used by the process definition must be the one that is already used by the organization. Many companies offer 'off-the-shelf' process descriptions which, in almost all cases may be destructive unless tailored appropriately for the organization. Terminology, technical nomenclature and even marketing words and phrases must be embedded into the core process model wherever appropriate to ensure that the maximum number of people can understand the process in an unambiguous way.

- **Awareness:** for people to use a process, they must be aware of the process in the first place. This sounds like basic common sense, but the simple fact is that if a process description is printed out and left on a shelf then, in many cases, that is exactly where it will stay. With today's technology and the ubiquitous nature of the internet and web browsers, it is a relatively simple matter to make process descriptions available to people via their desktops. Of courses, this will only work in places where people sit at computers but, even if people do not have computer access, the fact remains that the process descriptions must be readily available to the people who are supposed to using them. The process descriptions should also make people's lives easier, rather than being an overhead (in terms of time). It is not until people can see the benefit of having this information to hand that they will truly start to adopt the whole process ethos effectively.

- **Fear of failure:** a common complaint when it comes to any sort of process modelling and process description is that the whole exercise is a waste of time because 'we tried it three years ago and it didn't work'. Just because something has been attempted once and failed, does not mean that it will never work. The actual underlying cause of these failures needs to be investigated. In almost every case where this has happened, it is relatively simple to see that all the information required for the process description was not present or that the problems discussed in this section have occurred. One of the main aims of this book is to introduce and define a process meta-model that can be used as a checklist for ensuring a complete and effective process description. By using this meta-model as a basis for an investigation, it is very common to see exactly why the previous process exercise has failed – one or more of the views required by the process meta-model is missing or incomplete.

- **Perception:** the perception of the process is key. People must be aware of the value of effective processes. A lack of understanding here may be due to poor education in the application, use and consequent benefits of the process.

These are just some of the common reasons why the process modelling exercise fails. This book intends to minimize the potential time and effort that is wasted by many organizations in pursuit of their process modelling requirements. Remember, process modelling is not magic, but nor is it a mundane task. There is a deep level of understanding required in order to produce an effective process model and description.

Modelling techniques

There are many modelling techniques that have been used extensively, and with varying degrees of success, for many years. Many of these techniques are based on visual techniques or, to put it another way, drawing diagrams to represent processes. The list of these techniques includes, but is not limited to:

- **Flowcharts:** the classic graphical modelling language that most people have come across at some point in their lives, even if it has nothing to do with software. Although widely used, flowcharts are frequently misused and are poorly understood. The biggest problem with flowcharts, however, is that they only realize a single view of the process model and, as discussed later in this book, there are seven views required for effective and complete process modelling. See Chapter 8 for a more in-depth description of the application of flowcharts for process modelling.

- **RACI matrix tables:** RACI stands for 'responsible', 'accountable', 'consulted' and 'informed' and RACI matrix tables are used to relate process activity to stakeholder roles. According to the RACI approach, any activity within a process will have a number of stakeholder roles associated with it, and these roles may be responsible (they do the work for the activity), accountable (they are responsible for the success or failure of the activity), consulted (they are asked to participate in the activity) or informed (they have information concerning the activity distributed to them). Basic RACI matrix tables are just that – a simple table for cross-referencing between the roles and the activity. However, these tables are often used in conjunction with flowcharts but are often contorted to include some sort of behaviour which makes the tables more complex and adds little value.

- **BPMN:** the business process modelling notation. The BPMN is the result of the business process modelling initiative (BPMI), whose aim is to provide a notation that can be readily understood by all business users and that ensures that various business execution languages can be visualized (BPMI, 2002). The three main aims are to define the notation and its association semantics and to amalgamate all best practice modelling notations (interestingly enough, including the UML). Although this is an excellent initiative that has yielded very good results, the BPMN is far too narrow to meet the stringent requirements for process modelling identified in this book. The notation itself focuses entirely on the behavioural aspect of the process model which, although adequate for the scope identified in the BPMI, is not considered wide enough for the purposes of this book. Indeed, the introduction of the process meta-model will show that there are seven views that need to be considered – four of which are realized by structural diagrams, for which the BPMN has no facility. Also, the BPMN does not consider the requirements for a process that are essential for any sort of process validation. This means that, in total, the BPMN could only be used to realize two of the seven views required for effective and complete process modelling. See Chapter 8 for a more in-depth description of the application of the BPMN for process modelling.

This is just a small sample of some of the techniques that are available for use. Although the technique adopted in this book is the UML, the main focus of the book is a series of concepts that can be realized using 'any single notation or, indeed, combination of modelling notations' that is capable of meeting the modelling requirements of the process.

The UML

This book uses diagrams to help to visualize and understand processes at many different levels. These diagrams are not random and are actually part of a larger 'language'. The language chosen is the UML, which is a *visual modelling language*:

- **visual:** the results can be seen graphically or, to put it another way, it is a language of diagrams containing symbols;
- **modelling:** reality is simplified in some way so that it can be more easily understood;
- **language:** it is a means of communication.

The choice of the language itself has a certain rationale. The UML is the most widely used modelling language in the world today. Although the UML has its roots firmly in the software world, it is increasingly being used for wider, more systems-based applications.

There are also several pragmatic reasons for choosing the UML:

- **Widespread use:** the UML is the most widely used modelling language in the world. Up until relatively recently, there were more than 100 visual modelling techniques and notations available to software engineers. However, the UML has now superseded all of them – with the full assent of every methodologist in the world. Although the UML originated in the software world, the notation itself can be applied to almost any form of modelling.
- **Accepted internationally:** the UML is not just limited to a particular country or continent, but is a truly world-wide standard that is accepted just about everywhere. This means that when working with colleagues in different countries, there is a common medium on which to base discussions.

- **ISO standard:** the UML is now an ISO standard – ISO 19501 (2005), which gives it more credibility than it just being an industry standard. Many of the criticisms that were aimed at the UML were concerns about its lack of international credibility, which are now resolved.

- **UK government mandate, via eGIF:** as the UML becomes more widely accepted, it also becomes more formally accepted by world organizations, such as governments. One example of this is in the UK, where there is an initiative named *eGIF: The electronic government interoperability framework* (Cabinet Office, 2004). The main aim behind the eGIF is to define the technical policies and specifications governing information flows across government and the public sector. It covers interconnectivity, data integration, e-services access and content management. This initiative will apply not only to organizations who deal directly with government bodies, but also many of their subcontractors.

- **Intuitive:** the notation used by the UML is, when used properly, simple and intuitive. Some aspects of the UML are more intuitive than others, which is due in part to some elements of the UML looking like previous techniques, such as flowcharts and data flow diagrams. This familiarity increases the perception that something is easier to understand.

- **Extensive use in other aspects of the organization:** this final advantage of using the UML is often overlooked but can have a massive impact on issues such as training. Consider an organization where there are managers, engineers, technicians, quality assurers, marketers, directors and sales teams. If each of these has a very basic idea of the core elements of the language and is familiar with one or two of the diagrams, then there is a massive increase in communication effectiveness. Of course, different people in different jobs will naturally use different techniques and tools to perform their work, but if the core *knowledge* behind the work is defined in a common language, then this knowledge can be turned into effective value in the business. For example, using a single core notation in training will decrease the number of different techniques being used, hence enabling a single, common view to be communicated by and to all members of staff by an effective training unit or partner. Also, in the case of process modelling, if the core company knowledge is captured in a process model, then there is a ready-made training course for anyone who understand the basics of the UML language. After all, what better source for training material than the actual knowledge itself! The concept of modelling all parts of the organisation into a single entity is known as Enterprise Architecture and is discussed in more detail in Chapter 7 where it will be seen that the same modelling techniques can be employed for both process and enterprise modelling.

Therefore, the notation used in this book is the UML. You do not have to be an expert in UML to appreciate how it is used, nor to start using it – the expertise will come with time. Also, the use of UML in this book is limited to a very small subset of the actual language, which minimizes the learning curve. Providing that the core concepts of the rationale for modelling is understood, the use of the notation is relatively straightforward.

CONCLUSIONS

This chapter introduced and explained the background of process modelling. It briefly explored the concept of risk and introduced the application of process modelling to control risk. Central to this, the chapter discussed the idea of processes and why they are so important, together with some problems that are often associated with processes. In fact, processes are far more complex than meets the eye; hence, the need for process modelling. If processes are going to be modelled, an appropriate language is required and, from the various languages and notations available, the Unified Modelling Language, or UML, was identified as the one used for the modelling in this book.

The remainder of this book builds on these foundations to create an entire approach to pragmatic business process modelling that is based on best modelling practice and uses an internationally recognized standard notation for its realization.

2 The UML Diagrams

'Oo-bi-doo! I wanna be like you-oo-oo. I wanna walk like you, talk like you do!
King Louis, The Jungle Book, Walt Disney

INTRODUCTION

In order to understand the magic behind processes it is first necessary to have an effective analysis and communication tool available for the task. In this book, the tool used is the UML.

This chapter introduces the diagrams that will be used as part of the process modelling approach described in this book, all of which are part of the UML. The information in this chapter presents only a small subset of the UML and focuses on only the parts of the language that are relevant for process modelling.

MODELLING

The UML can be an intimidating language at first appearances, particularly to people who do not necessarily have a background in technology or modelling. However, like any other language, all parts of the language are rarely used at the same time and certain subsets of the UML lend themselves to particular applications. In this instance, we shall be looking at the small subset of the UML that applies to process modelling.

Before looking at the diagrams that will be used, it is first necessary to look at some basic concepts involved with modelling and, in particular, the UML.

When modelling any sort of system, it is important to understand a few requirements with which any decent modelling language should be able to cope. These are generic requirements for any form of modelling and are not specific to the UML.

Before looking at the four basic requirements for any sort of modelling, it is worth revisiting the reasoning behind modelling.

- A model is a simplification of reality.
- We model in order to:
  - increase our understanding;
  - identify areas of complexity; and
  - ease communication.
- We have to do this because, as human beings, we cannot comprehend complexity.

Bearing in mind the driving force behind modelling, it is important to have some sort of common language that can be used as a modelling medium. In order to choose an effective modelling language, it is first necessary to understand the four basic requirements of modelling any system, described below:

- **The choice of model:** there are many correct ways to represent any sort of system, but it is important to choose the most appropriate way. Almost everyone will remember back in their schooldays when teachers used to say (and still do) that you get the marks for the working out or, to put it another way, for showing your choice of approach. To put this into a process modelling context, a process is simply an approach to doing something, therefore choosing an appropriate process is crucial for getting something right, for running a successful project and for demonstrating quality. Choosing an inappropriate approach, or process model, can be very costly.

- **The abstraction of the model:** it is essential to look at any system at different levels of abstraction, or detail. For example, imagine looking at the plans for a house, where there would be an overall, high-level view of the house, maybe showing just the exterior and the surrounding area. Also, supporting this, there will be plans for each storey of the house, each room on each floor, the interconnections between floors, and so on. In fact, some aspects of the plan will be very low-level or finely detailed aspects of the house, such as an individual window fixing that may have a drawing all to itself.

- **The connection to reality:** a model is a simplification of reality and, because of this, there is an inherent danger with modelling – it is possible (and, in some cases, easy) to miss off either too much information or relevant information from a model.

- **Different views:** consider for one last time, the example of the house. Consider the different people that will be involved in its construction, such as builders, carpenters and electricians. Each of these different people will require different pieces of information – the electrician will only be interested in the wiring diagram and where the wires will run in the house, whereas the carpenter will be less concerned about the electricity but, rather, be more concerned with the doors, windows, and so on. Different people have different views and, hence, require different sorts of information. Paramount to this, however, is that all information must be consistent as each different piece of information is merely a different view on a common model and it is important to get the model correct by matching up the views.

It is now time to look at the language that has been chosen to carry out the modelling – the UML.

THE UML

The aim of modelling is to create a model that will help to identify and manage complexity, aid understanding and to improve communications. The UML provides a toolkit of 13 diagrams. Each diagram may be used to realize a number of views of the model. Each diagram represents a slightly different view of the model and is analogous to opening a small window onto the model. Enough of these windows must be opened to provide a full specification of the model and to provide enough confidence that the model is correct. In most cases, it is not necessary to use all the diagrams; rather, a small subset of diagrams is used. In the case of process modelling, we shall be looking at a subset of four diagrams: the class diagram, the activity diagram, the sequence diagram and the use case diagram.

Modelling using the UML

Real life is inherently complex and, therefore, in order to understand and be able to communicate any information concerning real life, it is important to model this information. As discussed previously, this modelling may take the form of mathematical equations, pictures, formal diagrams, text descriptions, and so on. However, even these simplified representations of reality – the models – are themselves very complex. In order to model effectively, it is important to have some sort of structure to the modelling notation adopted, which is where the UML comes in. The UML is used to visualize a model by drawing a number of diagrams to represent different views of the model.

Any model has two distinct aspects in the UML, the structural aspect and the behavioural aspect:

- The structural aspect of the model shows the 'what' of the model – what entities exist, what relationships exist between them, what each entity looks like and what each entity does.
- The behavioural aspect of the model shows the 'how' of the model – in what order things happen, under what conditions, timing concepts, sequencing and scenarios.

Each of these two aspects of the model *must* exist in order for the model to be fully specified and these two aspects *must* be consistent with one another. In order to visualize these two aspects of the model, a number of UML diagrams exist that are used to represent either structural or behavioural aspects of the model. Each of these diagrams will represent some sort of *view* of the model, and all these views will combine to form a complete specification of the model. Despite the fact the model is a simplification of the very complex reality, it must be borne in mind that this model, when considered in its entirely, still has the potential to be complex. Think of the model as a large, complex beast, consisting of ever-changing and shifting swirling lines, that is quite incomprehensible. Each time a diagram is created, it is like opening a window into a very small part of the complex model. Each time one of these windows is opened, a very simple representation of the view out of the window is constructed.

The UML language

The UML is a language that aids the understanding of a model by representing it graphically. Any UML model will be made up of a number of views of the system and each of these views will be realized using one or more of the diagrams that make up the UML language. In the UML, there are 13 different types of diagram, although, for the purposes of this book, we will only be looking at a subset of four diagrams: the class diagram, the activity diagram, the sequence diagram and the use case diagram.

The remainder of this chapter is intended to be used as a reference for future modelling and, although only four of the 13 UML diagrams are covered, there is still a lot of information for readers who are completely new to the field of modelling to take in. It is recommended, therefore, that if you have little or no modelling experience you should read this chapter in separate sittings, rather than trying to understand it all on one occasion.

Each diagram has the same basic structure, as they are made up of 'nodes' (usually shapes of some description) that are joined together via 'paths' (usually represented by lines of some description). Each diagram is described in terms of its modelling elements and then an example of the use of that diagram is introduced and discussed. You may find it easier to look at the graphical notation and the example at the same time, to enforce the connection between the modelling elements and how they appear on a diagram.

THE CLASS DIAGRAM

Class diagrams represent a structural aspect of the system and have many uses. They allow conceptual 'things' to be drawn and the relationships between these identified. Class diagrams form the backbone of any UML model and will have consistency relationships with all the other diagrams used for process modelling.

Class diagram concepts and notation

The graphical notation for the elements that make up a class diagram are shown in Figure 2.1.

The basic elements of a class diagram are the *class* and the *relationship*.

- A *class* represents a conceptual thing and is usually a noun. A good way to understand the nature of a class is to think of it as a template

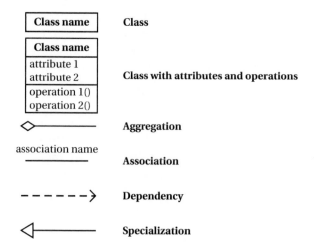

FIGURE 2.1   *Graphical notation for class diagrams*

for something. For example, the class 'Person' would represent all people generally, rather than a specific person. A specific person is known as an *instance*. Classes are represented graphically by rectangles and can be further described by identifying *attributes* and *operations*. Classes form the basic nodes in the class diagram.

- A *relationship* represents the identification of a conceptual relationship between one or more classes. A relationship is represented graphically by variations on a line, depending on the type of relationship. There are four types of relationship that are used for process modelling: the *association*, the *aggregation*, the *generalization/specialization* and the *dependency*. Relationships form the basic paths in the class diagram.

The class diagram can be defined in more detail, but these are the two basic elements at its core.

Representing classes

The graphical notation of a class is shown in Figure 2.2, in which there are two classes, each represented as a rectangle. This is a valid UML diagram, but one would have to question the value of a diagram where only two disparate classes are shown, although, as will be seen later in this book, the lack of information on a diagram can often be as revealing as the amount of information present.

FIGURE 2.2   *Graphical notation of a class*

In order to relate two or more classes together, a relationship is used. The most basic type of relationship is known as an association and identifies a simple conceptual relationship between one or more classes.

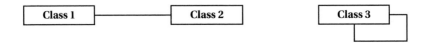

FIGURE 2.3   *Graphical notation of an association relationship*

The diagram in Figure 2.3 shows two examples of the graphical notation for an association relationship. On the left-hand side of the diagram, there is an association that is relating together 'Class 1' and 'Class 2'. This diagram would be read as 'Class 1 is associated with Class 2'. It is also possible to have an association related back to the same class, as shown on the right-hand side of the diagram. In this case, the diagram, would be read as 'Class 3 is associated with Class 3' or, 'Class 3 is associated with itself'.

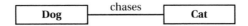

FIGURE 2.4   *Naming an association*

The association itself should always be described by a piece of text, as shown in Figure 2.4, to make the diagram easier to understand. This diagram should be read as 'Dog chases Cat' and this sentence, when read out loud, should make sense to a third party. However, as is the case in this diagram, an incomplete diagram can be open to misunderstanding. For example, there is nothing on the diagram to indicate which way the diagram should be read – left-to-right, or right-to-left. Although many people would automatically read left-to-right, in a diagram of any reasonable size or complexity, it is impossible to organize all the elements of a diagram in a left-to-right fashion. Also, by reading from left-to-right, people are often assuming a logical order of things occurring or happening, and this is not the information that is conveyed on a class diagram.

Figure 2.5 indicates the direction of the association with a small triangle, showing that the direction is left-to-right. Therefore, this

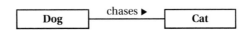

FIGURE 2.5   *Showing direction on an association*

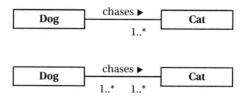

FIGURE 2.6   *Showing numbers on classes*

diagram definitely says 'Dog chases Cat' and cannot be read the other way around. However, there is room for ambiguity even on a diagram that is this simple. Consider the question 'how many cats and how many dogs?' At the moment, there is no indication of the ratio of cats to dogs, so this needs to be cleared up before the diagram can be read correctly.

Figure 2.6 shows the association between 'Dog' and 'Cat', but this time there are two variations shown that differ because of the numbers (or 'multiplicity') involved. Numbers are indicated on the ends of associations and use a simple, intuitive system.

- Numbers are represented as simple numerical characters, therefore, to indicate the number five, the digit '5' would be shown. The only exception to this is the situation where the number is one, and this can be indicated by either showing the digit '1' or by leaving the end of the association empty. Any association without a number indicated is assumed to be '1'.

- A range of numbers is represented as the extremities of the range with dots between. Therefore, to indicate a range between two and five, the association would have a multiplicity of '2..5'. A star can also indicate that a range is open-ended, which is useful, because it is very common. For example, to indicate one or more, the association would have a multiplicity of '1..*'.

- A series of numbers is represented by simple set of digits. Therefore, one, two or three is indicated as '1, 2, 3', six, nine, 11 or 20 is represented by '6, 9, 11, 20', and so on. The only exception to this is where there are two consecutive numbers in a sequence where the series or range syntax can be used. Therefore, to indicate zero or one, the multiplicity could be either '0..1' or '0,1'.

The upper half of the diagram, therefore, is read as 'Dog chases one or more Cat'. Note that no number is indicated on the 'Dog' side of the association, therefore the number is assumed to be '1'. It is important to understand that the numbers indicate a *ratio* rather than absolute numbers, so a more correct way to read the diagram would be 'each Dog chases one or more Cat'. The inclusion of the word 'each' here

FIGURE 2.7   *Examples of attributes for the class 'Cat'*

conveys the fact that there may be many dogs, each of which will chase a number of cats, rather than saying that there is only a single dog. This could represent anything from one dog chasing one cat, right up to a dog chasing a herd of cats.

The lower half of the diagram, although looking very similar, has a subtly different meaning and should be read as 'one or more Dog chases one or more Cat'. This could represent anything from a dog chasing a single cat, to a pack of dogs chasing a single cat, to a pack of dogs chasing a herd of cats, and anything in-between.

Classes can also be defined in more detail by identifying their features and their behaviour or, to put it another way, what each class looks like and what it does.

The features of a class are known as 'attributes' and are usually nouns that can have different values associated with them.

Figure 2.7 shows the class of 'Cat' with its features identified as attributes. In this example, three attributes have been identified: 'Name', 'Age' and 'Colour'. It is important that attribute names are chosen effectively and one way to ensure this is to think about the different sorts of values that an attribute may take, for example:

- 'Name' could be a text string.
- 'Age' could be a integer or a real number, depending on the requirements of the model. It may also be desirable to indicate a range here, so that 'Age' could be defined as an integer somewhere between zero and 20. This would be shown as 'Age:int(0..20)'.
- 'Colour' could be a text string, or a list of predefined colours, or a number to indicate the colour, a hexadecimal representation of the colour, and so on.

In fact, just by thinking about the sort of values that an attribute can take can really help in understanding the model. Consider, for example, if an attribute was identified as 'Black', would this be correct? In many cases, the answer would be 'no' as the attribute cannot take on different values – in fact it may very well be that the author of the model intended to represent 'Colour' but, instead, used the term 'Black'. However, there is also an argument that 'Black' is a correct attribute if the intention was only to find out whether the cat is black or not. In such a case, the attribute value would be Boolean. It may be that the model is intended to be used for customers who are all witches, in which case they are only interested in

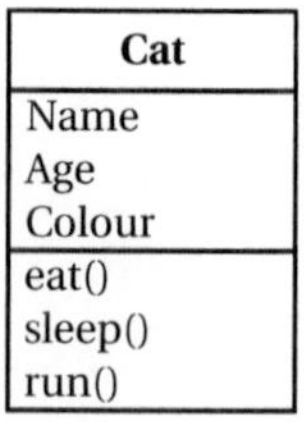

Cat
Name
Age
Colour
eat()
sleep()
run()

FIGURE 2.8 *Example of operations for the class 'Cat'*

whether the cat is black or not (witches, as any child can confirm, always have black cats!).

It is also possible to identify the behaviour of a class by identifying *operations*. An operation is usually a verb and represents something that the class does.

Figure 2.8 shows the operations that have been identified for the class 'Cat'. The operations represent what the behaviour is – *not how the class behaves*. Remember that the class diagram is a structural diagram and, as such, shows the 'what' of a system, not the 'how'. The operations are as follows:

- 'eat', which could be further described by stating what type of food is eaten, the amount, and so on, and which information can be shown in the brackets after the operation name; in this example, the operation may be further specified as 'eat(food_type, amount, frequency)';
- 'sleep', which may be further described by stating the length of the sleep, the location, and so on, for example 'sleep(duration, location)';
- 'run', which may be further described by stating the speed, direction, and so on, for example 'run(speed, direction)'.

Of course, it is entirely possible to leave the brackets empty and, in reality, this is often the case with process modelling, but the mechanism for further specification is there if required.

Representing relationships

In the same way that classes can be described in more detail by adding attributes and operations, it is also possible to define relationships in more detail by considering different types of relationship. These basic different types of relationship are defined as part of the standard UML language. The four basic relationship types that will be used are: associations, aggregations, specializations and dependencies.

Association

An association is the most basic type of relationship and is used for expressing simple conceptual relationships between two classes.

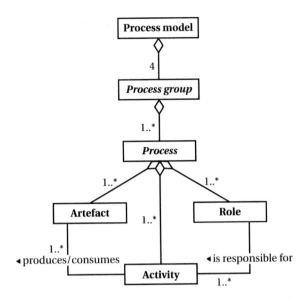

FIGURE 2.9   *Example of the aggregation relationship*

The association relationship has been used several times already in this chapter and can be seen in Figures 2.3, 2.4, 2.5 and 2.6. An association allows classes to be related together and should be very easily read and understood by anyone looking at the diagram.

Aggregation

An aggregation allows an 'is made up of' relationship between classes and allows the structure of a class to be broken down into a number of component classes. This is a very powerful mechanism that allows hierarchies and structures to be expressed, at several levels, on a single diagram.

Figure 2.9 shows a number of aggregation relationships that depict the hierarchy of the structure of the main class 'Process model'. The diagram shows that the main class 'Process model' is made up of one or more 'Process group', each of which is made up of one or more 'Process'. Note how numbers are indicated in exactly the same way as with a standard association. At the bottom of the diagram there are three aggregation relationships, all from the class 'Process' to the classes 'Role', 'Artefact' and 'Activity'. Although there are three aggregations on this diagram, it is usual to overlap them, as has been done on Figure 2.10, to facilitate reading the diagrams.

Figure 2.10 has exactly the same meaning as Figure 2.9, the only difference being that the three aggregations in that diagram have been overlaid so that they appear as a single aggregation with three branches.

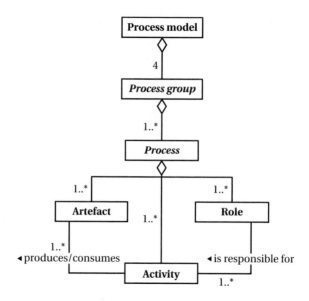

FIGURE 2.10   *Overlapping aggregations to tidy up a diagram*

Specialization

The specialization relationship allows a 'has types' relationship to be defined, which can be used to classify classes into different 'types of groups. This is a natural way to express information, particularly when different elements of a similar nature need to be differentiated in some way. This relationship is indicated graphically by a triangle symbol which should be read as either 'has types' if reading the diagram downwards, or as 'is a type of when reading upwards.

Figure 2.11 shows four specializations from the class 'Process group'. This diagram is read as: 'Process group has types of: Enterprise, Project, Agreement and Technical' if reading from top-to-bottom. If the diagram was being read from bottom-to-top, then it would be read as 'Enterprise, Project, Agreement and Technical are all types of Process group'.

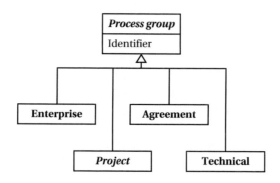

FIGURE 2.11   *Example of the specialization relationship*

It is possible to have many levels of nesting in the specialization hierarchy that make use of a feature known as *inheritance*. Inheritance specifies that any features of a parent class are inherited by all its child classes. A parent class is a class that has subtypes defined below it, whereas a child class is a class that is a subtype of a parent class. It is possible for a class to be both a parent of one class and a child of a different class, as shown in Figure 2.12.

Figure 2.12 shows a classification hierarchy with many levels, all related by specialization relationships. In this example, there are two types of 'Project' defined: 'Support' and 'Management'. The class 'Management' also has three further types defined as 'Project management', 'Resource management' and 'Risk management'. Consider, as an example, the class 'Resource management'. This class is a type of 'Management', which is a type of 'Project', which is a type of 'Process group'. Therefore, it follows that 'Resource management' is actually a type of 'Process group', albeit via seveal levels of nesting. 'Process group' has an attribute of 'Identifier' defined and this attribute is inherited by all its child classes. Therefore, the classes 'Enterprise', 'Project', 'Agreement' and Technical' all inherit the attribute directly from 'Process group'. The classes 'Support' and 'Management' also inherit the same attribute from 'Process group', this time indirectly via the class 'Project'. Finally, the three classes 'Project management', Risk management' and 'Resource management' all inherit the same attribute.

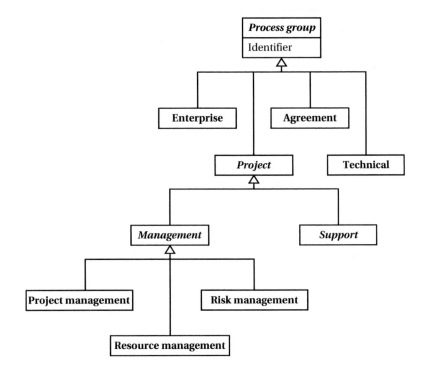

FIGURE 2.12 *Example of inheritance*

Inheritance also works for operations and any structures that are defined for a parent class, such as an aggregation. This is something that will be explored later in this book.

Notice how several of the classes have their names italicized, such as '*Project*' and '*Management*'. This indicates that the class is 'abstract' in that it has no instances. This is usually used when a class is showing a classification or grouping and has no real-life instances.

The term 'specialization' is often used with the term 'generalization' – either with the two terms used at the same time (specialization/generalization) or one term being used in preference to the other. This is because the specialization relationship can be read either top-down or bottom-up and each term reflects this. If the diagram is read from top to bottom, the classes get more specialized the further down the hierarchy that they occur. Likewise, if the diagram is read from the bottom to the top, then the classes get more generalized the further up the hierarchy they occur.

Dependency

The final type of relationship is the dependency. A dependency is used to relate two classes in a tightly coupled way, which implies that as one class changes, so will its dependent classes. There are many uses for this, one of the main uses being to express instances of classes.

A dependency is shown graphically by a dashed directed line between two classes. The class with the arrow next to it is the dependent class and, conversely, the one without an arrow is the governing class (see Figure 2.13).

Figure 2.13 shows three dependencies that are related to the 'Stakeholder requirements' class. The dependency relationship is used in different ways here:

- **To represent instances of a class:** the two elements 'Project X :Stakeholder requirements' and 'Project Y :Stakeholder requirements' represent instances, or real-life examples, of the class 'Stakeholder'. In order to differentiate between one of these instances (also known as objects) and a normal class, the text in the instance box is underlined and a colon precedes the name of the class. It is also possible to provide an identifier for each instance; in this case the identifiers 'Project X' and 'Project Y' have been used. Remembering that classes are abstract and define templates for real-life things, the instances represent these real-life things. Therefore, in the example shown in Figure 2.13, the class represents the template for the process known as 'Stakeholder requirements', whereas the two instances represent real-life examples or executions of this process. This instance relationship is also shown here with the dependency relationship (the dotted line) by the word 'instance' with

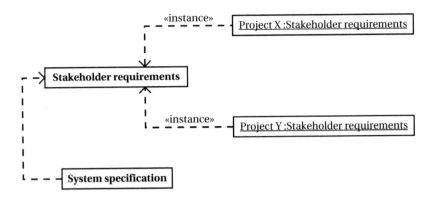

FIGURE 2.13 *Example of dependencies*

chevrons around it. In summary, therefore, the <<instance>> dependency relates instances and classes – the real to the abstract.

- **Normal dependency:** the second type of dependency used in Figure 2.13 is just a simple dependency that implies that the two classes have a very strong relationship. In this case, the class 'System specification' is dependent upon the class 'Stakeholder requirements', as they share some of the same content, which is generated by the 'Stakeholder requirements' class. Therefore, when the 'Stakeholder requirements' class changes, so does the 'System specification' class – hence the dependency relationship. In summary, therefore, the normal use of dependencies relates two classes – abstract to abstract.

Dependencies should be used sparingly in class diagrams as it is easy to misuse them when a normal association would be more appropriate.

Using class diagrams for process modelling

Class diagrams are used to realize four of the views from the process meta-model, which are:

- **the process structure view,** where classes are used to define the basic terminology and process structure for the whole process model;

- **the process content view,** where classes are used to represent actual processes, with their relevant artefacts and activities represented as attributes and operations respectively;

- **the stakeholder view,** where classes are used to represent the stakeholder roles in the system, along with relationships between them;

- **the information view,** where classes are used to represent the artefacts in the system and the relationships between them.

Each of these diagrams will be explained in more detail in Chapter 4.

29

THE ACTIVITY DIAGRAM

The activity diagram realizes a behavioural aspect of the overall model and is used to model low-level, or detailed, behaviour. The activity diagram has strong relationships with the class diagram. Activity diagrams look familiar to many people, as they are derived from flowcharts. Most people will have seen a variant of a flowchart at some point in their lives, hence many people find the activity diagram a friendly diagram to work with.

The activity diagram shows the 'how', or the behaviour, of a single class. A class diagram identifies attributes and operations, but doesn't specify in which order operations are executed, nor the information flow. The activity diagram does both of these and more. One key feature of an activity diagram, essential for process modelling, is that it enables the definition of responsibility for activities within a process.

Activity diagram concepts and notation

The basic graphical notation for the activity diagram is shown in Figure 2.14.

The basic elements within the activity diagram are:

- **The activity invocation:** an activity invocation is the execution of an operation taken from its owner-class (the class whose behaviour is being defined by the activity diagram). An activity invocation must exist for each operation from the owner-class, and vice versa. An activity invocation is represented graphically by a soft box (a rectangle with four straight edges but for rounded corners) or, to put it

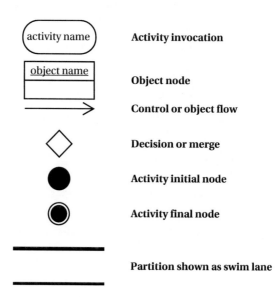

FIGURE 2.14 *Graphical notation for activity diagrams*

another way, a sausage shape. Each activity invocation represents the processes of some sort of information and it is also possible to represent activity invocations that receive, or send, messages from, and to, the outside world. These are known as *signals*. These signals are represented graphically by irregular pentagons with one end being either convex (to represent an outgoing signal) or concave (to represent an incoming signal). The activity invocations form the basic nodes in the activity diagram.

- **Control and object flows:** activity invocations must be executed in a particular order, and the control and object flows define this order, by relating activity invocations together in an ordered flow. Both control and object flows are represented graphically by directed lines, the ends of which attach to activity invocations. The control and object flows form the basic paths in the class diagram. Control and object flows differ conceptually if not graphically, as a control flow shows pure sequence, whereas an object flow represents the flow of information (in the form of an object) around the diagram.

- **Control fork and joins:** the flow of control, represented by the control flows, can be split up in concurrent flows using control forks and joins. A control fork splits a single flow into any number of concurrent flows that may, or may not be executed in parallel. These split flows can then be joined back together using the control join. The activity diagram uses the concept of 'token flow', which means that, for each flow, there is a conceptual token that can be used to track its current progress. In order for a set of flows to be joined together, each must present its token to the control join before the overall flow can progress. Another way to think about this is to imagine that all concurrent control flows must complete before they can be rejoined. Both control forks and joins are represented graphically by thick black lines with a single flow entering and multiple flows leaving (in the case of the fork), or multiple flows entering and a single flow exiting (in the case of a control join). Control forks and joins form nodes in the activity diagram.

- **Object nodes:** objects are used to represent information flow within the activity diagram, which is useful for showing the inputs and outputs of each activity invocation. They can be represented as instances on the diagram (a rectangle with the class name underlined and a preceding colon) or by simply showing text on a line. The choice between which to use is usually dependent on which makes the diagram more readable. For example, text is easier to use for showing simple information flow between two activity invocations. If, on the other hand, the information flow is coming in from somewhere else in the system, it is more usual to show the full graphical syntax of the rectangle.

- **Start and end states:** each activity diagram must start and end. This represents the creation and destruction respectively of an instance of the owner-class. A start state is represented graphically by a filled-in circle, whereas an end state is represented by a bulls-eye symbol.
- **Swim lanes:** swim lanes represent regions on an activity diagram and are used for allocating responsibility to activity invocations. A swim lane is represented graphically by two parallel lines that partition the diagram and encapsulate a number of activity invocations. Note that responsibility is allocated to the activity invocations, rather than the objects that flow in and out of them.

Figure 2.15 shows an example of an activity diagram. The diagram is divided into a number of swim lanes that are represented by the vertical lines that divide up the diagram and that each have the name of a stakeholder at the top. In this way, any activity invocations that are contained within a life line are under the responsibility of the stakeholder at the top of the swim lane. Each activity invocation represents a calling of

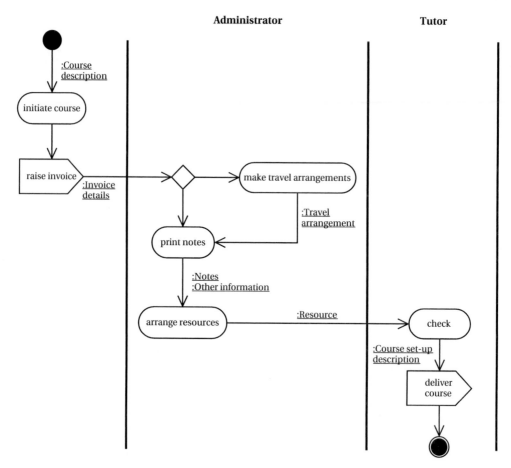

FIGURE 2.15 *Example of an activity diagram*

an operation from the parent class and is represented by a sausage shape on the diagram. Inputs and outputs to each activity invocation can be shown by objects, that may be represented graphically by boxes or, in the case of complex diagrams, by simple text associated with each transition.

The activity diagram shows the logical control and information flow through an instance of a class and also assigns responsibility for each activity invocation.

It is also possible to show where messages are transmitted or received by the activity diagram as signals – a transmit signal is represented by a pentagon with a convex edge, whereas a receive signal is represented by a pentagon with a concave edge.

Other concepts, such as concurrent execution of control, can be shown using flow forks and joins, where the flow is split between different threads that may be executed concurrently.

Using activity diagrams for process modelling

Activity diagrams are used to realize the 'process behaviour view' from the process meta-model. The process behaviour view is a set of activity diagrams, each of which describes the behaviour of a single process. The activity diagram is used exclusively for the 'process behaviour view' in the process meta-model, and is related directly to classes from the 'process content view'.

THE SEQUENCE DIAGRAM

Introduction

The sequence diagram realizes a behavioural aspect of the overall model and is used to model high-level behaviour. The sequence diagram is an excellent diagram for tying different views of the system together and forms the basis of the process validation of the process meta-model.

Sequence diagram concepts and notation

The graphical notation for a sequence diagram is shown in Figure 2.16. The basic elements within a sequence diagram are:

- **Interactions:** an interaction is a representation of an ordered set of activities that are executed in order to fulfil a particular requirement or, to put it another way, an interaction is a scenario. Each interaction is defined using a sequence diagram and each sequence diagram has a frame around it that identifies the particular interaction. Any one of these interactions can now be called up during any other interaction so that interactions may be nested. When an interaction is called up during another interaction, it is called an 'interaction occurrence'. The graphical notation for an interaction is a large box that contains the sequence diagram, with a small pentagon in the top left-hand corner containing its name. An interaction occurrence has the same

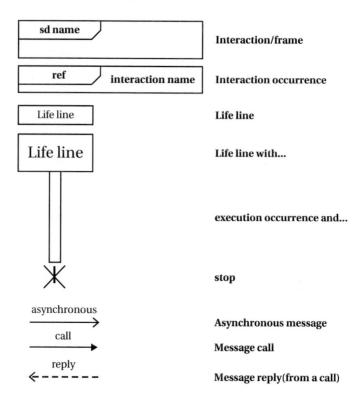

FIGURE 2.16   *Graphical notation for sequence diagrams*

graphical symbol except, this time, there is no sequence diagram within it. Therefore, the symbol is far smaller. Instead of the name of the interaction in the label box, the term 'ref is used to indicate that this interaction is defined elsewhere, and the name of the interaction is written in the main body of the symbol, where the sequence diagram is usually located. Interactions may be represented by an entire sequence diagram or, indeed, may be called up as single interaction occurrences that are defined on other diagrams.

- **Life lines:** a life line represents an instance, or collection of instances, of a class. A life line is represented graphically by a box with the name of the parent class in it, with a dashed vertical line underneath it. This line represents time, going down the page. A life line represents a graphical node on the diagram.

- **Messages:** a message is the basic communication mechanism between life lines and can represent almost any form of information exchange. This could be a true data exchange or may be a simple control message exchange. These messages may be as simple or complex as required but, in the examples shown here, will be kept deliberately at quite a high level.

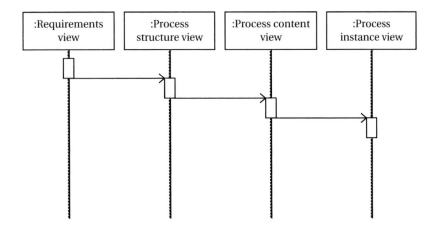

FIGURE 2.17   *Example of a sequence diagram*

Figure 2.17 depicts a simple sequence diagram. The boxes across the top of the diagram represent the instances of classes, or life lines, as they are known. Each lifeline has a dashed line going down the page underneath it, that represents time going down the page – the top of the line representing the earliest time and the bottom of the line representing the latest time. Interactions between life lines are represented by messages that are passed between the dashed lines, and are described by a text identifier on top of the line. This identifier may also include any important information that is required by the message, shown in brackets after the identifier name. It is also possible to show conditions that may have to be met before a message can be sent or received by showing the logical condition in square brackets.

In this way, it is possible to describe the sequence of events (going down the page), the messages passed between the life lines, and any logical condition or any information that is passed between the life lines.

Using sequence diagrams for process modelling

Sequence diagram are used in the process meta-model to realize the process instance views. These process instance views are used to represent *scenarios* associated with particular requirements that are used to validate requirements. This is discussed in more detail in Chapter 4.

THE USE CASE DIAGRAM

The use case diagram realizes a behavioural aspect of the overall model and is used to model the behaviour of the system at its highest, or context, level. The use case diagram is used exclusively for modelling requirements and context in the UML and, although very simple to look at, it is perhaps the most difficult diagram to get right.

Use case diagram concepts and notation

The basic notation for the use case diagram is shown in Figure 2.18.

The use case diagram has the following main elements:

- **Actors:** an actor represents a stakeholder role and is represented graphically by a 'stick person'. The stick person symbol is particularly confusing as, not unreasonably, many people assume that it represents a person, but this is not the case. The stick person, or actor, represents the *role* taken by a person, thing, organization or place and, as such, is not actually a person in real life. Caution must be exercised when identifying and defining actors in a use case diagram. All actors sit *outside* the boundary of the system that is being modelled and interact in some way with the system, in that each actor will have some relationship with an aspect of functionality of the system, which is represented by 'use cases'. Actors represent graphical nodes in a use case diagram.
- **Use cases:** a use case represents some aspect of functionality of the system, or capability, and is typically representative of some sort of requirement of the system. These requirements may be business requirements, functional requirements or non-functional require-ments. Use cases, together with actors, represent graphical nodes in the use case diagram.

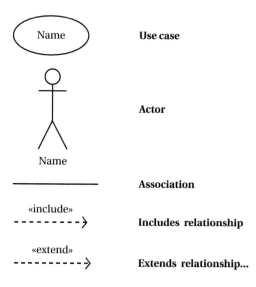

FIGURE 2.18 *Graphical notation for use case diagrams*

- **System boundary:** the system boundary, which is represented by a large rectangle in a use case diagram, indicates the divide between the functionality within the system and the actors outside the system. Any diagram that has a system boundary may be thought of as a *context* of the system. Each context of the system represents a view point of the system from a particular stakeholder's point of view and, typically, any system will have a number of contexts defined for it. For example, it is quite common to find a *business context* defined for a system, that represents the high-level business requirements of the organization, as well as a *system context* that represents the individual requirements of a particular project. Also, the *system context* will often be made up of a number of view points, such as the *product context* that represents the require-ments of the end product, and the *project context* that represents the requirements for running the projects. All these contexts must be consistent with each other while individually adding value to the understanding of the project. In the case of process modelling, the context defined is known as a 'requirements view' on the process meta-model. Potentially each stakeholder has its own context and, hence, its own set of requirements.

- **Relationships:** there are three basic relationships that are defined in the UML language, which are the *association*, the *include* dependency and the *extend* dependency. The basic association simply identifies some sort of relationship between an actor and a use case. Unlike conventional associations, associations on use case diagrams should not be named, nor is a direction indicated on them. The actual nature of the association is defined in more detail using UML interaction diagrams, such as the sequence diagram. The two types of dependency that are predefined in the UML are the include and extend relationships. Relationships represent the graphical paths in the use case diagram.

A use case diagram is unique compared to the other UML diagrams in that it has two specific usages, which are often abused. A use case diagram may be used to model either a context of a system or a set of requirements that has been decomposed from a higher-level requirement and will, ultimately, be traceable back to a context.

Figure 2.19 shows a use case diagram that models a context. The visual indicator that the diagram is a context, rather than a decomposition of some higher-level requirement, is the system boundary, represented by the large rectangle that contains the use cases (ellipses). The actors are outside the boundary of the system and are connected to the use cases by associations. These associations not only relate actors and use cases but each time an association crosses the system boundary, it represents an interface between the system and the outside world.

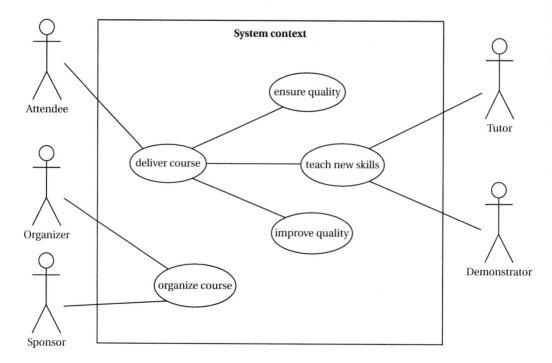

FIGURE 2.19 *Example of a use case diagram showing a context*

All use cases in a context should be related to actors outside the system boundary either directly or indirectly. A direct relationship is represented by a dedicated relationship between the use case and one or more actors, whereas as an indirect relationship may be an inherited relationship via a specialization, include, extend or constrain relationship, described in more detail below.

The other use for the use case diagram is to decompose one of the higher-level requirements into its own diagram. The use case diagram in Figure 2.20 shows the decomposition, or breakdown, of a high-level requirement – in this case the 'organize course' requirement – from the context diagram.

Notice how, in Figure 2.20, the relationships between the use cases have been specified in terms of the special nature of the relationship. There are three basic types of relationship specified within the UML, which are:

- **The specialization relationship:** This is exactly the same as the specialization relationship that is used in class diagrams and, similarly, is read as 'has types'. Therefore, in the diagram, the requirement 'organize course' has two types: 'organize in-house course' and 'organize external course'. The specialization also allows inheritance, which means that the two child requirements ('organize in-house course' and 'organize external course') both

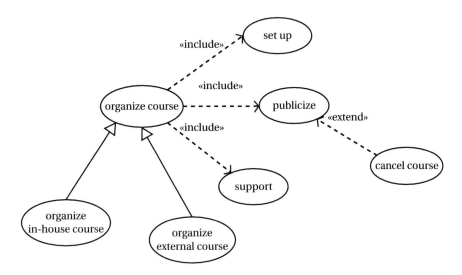

FIGURE 2.20 *Example of a use case diagram showing a decomposition of a higher-level requirement*

inherit the structure of the parent requirement ('organize course'). Therefore, the three requirements included in the parent requirement are inherited by the two child requirements.

*   **The <<include>> relationship:** the <<include>> relationship states that any use cases on the directed end of the dashed line are *always* part of the use case on the other end of the line. Therefore, the use case 'organize course' always includes: 'set up', 'publicize' and 'support'. This is how composition is indicated on a use case diagram.

*   **The <<extend>> relationship:** the <<extend>> relationship states that any use cases on the directed end of the dashed line are *sometimes* part of the use case on the other end of the line. Therefore, the use case 'cancel course' extends the functionality of the use case 'publicize', depending on certain conditions.

There is a fourth type of relationship that is frequently used in use case diagrams, known as the <<constrain>> relationship. Although not a standard part of the UML notation, the UML is often extended to include such a relationship.

Figure 2.21 shows a <<constrain>> relationship, that is used to relate functional and non-functional requirements together. A functional requirement represents some function of the system into which users or operators are directly inherited, whereas a non-functional requirement represents a requirement that will constrain the way that a functional requirement can be realized. In the context of process modelling, non-functional requirements will include requirements such as:

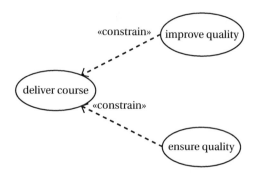

FIGURE 2.21 *The <<constrain>> relationship*

- **Quality requirements:** this will often consist of meeting a particular standard or set of standards. This can be very important and can also be one of the most unrealistic non-functional requirements of a system. It is not uncommon to see well over 50 standards referenced as being 'essential' to the successful implementation of a system. Of course, in reality, it is quite unrealistic to demand that so many standards should be complied with, unless the project is directly related to standards compliance.
- **Implementation requirements:** some non-functional requirements will constrain other requirements by insisting that a particular technique, tool or technology is used as part of the system development. Of course, dictating any of these will limit the way that the system is developed.
- **Environmental requirements:** any system has to operate in some kind of environment, whether it is the natural environment, an artificial environment or whatever. In almost all cases, the type of environment in which the system lives will have some constraining effect on the system.

These non-functional requirements are just as important as the actual functional requirements but can often be far more difficult to quantify and, hence, to validate.

Using use case diagrams for process modelling

Use case diagrams are used to realize the 'requirements view' of the process meta-model, which consists of a number of use case diagrams, each of which represents a context of the system from the viewpoint of one stakeholder or a stakeholder group.

It is often argued that a requirements view is the most important single view of a system, as it is the view to and from which all other views will be traceable. It is crucial, therefore, that the requirements view is both correct and an accurate representation of real life.

CONSISTENCY BETWEEN THE DIAGRAMS

It must be remembered that each of the diagrams is simply a small view of the overall model. This model is a large, complex beast that is difficult to understand. Therefore, breaking the model down into a number of simpler views, each of which is realized visually by a number of diagrams, makes understanding easier. However, in order to have the confidence that the model itself is correct and that our understanding is valid, it is essential that the model is checked for consistency by relating elements of different diagrams together.

The UML is more than just a random collection of drawing elements brought together into a set of diagrams, as every element in the UML is related to another element in some way. These interrelationships are defined in what is known as the *UML meta-model*. The UML meta-model is fully defined in the UML standard (available from www.omg.org) and is, in a nutshell, a UML model of the UML. In order to keep things simple in this book, all relevant consistency relationships have been abstracted into tables in Chapter 4.

CONCLUSIONS

This chapter has presented the basic syntax and notation of four of the 13 UML diagrams that are used for process modelling. The basic concepts have been addressed here generally, but each will be discussed in more detail, with process modelling specifically in mind, in the chapters that follow.

The information presented here is by no means an exhaustive definition of the syntax for each of the UML diagrams, but represents the key elements of each diagram that will be used in the remainder of this book. It is possible to carry out all process modelling activities with this simple notation but, for a more complete description of the UML syntax, semantics and rules, see any of the excellent reference manuals that are generally available (for example, Holt, 2004; Rumbaugh *et al.*, 2004).

3 Requirements for Process Modelling

'Those that don't ask, don't want – those that ask, don't get'

Christine Holt (author's mother)

INTRODUCTION

The previous chapter introduced the UML as the tool that will be used to de-mystify the world of processes. This chapter investigates just why process modelling is so deceptively complex and difficult to get right and identifies a number of problems associated with understanding and communicating processes.

The fact that we are modelling processes means that we are simplifying reality. This means that, by necessity, we will have to miss out some information. A full process specification will consist of the model and an important part of that model is the textual descriptions that accompany all its key elements. This chapter looks at the various requirements for modelling processes effectively and efficiently. Each major point is discussed in the next section.

SPECIFIC PROCESS MODELLING REQUIREMENTS

Complete information

One very real danger that occurs when modelling anything, not just processes, is that too much information may be inadvertently missed out. A process model that is too simplified will not add the amount of value that an appropriately modelled one will and, likewise, a process model containing too much detail will be riddled with complexity and all its associated problems. Reaching the appropriate level of abstraction can be very difficult to achieve, therefore some guidance is required for obtaining the correct level of detail. This is one of the features of the process meta-model that is introduced at the end of this chapter.

Realistic processes

Another problem that occurs with process modelling is one of ensuring the process really reflects the practices carried out in real life. This occurs because processes are usually modelled as abstract notions that are thought about theoretically before being put into practice. This is all well and good, but it is just as important to think about the real-life execution of such processes, which are referred to as 'process instances'; in other words, real-life examples of the processes being executed in the organization.

Process partitioning

Any process model has the potential to contain a very large number of processes and it is important to be able to partition them in some way. The approach to partitioning processes into groups can take many forms. For example, many organizations will take an international standard as the basis for the main process partitions. Rather than using an international standard or best practice model, processes are also often grouped in terms of their functionality, or in terms of areas of responsibility. The actual approach taken will depend on the organization and the nature of the applications of the process, but this decision must be made and recorded in some way.

Process iteration

When processes have been identified and the key features defined, it is important to be able to define how the activities in the process are carried out – the order in which they are executed, the conditions under which they are executed and any timing constraints that may come into play. Very often, the internal workings of a process will be defined as a linear set of activities, whereas, in real life, many processes will exhibit a high degree of iteration. For example, most processes will have decision points and, by the very nature of a decision point, there will be more than one option based on a decision. These different options result in different paths of flow through a process causing a high degree of iteration. Caution must be exercised when identifying iteration, as the more iterations within a diagram, the higher the level of complexity.

In real life, it is possible to execute many instantiations of a single process at the same time. Consider any transaction-processing system where it is a key feature of the system to be able to process transactions in parallel, rather than in a simple sequence.

Complexity and interactions

Interactions exist at many levels in a process model, both in its structural definition and its behaviour. These interactions can be identified visually by looking at the graphical paths (lines) on any diagram that connect the graphical nodes (shapes). It is these relationships and interactions between elements that lead to complexity, rather than the elements themselves. Imagine a set of five elements represented as five classes, as shown in Figure 3.1, which illustrates why relationships and interactions lead to complexity.

First, consider the pattern shown as Figure 3.1a, where there are five classes with no relationships between them. Clearly, this is simple and would be perceived as easy to understand by anyone looking at the shapes, as the level of interaction between the elements (also known as the *coupling*) is zero. This is very often the perception when presented with a text list of things. In reality, however, there are usually relationships between the various elements in a diagram or in a list. This is represented in Figure 3.1b, where each element is now related to the other elements in some way. It is quite clear that Figure 3.1b is more complex than Figure 3.1a. Although both have exactly the same number of elements, in Figure 3.1b the interactions, or the coupling, between these elements is higher than in Figure 3.1a. Finally, consider the case when there are yet more interactions between the same set of elements, as illustrated in Figure 3.1c. Clearly, this is more complex than Figure 3.1b and it is orders of magnitude more complex than Figure 3.1a. Again, it has the same number of elements as Figures 3.1a and b, but the increased number of interactions leads immediately to an increased level of complexity.

Complexity, therefore, is very much a function of the relationships between elements of a diagram, rather than of the number of elements themselves.

A structural diagram has been used in Figure 3.1 – in this case a class diagram – but the same principle applies to any of the diagrams discussed in this book. Also, as these interactions and complex relationships exist on all the different diagrams, they can exist in all views of the system and at all levels of abstraction, for example:

- A very high level of abstraction, such as between the system and the user of the system, or between systems. In terms of process modelling, this manifests itself as requirements for the process.
- A high level of abstraction, such as between subsystems of an overall system, where the elements or components of a system interact to

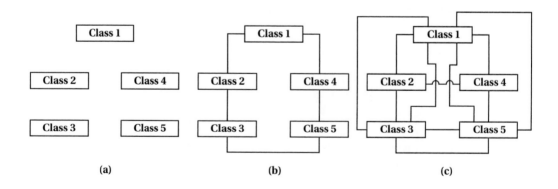

FIGURE 3.1 *The complexity of relationships*

deliver complex behaviour. There will usually be several levels of high abstraction and, in terms of process modelling, this will manifest itself as process executions interacting in different situations.

- A medium level of abstraction, where individual elements are modelled and the interactions represent internal relationships and interactions. In terms of process modelling, this will manifest itself as the definition of the behaviour inside a process.
- A low level of abstraction, where the model represents individual activities, or algorithms, that cannot be decomposed any further. In terms of process modelling, this will manifest itself as defining the behaviour of activities within a process.

When looking at elements within a system, the information is deceptively simple. To get a more realistic view of the system, it is essential to visualize the relationships between these elements.

Traceability

One of the most important goals for any quality system is that of traceability. It is essential to be able to trace from any point of any life cycle back to the original project requirements. For example, during an audit, the auditor may point at any part of the system that is being developed and ask which of the original requirements that part of the system is meeting. The same is true for the process model: it is essential that all the artefacts are not only identified, but that they are also fully traceable. For example, a delegate booking process may require an invoice to be produced and sent out to a customer, but if there is no traceability between the booking process and the associated invoicing process then the whole process will fail.

MEETING THE REQUIREMENTS THROUGH MODELLING

The requirements identified and discussed above can all be met by appropriate use of UML modelling. This section aims to look at each of these requirements and then to relate them to different UML modelling mechanisms to get an idea of how each of them can be visualized using the UML.

We have already seen that a process defines an approach to doing something, therefore there is a clear need to be able to model:

- the name of the process itself;
- the inputs and outputs of the process;
- the activities that are executed in order to achieve the aims of the process.

Another important aspect of process definition is that each of the activities that is identified must also have responsibility defined for it, in

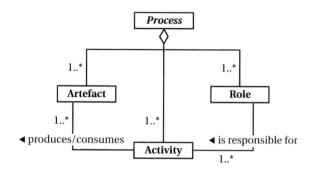

FIGURE 3.2 *Simple definition of a process*

terms of a stakeholder role. This information can be represented using a simple class diagram.

Figure 3.2 shows a simple definition of what a process is and how it must be represented. The diagram is read as follows: a 'Process' is made up of one or more 'Role', one or more 'Activity' and one or more 'Artefact'. Also, each 'Activity' produces/consumes one or more 'Artefact' and each 'Role' is responsible for one or more 'Activity'. This is the terminology that will be adopted for the rest of this book.

This diagram is very useful for two reasons:

- It defines the basic structure of the process model itself. This diagram will be expanded later and will form the 'process structure view' in the process meta-model.
- It defines the key terminology to be used throughout the process model. For example, the term 'artefact' has been used here to represent inputs and outputs, but this term could quite easily have been defined as something else, such as 'deliverable', 'work product' or, indeed, 'input' or 'output'. The same is true for the other terms: 'activity' could have been defined as 'task', 'action', and so on, and 'role' could have been defined as 'stakeholder', 'responsibility', and so on.

This diagram is useful for defining the structure and terminology, but it would be impractical to use the same structure to represent *actual* processes, as any process will have a number of activities, artefacts and stakeholders, each of which would be represented by a class on a diagram like this one. Therefore, the diagram is simplified by representing the whole process as a single class. Remembering back to the UML element of the class, a class can be further described by a number of attributes and a number of operations. An attribute describes a feature of a class, which is comparable to the artefacts of a process. Likewise, an operation describes something that is done in a class, which is comparable to the activities in a process. Therefore, it is possible to represent a process, together with its

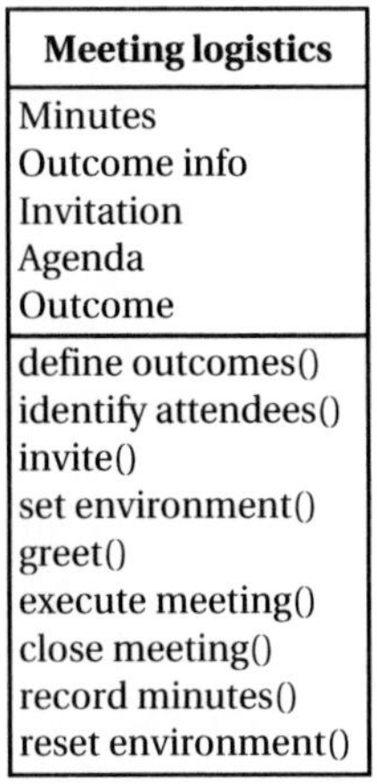

Meeting logistics
Minutes
Outcome info
Invitation
Agenda
Outcome
define outcomes()
identify attendees()
invite()
set environment()
greet()
execute meeting()
close meeting()
record minutes()
reset environment()

FIGURE 3.3   *Compact definition of a process*

artefacts and activities, as a single class that exhibits attributes and operations.

Figure 3.3 shows a class that represents the process 'Meeting logistics', which is executed in order to plan and run meetings. The name of the class is the name of the process, in this case 'Meeting logistics'. The attribute names, shown in the second box, represent the names of the artefacts that are produced and consumed as part of the process. The operation names, shown in the third box, represent the activity names that are the individual steps in the process that produce and consume the artefacts.

So far, the information on the diagram has shown two of the three things that need to be specified – the artefacts and the activities – but has not shown the stakeholders. The stakeholders can be represented on a different class diagram, but one that is dedicated to identifying the stakeholders as classes and the relationships between them. This class diagram represents a stakeholder view of the system and forms part of the process meta-model.

TAILORING PROCESSES

No matter how well understood a process is, how often it is used or how well specified it is, processes always need to be tailored. Tailoring a process means specializing it in some way, which could be for any number of reasons:

- **A natural evolution of the process due to change in internal process requirements:** All processes must be reviewed periodically to ensure that they are still fit for purpose. As time goes on, the process itself may evolve in terms of the way that it is being implemented by the people in the organization. Perhaps a new software tool is being used that makes the process easier to follow by automating one or more of the steps. In such a case, the process must be revisited and re-verified.

- **A natural evolution of the process due to a change in the organizational requirements of the process:** in many instances, the process must evolve due to a change inside the organization. Maybe the business of the organization has evolved and the processes need to be checked to make sure that they meet the new requirements – in other words, validation. For example, consider a company that suddenly starts to create real-time or safety-critical systems which previously had only been involved in basic systems. Although the original process itself still works (verification), it no longer meets the organization's new requirements (validation).

- **A forced evolution of the process (change in external require- ments):** As well as the internal, organizational requirements for a process changing, there can also be external, or outside, influences that affect the process. For example, there may be a change in law, best practice standards, and so on, that will impact on the product associated with the process, or the process itself directly, which means that the process may have to be tailored in some way. For example, consider the case of electro-magnetic compatibility (EMC) regulations that now affect just about every electronic product on the market. It is no longer good enough to make an excellent TV set, for example; if the TV set does not meet the EMC regulations, then it cannot be sold – regardless of how it may be perceived to be. In such a case, the processes must be checked against external requirements (validation) even though the process itself still functions as was originally intended (verification).

- **New applications/projects:** As time goes on, any organization will evolve in terms of the way that it operates, the products that it produces, and so on. As the organization evolves, then so must the products. For example, an organization involved with developing mobile phones may branch out into personal electronic organizers, which would result in the processes needing to be validated once more.

- **Off-the-shelf process:** The process may be an off-the-shelf process that can be bought from a specialist company, such as the content of a book or standard or, in some cases, a shrink-wrapped product. Any predefined process will invariably not meet every requirement of any organization. Such an off-the-shelf process is an excellent *basis* for a bespoke process model but, as is the inherent nature of any bespoke system, it must be tailored to meet specialized requirements. Every organization or business unit within an organization will have its own specialized requirements. Even organizations that look on the surface as if they are very similar will have some differences and it is these differences that cause many of the headaches associated with processes. In fact, many of these off-the-shelf solution providers are very open about what their processes can and cannot do and they are, indeed, sold as a small part of an overall package that includes specialist consultancy and tailoring services provided by the vendor. The danger arises, however, when the vendor is so arrogant as to claim that their product, in its off-the-shelf form, will meet all the requirements of any potential customer organization. (Remember that this book states, quite explicitly, in Chapter 1 and in later chapters, that the process meta-model provided as the cornerstone of the book must be tailored to meet the needs of an organization – which is one of the reasons for this section.)

There is a need, therefore, to be able to tailor a process to meet changing requirements or an evolution of the organization or business. Any process that is represented by a single class in UML can be tailored very easily, as there is a basic mechanism in the UML for tailoring a class, known as *specialization*. Specializing a class, is, in effect, tailoring that class for a specific usage.

Consider a process that is defined in terms of its artefacts and activities, represented in UML by a class with attributes and operations. This process may be intended to be appropriate for a specific type of project, but what happens when the requirements change?

Figure 3.4 shows an example system design process where the artefacts and activities are represented by attributes and operations respectively. This process may very well have been used for some time within the organization and may have been used very successfully. However, what would happen if the requirements for the process were to change? For example, the requirements for producing architecture will differ quite significantly if the architecture is for a real-time system or a safety-critical system. In such cases, there is a need for additional information to be

System design
Architecture framework
Operational view
Technical view
Process view
Design document
Review record
Traceability matrix
produce architecture()
document design()
review()
check consistency()
establish traceability()

FIGURE 3.4   *Example process: 'System design'*

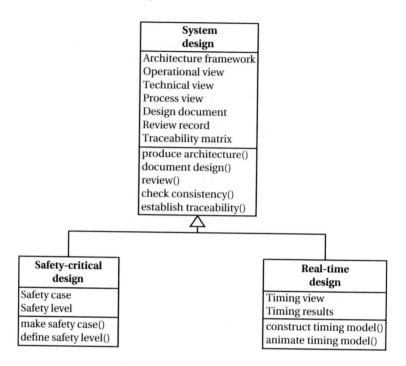

FIGURE 3.5   *Tailored processes*

added to the basic process. Maybe more artefacts are required, such as a safety case in the example of the safety-critical systems, which will also result in the definition of an additional activity to generate the safety case. The specialization mechanism in the UML allows exactly this sort of tailoring to be defined.

Figure 3.5 shows how the specialization mechanism can be used to tailor a basic process by adding in extra artefacts and activities in its tailored child class. Note that, because of the rules of inheritance, all the existing artefacts and activities for the basic 'System design' process will be inherited by the child classes of 'Safety-critical design' and 'Real-time design'. Also note that, as the behaviour of the process has been changed (more operations, hence activities, have been added), the process requires a new behavioural view to specify exactly how the new activities behave within the process.

This specialization mechanism allows any process to be tailored so that this new information can be retained within the process model.

THE PROCESS META-MODEL

The requirements for process modelling have been discussed together with how each of them may be realized using the UML. However, this is still not enough, as all this information must be brought together in a format that is of practical use for process modelling practitioners. This bringing together of different concepts and realizations results in the process meta-model. This meta-model will form the main discussion for the remainder of the book and, indeed, Chapter 4 is devoted to describing each element in detail.

The process meta-model has two main aspects:

- **The process concept view:** shows the main concepts involved with process modelling.
- **The process realization view:** shows how to realize these concepts using the UML.

Each of these views is introduced briefly below.

Figure 3.6 shows the process concept view of the process meta-model. This view shows the main concepts involved in process modelling and highlights some of the problems associated with the subject. The whole of the process meta-model is a generic model that is intended for use by almost any organization. Naturally, as with all things generic, it will not meet everyone's requirements all of the time, but will serve as a starting point for developing a bespoke meta-model for any particular industry or organization. For example, it is often the case that the terminology used here will be inappropriate, depending on the industry or organization, or that there already exists a well-known set of terms for process modelling. In many cases, although the actual words on the process meta-model change, the pattern of the meta-model (the layout of the shapes on the page) stays largely unchanged. This diagram is discussed in depth in Chapter 4.

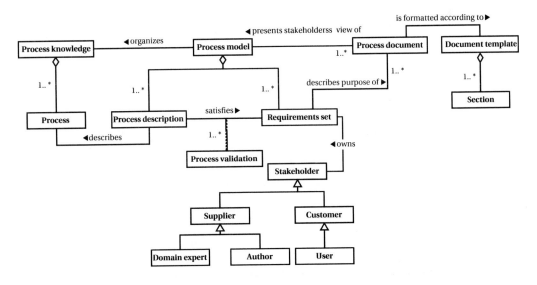

FIGURE 3.6 *Process meta-model: Process concept view*

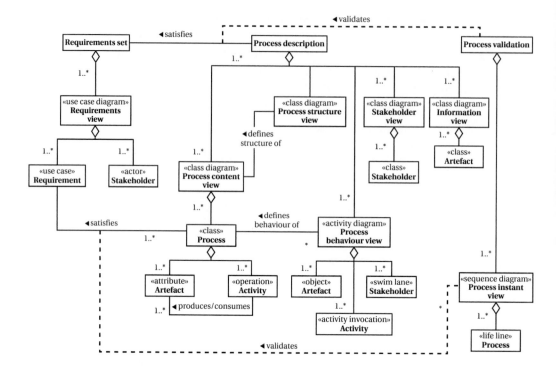

FIGURE 3.7   *Process realization view*

Figure 3.7 shows how the concepts from Figure 3.6 may be realized using the UML. Each concept has been broken down into more detail and UML modelling concepts associated with each one.

This process meta-model, when viewed in its entirety, forms a practical yet very effective tool when it comes to modelling any sort of processes in real life.

CONCLUSIONS

This chapter introduced a set of practical requirements for process modelling that must be met before a correct and robust process model can be specified. Each of these requirements may be realized by using effective modelling – in the case of this book, the modelling notation adopted is the UML. By bringing all this information together, it is possible to specify a process meta-model that not only identifies the key concepts involved with process modelling, but also specifies how each one may be realized using the UML.

Chapter 4 takes a detailed look at the process meta-model and how it can be used for practical and effective process modelling.

4 The Process Meta-Model Expanded

'Da dah, da da da dah, da da da da da-da-da-da, da da da-da-da-da-DAH-DAH'
Theme tune to *The Magnificent Seven*, UA/Mirsch-Alpha

INTRODUCTION

The secret of any card trick relies on the fact that the audience is presented with only a single view of the trick – the one that they are intended to see. What the audience does not see is the preparation, the set-up, the confederates in the crowd, the sleight-of-hand, the sneak glimpses and the general deception employed by the magician. In order to understand such a trick, it is important to look at it from many different angles, or viewpoints. The same is true of process modelling: the secret is to look at any process from a number of different views – the number being seven. The views, when combined, form the process meta-model.

The concept of the meta-model has been introduced in previous chapters and this chapter provides a full description of the process meta-model. A meta-model is, quite simply, a model of a model. Therefore, the process meta-model is a model of a model that is used for process modelling. The process meta-model itself has two views:

- **The process concept view:** shows the key concepts associated with process modelling and draws relationships between them.
- **The process realization view:** shows how the conceptual view may be realized using the modelling techniques introduced in this book. This realization view is indispensable as, among other things, it serves as a checklist when specifying and analysing processes.

The next section describes the process meta-model in more detail. The following two sections then look at ensuring consistency in a process model and give some example uses of how the meta-model may be used to add value to a process modelling exercise.

PROCESS CONCEPT VIEW

This section provides an overview of the process concept view (see Figure 4.1).

Figure 4.1 shows the process concept view. To begin with, we consider the diagram and the concepts that it conveys. These are then used as a basis for discussion.

In the top-left corner of the diagram, there is a class named 'Process knowledge' that is made up of one or more 'Process'. This process knowledge and its associated processes represent any sort of process knowledge whatsoever, in its raw form. For example, this process knowledge may be tacit knowledge inside someone's head that may need to be extracted in order to understand it properly. Otherwise, it may be written down in a book or process document. Basically, this process knowledge could be almost any sort of information relating to processes.

On the right-hand-side of the diagram, there is a class named 'Process document' and an associated class named 'Document template'. The process document class here represents the final manifestation of the process definition in some sort of document. This could be a standard, procedure or work practice, which could be a hard-copy document, electronic copy (such as a word-processing file) or some sort of web-based document. This document is formatted according to the document template, which will probably reflect some in-house or corporate style for document presentation. This document template is made up of a number of specific sections, subsections, and so on, represented on the model simply as the class 'Section'.

Between the raw process knowledge and the final, deliverable process document lies the 'Process model' and it is this process model that represents an ordered, structured and consistent representation of the process knowledge. The process document is based directly on this process model.

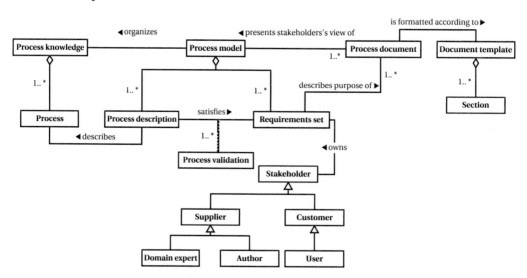

FIGURE 4.1   *Process meta-model: Process concept view*

In fact, it is possible to redraw the same diagram but, this time, to group the diagram into three main sets of information, as shown in Figure 4.2.

The main discussion point for the diagram in Figure 4.1 is the relationship or, more to the point, the lack of relationship, between the source information in the form of the process knowledge and the presentation of the output, in the form of the process document. This is the most contentious point on the diagram, but is also the most important.

Problems with processes have been discussed previously in this book, and this lack of relationship represents one of the biggest and most common of these problems. There is *no* direct relationship between the two. When there is a direct relationship, then this is where the major problems start to occur. The source information is raw, disorganized and often chaotic information contained in someone's head or in a document that exhibits the three classic 'evils of life':

- **Complexity:** as the information is unstructured, it is very easy to hide or overlook complexity. As mentioned in Chapter 3, it is the relationships between things that cause complexity.
- **Lack of understanding:** very often, the source information is poorly understood and, therefore, prone to error. Even processes that work very well are often misunderstood and, hence, not very robust to change or tailoring.
- **Poor communication:** if the process knowledge exists within someone's head, it is often very difficult for them to communicate this information to someone else, particularly if the process knowledge is something that someone does every day and has become a part of them. The same is true for written information, where badly written text can lead to problems of both complexity and lack of understanding.

The document template is often perceived as the answer to these three problems but, as is often the case, these templates can be a pain rather than a boon:

- **Complexity:** although many people see templates as a way to simplify a document, the headings are often too generic and can lead to people putting information anywhere, particularly if the information that they want to record is not a direct fit for any of the headings. Also, people will tend to be driven by the headings and simply pour all their process knowledge under each heading, rather than thinking about what they are writing.
- **Lack of understanding:** many people assume that because something is well set out (it has headings), the information is correct. By simply following a template, it is very easy for people to not think about what they are writing. One advantage of an

approach such as the meta-model approach is that it forces people to think about what they are doing and makes it far more difficult to gloss over tough issues and decisions.

- **Poor communication:** a poorly thought-out template can easily communicate the wrong information or lead to a false sense of security, as suggested in the previous two points. One common problem is that many templates are based on other templates, which results in the same information being generated for different types of artefact. It is crucial that the appropriate information is communicated by each artefact in the system.

Another key element of this diagram is the relationship between 'Process document' and the 'Requirements set' and, in particular, the numbering ratio between the two. Note that the diagram reads as: each 'Requirements set' describes the purpose of *one or more* 'Process document'. It is the 'one or more' that is of specific interest here. It is quite often the case where different process documents, for example, standards, are produced based on the same information. Bear in mind that the diagram also says that the 'Process document' presents a stakeholder's view of the 'Process model', which means that each stakeholder has their own view on the process model. Imagine, for example, a process model that describes the processes involved with using a rail system. Although it is a single system, the processes for, say, a passenger compared to those of a driver will be completely different. Therefore, the same set of processes in the 'Process description' may represent a completely different 'Requirements set' for each stakeholder. Therefore, it is possible for a single process model to be realized in a number of process documents that, although based on the same source information, will represent a different stakeholder's point of view.

Figure 4.2 shows exactly the same information as Figure 4.1, except, this time, the information has been grouped into three main headings:

- **Source:** represents any raw process information. This knowledge may be in someone's head or documented, for example, in the form of a standard.
- **Understanding:** a grouping that represents the model of all the process knowledge and forms the basis for the final document.
- **Presentation:** a grouping that represents the final presentation of the process model, such as a standard, a procedure, and so on. Chapter 8 discusses presentation in more detail and considers the use of several different notations.

Therefore, to summarize, the 'Source' information is the raw process knowledge, the 'Understanding' represents the ordered, structured and consistent model of this information and, finally, the 'Presentation' represents the final manifestation of the process knowledge.

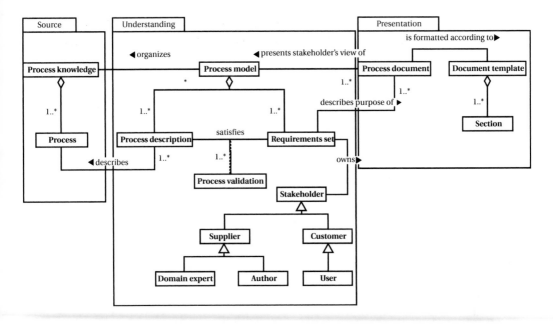

FIGURE 4.2 *Process concept view with groupings*

The 'Source' information is out there in the real world and can be obtained from any number of sources. The 'Presentation information' is the intended output of a process generation exercise, whereas the 'Understanding' forms the focus of this book. This 'Understanding' information, in the form of the process meta-model, is expanded upon in subsequent sections of this chapter.

PROCESS REALIZATION VIEW

This section introduces the process realization view and describes each of its part in detail. An example is used throughout to illustrate what each of the different views should look like. Also, of critical importance is the concept of consistency between the different views and this is dealt with in the next section. Following this, a discussion on the uses of this meta-model is presented together with some typical scenarios that demonstrate practical uses for these techniques.

The process realization view shows how the information introduced by the process concept view may be modelled using the UML. This section looks at each of the main elements of the process model in more detail. This is then related to the UML and the different elements of the language that may be used for each part of the realization view.

Figure 4.3 shows the process realization view, in which the main elements of the process model introduced in Figure 4.1 are broken down into further detail. In this diagram, a new modelling element has

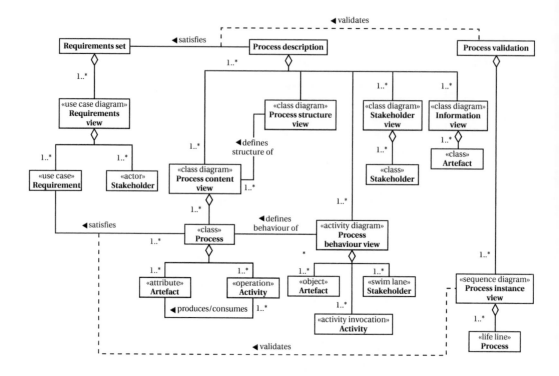

FIGURE 4.3   *Process realization view*

been introduced – that of UML *stereotypes*. A stereotype is a way of tailoring the UML language for a particular application; in this case the language has been tailored to relate UML concepts to the process modelling concepts. Any class that has words written above it in chevrons <<>> is not a regular UML class, but is known as a UML stereotype. In Figure 4.3, whenever there is a class name with a word in chevrons written above it, the word in chevrons represents the element of the UML language used to realize the concept represented by the class. For example, the concept of a 'Requirements view' (indicated by the class 'Requirements view') is realized in UML using a use case diagram (indicated by <<use case diagram>>). Of course, other notations may be used (as discussed in Chapter 8) but for the purposes of this book, the UML is the chosen notation.

   A complete set of these views is required for a full specification of any process – the omission of any single view can lead to problems. There are some situations where not all views are required, but these situations usually relate to process models that are deliberately incomplete. For example, most international standards will specify 'what' to do, but not 'how'. This results in a subset of the views being produced with an emphasis on structure rather than behaviour. However, even in situations such as these, it is still often the case that all views, including the behavioural views, need to be considered in order to get the subset of the views correct. This is discussed in more detail later in this chapter.

There are seven views in the process meta-model: the requirements view, the process structure view, the process content view, the stakeholder view, the information view, the process instance view and the process behaviour view. Each of these views is now discussed in more detail.

THE SEVEN VIEWS OF THE META-MODEL

The requirements view

The requirements view specifies the overall aims of the process document and is realized, in the UML, by a use case diagram. It is possible to have a number of different requirements views for a single process model, depending on the number of stakeholders involved. Typically, each process document is aimed at a particular set of stakeholders and each one of these stakeholder sets has its own requirements set. Theoretically, it is possible for every stakeholder in the system to have their own process document, written specifically for them, but this is impractical in terms of the sheer number of process documents required, so the process documents are almost always geared towards groups of stakeholders, rather than individuals.

The requirements view is also very important as it forms the basis for validating each process. It is quite often the case that a set of processes is defined that is fully verified, but that is not validated. The difference between the two is defined, for the purposes of this book, as follows:

- **Process verification:** concerned with ensuring that the process works properly – that it is correct, consistent and will respond to a set of inputs in a predictable fashion.
- **Process validation:** more subtle than process verification, as process validation asks whether the process actually achieves what it is supposed to. It is perfectly possible for a process model to be correct and working (verified) but not to meet the requirements for the process model, in which case the process model is useless.

It is the requirements view that provides an understanding of exactly why the process model is needed in the first place. If the requirements for the process model are not known, then how on earth can a process model be validated? The answer, of course, is that validation is impossible without an understanding of what the requirements are.

One of the features of a robust process model is its ability to remain valid over a long period of time. In order to do this, the process model must evolve to react to the changing environment in which it lives. As time goes on, changes will occur in the surrounding environment, so it is important that this can be captured in some way, and it is the requirements view that achieves this. Examples of changes include:

- **Changes in related process models:** invariably, a process model does not exist in isolation and has to co-exist with a number of other process models, such as related standards, procedures, and so on. It is quite possible, and, indeed, quite common, for these external process models to change in some way and to render elements of the actual process model redundant, incorrect or simply out of date.
- **Changes in the business:** businesses are living entities and, as such, are subject to change due to any number of factors, such as technology changes, best practice changes, new business areas opening up, automation of production, and so on. As the business evolves, then so must the process model to reflect this.

These changes are nothing new but, in many instances, they often go unnoticed as the process model still functions in a correct fashion, but it can no longer meet its new requirements. This is analogous to verification and validation:

- *Verification* means that something works correctly and without problems. Clearly, it is important that any process model can be verified.
- *Validation* means that something does what it is supposed to do or, to put it another way, that it meets its requirements. Clearly, it is also important that any process model can be validated.

It is the combination of these two, however, that delivers a good process model, as it is quite common for a process model to be verified and validated when it is first defined. However, as time goes on, the requirements change, as discussed above, which leads to a non-validated, yet still verified process model. It is the fact that the process model remains verified that leads to complacency. Therefore, it is crucial that any process model is continuously assessed on a regular basis, maybe once or twice per year, in order to make sure that the requirements for the process model are still accurate and that the process model itself can be validated against these requirements.

The requirements view, therefore, is essential for ensuring that the process model is correct and can be validated over a period of time, and that it evolves to reflect any changes in the environment.

Figure 4.4 shows an example requirements view for an invoicing process. The main requirements for the view are shown visually by the use cases and the related stakeholders are shown by actors outside the boundary of the system. Each time there is a relationship identified between a use case and one or more stakeholders this signifies that an interface exists between the process and the stakeholders.

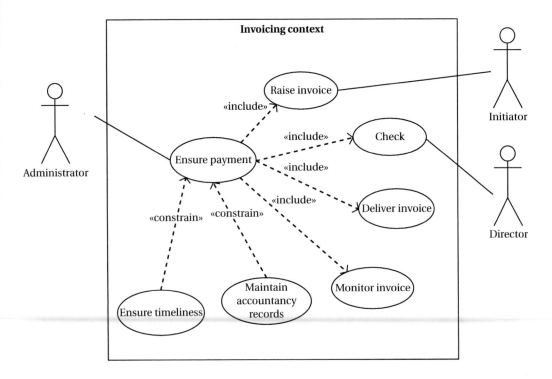

FIGURE 4.4   *Example requirements view for an invoicing process*

In this example, the main requirement is to 'Ensure payment', which includes four lower-level requirements:

- 'Raise invoice', which represents generating the invoice.
- 'Check', which represents the requirement for ensuring that all the invoice details are correct – bearing in mind that incorrect invoices do not get paid.
- 'Deliver invoice', which represents the requirement for making sure that the invoice gets to the right person and place.
- 'Monitor invoice', which represents the requirement for continuously checking the progress of the invoice through the customer's invoicing process.

Note that there are also two large constraints on the main requirement, which are:

- 'Ensure timeliness', which makes sure that invoices are paid on time.
- 'Maintain accountancy records', which restricts the main requirement in that however the requirements are met, there must be an established audit trail.

Consider now how these requirements may change over time. For example, an additional constraint may be added that relates to using a particular accountancy methodology (such as accrual or pre-payment accounting for VAT) or tool. Requirements may also change because of problems or ambiguities with the current process. For example, it may become an issue that the checking requirement needs to be carried out by someone independent of creating the invoice, or maybe specifically someone at, say, director level. All of these subtleties must be built into the requirements view if they are major concerns for the process.

To summarize, there must always be a requirements view for a process. A process without any defined requirements may be verified but will *never be validated.* It is usually the case, rather annoyingly, that the requirements view has not even been considered for the purposes of process modelling.

The process structure view

The process structure view shows a high-level representation of the basic structure of, and the terminology used throughout, the process and is realized using a class diagram. This view only needs to be generated once and then it will dictate the basic structure of all the subsequent processes.

Typical decisions that need to be made here include obtaining a consensus on the terminology to be used throughout the project and identifying the high-level classifications, or groupings, of processes.

This view is very useful for mapping between different process models at a high level, resulting in a basic correlation between the terminology used between process models, which can be invaluable when it comes to audits and assessments. This is explored fully in Chapter 5, which is concerned with process mapping and metrics.

The process structure view is realized using a class diagram in the UML, with each class representing one of the main concepts within the standard, an example of which is shown in Figure 4.5.

Figure 4.5 shows a simple process structure view that defines the key terminology to be used in the example process model. It can be seen that the 'Process model' is made up of four 'Process group', each of which is made up of one or more 'Process'. Each 'Process' is made up of one or more 'Artefact', one or more 'Activity' and one or more 'Role'. Furthermore, each 'Role' is responsible for one or more 'Activity' and each 'Activity' produces/consumes one or more 'Artefact'.

Therefore, the basic terminology, together with the relationships between the terms has been identified and can be used as the basis for the process model glossary. This is the terminology that will be used throughout this book, as the view has already contributed to the understanding of process modelling.

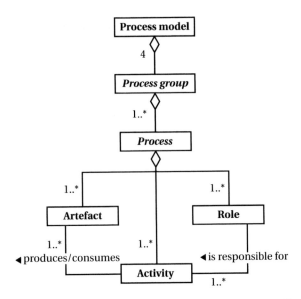

FIGURE 4.5   *Simple process structure view*

It is also possible to add more detail to this view; for example, Figure 4.5 identifies four different types of 'Process group' but there is no indication of what these groups are. Therefore, a more detailed view may be produced.

Figure 4.6 shows a more detailed process structure view, this time with the additional definitions concerning the process groups. In this view, the four types of process group are identified as: 'Enterprise', 'Project', 'Technical' and 'Agreement'. The structure of each of these process groups

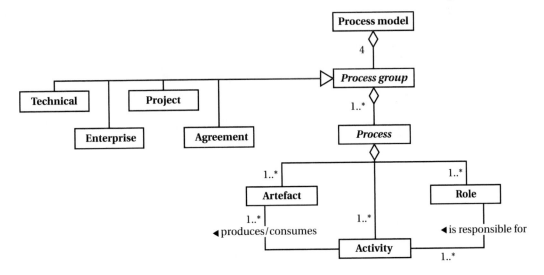

FIGURE 4.6   *More detailed process structure view, highlighting types of 'Process group'*

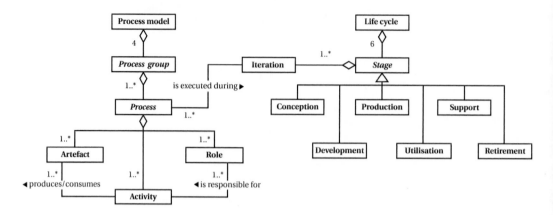

FIGURE 4.7 *More detailed process structure view, highlighting life cycle concepts*

is the same – they all inherit the structure of each 'Process group' and hence each is made up of one or more 'Process', and so on.

It is also possible and, in most cases, desirable to expand the process structure view to include life cycle concepts. Figure 4.7 shows a more detailed process structure view that, this time, has been expanded to include life cycle concepts. It can be seen from this view that there is a concept of a 'Life cycle' that is made up of six types of 'Stage'. These types are identified as: 'Conception', 'Development', 'Construction', 'Transition', 'Operations' and 'Retirement'. Each of these stages is made up of one or more 'Iteration'. It is this iteration that provides the link between the process model and the life cycle concepts, as one or more 'Process' is executed over each 'Stage'.

The types of process group have not been shown in Figure 4.7, purely to make the diagram easier to read. Indeed, although it is possible to amalgamate Figures 4.6 and 4.7 into a single diagram, it is often easier to communicate this information by splitting the diagram into two, or three, smaller views that are consistent with one another.

In some cases, the process structure view can be relatively simple, yet in others the view can be quite complex. As an example of this, the model in Figure 4.8 shows the process structure view for the Welsh National Curriculum which is the standard for education in Wales. This process structure view contains many concepts and is, in comparison to Figure 4.5, relatively complex.

It is interesting to note that, in the UK, there exist several standards for school education, all of which fall under the banner of the *National Curriculum* but each of which has a slight difference in content. For example, in Wales, there is a subject order for learning the Welsh language, which does not exist in the English version of the standard, but that is in the *content* of the standard rather than the structure of the standard, as illustrated in Figure 4.8. In fact, the process structure view for

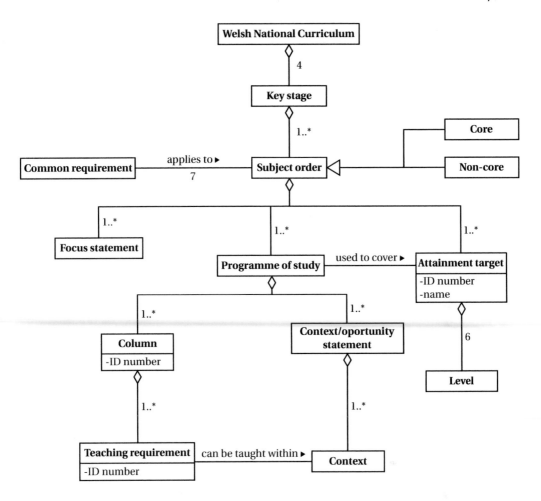

FIGURE 4.8   *Process structure view for the Welsh National Curriculum*

both variations on the standard are *identical,* except for the name of the standard itself. The ability to be able to compare and contrast different standards from different view points, using the meta-model, can be quite revealing and is a very powerful analysis technique.

There is another reason why this view is particularly powerful that is not immediately apparent from looking at Figures 4.5, 4.6 and 4.7 and this is the concept of hidden complexity. When a process model is defined without a process structure view, it is very easy to over-decompose processes. To illustrate this, consider Figure 4.9, which shows a process structure view that has the potential to lead to many problems within the process model. The main reason for this is that this model shows the situation where it is possible to decompose a process into a number of subprocesses and there is no limit on the number of decompositions that may occur. The process structure is the same as the one in Figure 4.5 until the 'Process' itself is defined. Whereas previously the process had been

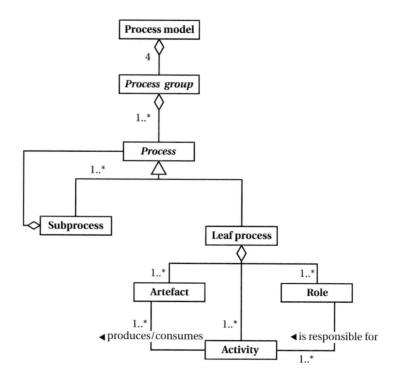

FIGURE 4.9 *Example of a potentially dangerous process structure view*

defined as being made up of one or more 'Artefact', 'Activity' and 'Role', in this view a process has two types:

- A 'Subprocess', which can be made up of one or more 'Process', which allows a process to be decomposed into another level of detail, which may then be decomposed into another level of detail which, in turn, may be decomposed into another level, and so on.
- A 'Leaf process', which is the lowest level of decomposition permitted in this structure and, hence, is made up of one or more 'Artefact', one or more 'Activity' and one or more 'Role'.

The danger exists here because it is possible to have one set of processes that can be decomposed over many, many levels, whereas other processes are not. This unevenness of the process decomposition often leads to an imbalance of the process model and can lead to processes either being too high level or overly detailed. A possible solution, in this case, would be to impose restrictions on the number of levels permitted that would avoid this problem. This process structure is redeemable, although potentially dangerous, whereas the example in Figure 4.10 is simply downright dangerous.

Notice that the difference between Figure 4.10 and Figure 4.9 is simply where the definition of the artefacts, activities and roles lies. In this case,

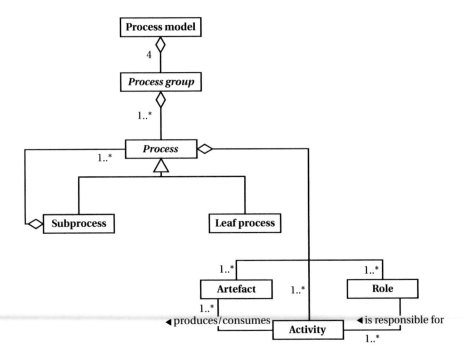

FIGURE 4.10   *Example of a dangerous process structure view*

it is possible to define roles, artefacts and activities for a subprocess as well as a leaf process – as the structure of the class 'Process' is inherited to both 'Subprocess' and 'Leaf process'. This leads to the very real possibility that a subprocess may be defined in terms of its activities and artefacts and *in addition to this specification* the subprocess may then be further decomposed into many other nested levels of process definition. This is a surprisingly common mistake to make and all but destroys any consistency in a process model.

When defining a process structure view, it is essential to think about how many levels of nesting or decomposition are required and then to specify this explicitly in this view. Like the stakeholder view, the process structure view is often omitted which means that there can be no confidence in the consistency of the model. Indeed, it will be seen in Chapter 7 that the process structure view is analogous to the ontology in the world of enterprise architecture, which is essential for modelling enterprises.

The process content view

The process content view shows the actual content, in terms of activities and artefacts, by representing each process as a single class. Due to the large number of processes within an organization, it is usual to produce a process content view for each classification, or process grouping, from the process structure view. Consider, for instance, the example that was used in Figure 4.6 that identified four types of process category. In this case, it is far more practical to produce four process content views – one for each process category – rather than trying to fit all processes onto a single diagram.

The process content view is realized in UML by a class diagram, and is very closely related to the process structure view in that it is the process content view that shows the *actual* activities and artefacts (adopting the terminology from Figure 4.5) exhibited by each process. Each process has a class to represent it and the process artefacts are represented by class attributes, whereas the process activities are represented by class operations. An example of this is shown in Figure 4.11.

Figure 4.11 shows an example of a process expressed in the notation described above. In this view, the process to be described is called 'Meeting logistics' and is intended to describe the set-up and running of a meeting within an organization. The name of the process is expressed as the name of the class. There are five artefacts for this process, each one represented as an attribute on the class 'Meeting logistics'. There are also nine activities for this process, each indicated by an operation.

By adopting this presentation style, it is possible to represent an entire process by a single class, while showing all of its artefacts and activities. This notation is not only simple and concise, but also allows an idea of the complexity of each process to be ascertained, albeit at a very high level, simply by looking at the number of attributes and operations and the ratio of their numbers. Consider the processes described in Figure 4.12, which shows a more-populated process content view showing the higher-level framework of the process model that has been abstracted from the

Meeting logistics
Minutes Outcome info Invitation Agenda Outcome
define outcomes() identify attendees() invite() set environment() greet() execute meeting() close meeting() record minutes() reset environment()

FIGURE 4.11   *Process content view: Example process*

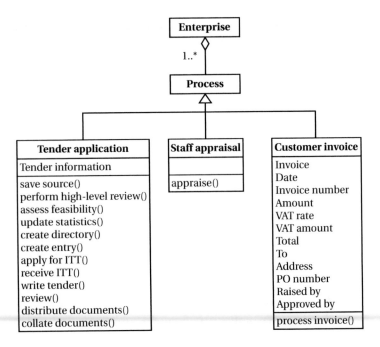

FIGURE 4.12   *Process content view: Warning signs*

process structure view. The process group 'Enterprise' is made up of a number of processes, three of which are: 'Tender application', 'Staff appraisal' and 'Customer invoice'.

An ideal, well-balanced process should contain about seven attributes and operations. This is because the number of things that a human can remember at any one time is defined as seven, plus or minus two – quite by coincidence, this is also the number of views in the process meta-model. Bearing this simple rule in mind, there are a number of issues with the three processes presented here:

- **Too many activities:** if a process exists with far more than nine (seven plus two) activities, such as the 'Tender application' process in Figure 4.12, the chance of someone being able to understand this process begins to diminish as the number of activities increases. There are simply too many steps involved in this task, which will, potentially, lead to complexity when the process is executed (this is discussed in more detail below in 'The process behaviour view'). This high number could be due to the fact that the activities represent very small steps of activity, which means that the level of granularity of the activities should be changed so that fewer activities represent the same behaviour. This high number could also be due to the fact that there is simply too much going on in this single process, and maybe the process should be broken down into two or more simpler processes that describe the same behaviour. Which of these two reasons is the cause will become more apparent when we examine another view – the process behaviour view – for this process.

- **Too many artefacts:** the same principles can be applied when the number of artefacts, represented by attributes, is excessive. An excessive number of artefacts (represented by attributes) may be due to the fact that the individual artefacts are too detailed and that the level of granularity of information needs to be raised. For example, in the 'Customer invoice' process, many of the attributes could be represented by a single artefact, which would decrease the number of overall artefacts.

- **Too few activities:** the situation where the number of activities defined is very low, typically one or two, can mean one of three things. First, the activities are identified at a very high level. In the example in Figure 4.12, the 'Customer invoice' process has a single activity identified named 'Process invoice'. This is practically useless as it does not convey enough information about the steps involved in processing the invoice – it would be just as easy to write 'execute process' as the activity name in all processes and hence make the whole model far simpler. Second, the process itself may be too detailed and may need to be abstracted into another, related process. The third possibility is, of course, that the diagram is correct, but this is quite unlikely, bearing in mind the first two possibilities.

- **Too few artefacts:** following on from the previous point, too few artefacts result in exactly the same problems but, this time, the danger lies in over-simplifying the artefacts of the process. For example, the end result of the 'Customer invoice' process is a single invoice with a number of details, but this could be represented as a single artefact named 'Invoice' and the diagram greatly simplified. However, in this case, the process has become so simplified and over-abstracted that it is no longer adding value to the process model and, hence, the organizational knowledge.

- **No activities or no artefacts:** if the situation arises where the number of artefacts or the number of activities is zero, alarm bells should start to go off immediately. This is wrong. Consider the situation where activities exist, yet there are no artefacts. In this case it means that it is impossible to demonstrate that a process has been executed – there is no evidence identified for any of its activity execution. Also, consider the situation where there are artefacts but no activities – where do the artefacts come from? It may be that the artefacts are part of a data store, in which case the owner class is not a process, but some sort of *storage element*. It should be noted here that it is possible to have a process grouping or classification in UML that has neither artefacts nor activities but, again, this is not a process as such.

- **Out of balance ratio:** considering the ratio of the artefacts to activities on the class is a quick, yet often accurate way to judge how well balanced a process is. Although there are no hard rules for this, an ideal process should have between five and nine of both artefacts and activities. It is also possible to gain an appreciation of how well thought-out a process is by looking at the ratio.

The process content view encapsulates all of the processes that exist within the process model and, therefore, gives a good overview of the scope of the capability of an organization in the various process groups. The process content view may be thought of as a library of processes that are available for the business.

The process behaviour view

The process content view identifies all the processes of interest for a system. For each of these processes, the activities and artefacts are also identified. In terms of modelling, the process content view is a structural view of the process and, therefore, there must be a corresponding behavioural aspect of the model. One of the views in the behavioural aspect of the model is the process behaviour view, which describes the behaviour, or the *how*, of a single process. Remembering the rules of UML, any class that exhibits behaviour (has operations) must have an activity diagram to describe its behaviour. As the process content view has already identified a number of processes that are represented as classes, and each of theses classes has at least one operation, then it follows that each of these classes must have an associated behavioural view. This means that each process from the process content view will have a process behaviour view associated with it – this relationship can be seen in Figure 4.3.

Each process behaviour view is realized in UML by an activity diagram that describes the behaviour of a single class or, in this context, a process. The activity diagram is made up of a number of elements, three of which are directly related to other parts of the meta-model:

- **The activity invocation:** represented by a sausage shape, this represents an activity from the process model, when using the terminology defined in Figure 4.5.
- **The object:** represented either by a box or by simple text, this represents an artefact.
- **The swim lane:** represented by two parallel lines and a label, this represents a role.

The activity diagram shows the order or execution of the activity invocations, together with any logical conditions associated with this order.

It also shows the information flow, represented by the production and consumption of artefacts, around the flow of activity. Finally, the responsibility for each activity can be shown by using swim lanes that correspond to roles.

Figure 4.13 shows an example of a process behaviour view, in this case the one for the 'Meeting logistics' process shown in Figure 4.11. In this example, there are four swim lanes that represent the four responsible roles for this process. Each swim lane is responsible for the activities contained within it and the general flow of execution is shown by the order of execution of these activities.

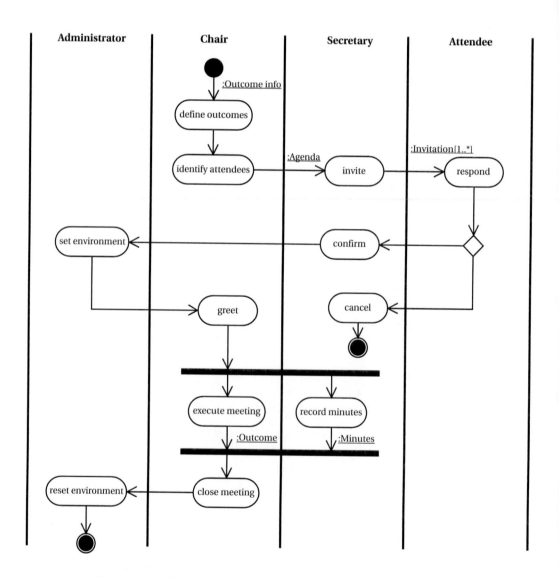

FIGURE 4.13 *Process behaviour view for the 'Meeting logistics' process*

The process behaviour view should be as simple as possible while still adding value to the process model. There are a few warning signs to look out for, however:

- **A single swim lane:** although this is certainly possible, it can often be an indication that the role identified is either the name of a person (rather than the stakeholder role name) who holds many roles, or that the role has been taken from too high in the hierarchy of the stakeholder view.

- **Too many possible execution paths:** remembering that complexity manifests itself through relationships rather than the nodes in the diagram, a diagram that is too messy or looks like a spider's web, should be avoided. In many cases this is the sign of a poorly understood or uncontrolled process. Bear in mind that some structure should exist within the process, so having every activity invocation related to every other one is needless.

- **Single execution path:** some processes are truly linear in their behaviour with no possible deviation from the single thread of execution defined. Although this is possible, it is very unlikely in all but the most trivial of processes. Bear in mind that many processes will have at least one decision point involved – certainly any process that contains any sort of review, checking or testing activity will have at least two possible outcomes in each case. Where this is the case, there will be different paths of execution and iterations.

It is also possible to show any other roles that are involved, yet not responsible. This is done by showing participating roles in the activity invocation in brackets – for example '(Project manager)' – or may even be indicated by an actor (a stick person) with an association to the relevant activity invocation.

The information view

The information view is concerned with identifying the key artefacts from the system and then identifying their inter-relationships. This viewpoint is crucial for two main reasons:

- **Inter-process consistency:** a large part of the complexity involved with process models is derived from the interactions between the processes, rather than the internal working of each process. In order to make sure that processes are compatible (for example, that their respective inputs and outputs match up), it is vital to have an understanding of both the main artefacts of the processes and their inter-relationships.

- **Process automation:** if the process model is going to be used at a practical level by a group, or several groups, of people, then process automation is a point worth considering. In order to automate processes, it is important to understand what each artefact looks like (maybe a template will be defined for each one) and how these artefacts relate to one another. In fact, very often it is individual parts of each artefact that relate to other parts of artefacts, rather than the entire artefacts relating to one another.

The information view in Figure 4.14 may be modelled at several levels of abstraction in order to represent the elements and their inter-relationships, and also the individual structure of each artefact. The information view forms the basis for all traceability checking which is essential for quality assurance purposes for any business.

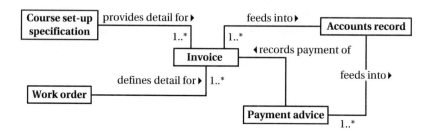

FIGURE 4.14   *Example information view showing relationships between artefacts*

The stakeholder view

The stakeholder view represents a simple classification of the different types of stakeholder roles that are involved with the process. The stakeholder view is realized in UML with a class diagram, with each stakeholder being represented by a single class.

It is typical for a single stakeholder view to be drawn up that represents many or, in some cases, all stakeholders in an organization, rather than creating one on a project-by-project basis. This is a tremendous help when it comes to trying to get an idea of the 'big picture' of an organization and can be invaluable when it comes to making sure that processes are consistent with one another.

The biggest mistake made by people when defining stakeholders is that they refer to stakeholders by individual names, such as the name of a person or an organization. It is the *role* of the person or organization, rather than the actual name that is of interest from the modelling point of view. There are several reasons for this:

- **Multiple roles:** it is possible and, indeed, very common for a single person to have more than one role. Consider the roles taken on by any single person in an organization and, in the vast majority of cases, each person will play more than one role. This is important as the roles played by an organization, for example, can be vastly different, yet have the same name associated with them.

- **Multiple names:** it is equally common for a single role to have many names associated with it. In some cases, particularly when it comes to users of a system, there can be millions of names associated with a single role.
- **Robustness:** by thinking of roles, rather than names, a model that is robust towards change is generated. Imagine how unmanageable the model would be if, every time that the name associated with a role changed, the model had to be changed. Not only is this impractical simply from people moving jobs (particularly in large organizations) but it is also possible that the number of names associated with a single role will increase as the project progresses through the development life cycle.

Therefore, always think of the role, rather than names when looking at stakeholders.

When generating a list of stakeholders, it is very easy to get things wrong for two totally different reasons. The first reason is that, invariably, if you were to write down a list of stakeholders associated with a process, there would be some missing. On the other hand, there will also be some stakeholders on the list who are not involved at all with the project. The only way to have any confidence that the stakeholder list is correct is to look at how and when the stakeholders occur on the different views of the process meta-model – a task that is straightforward, thanks to the diagram in Figure 4.3.

It is also difficult to know where to start thinking about stakeholders. Therefore, consider the very simple generic stakeholder view shown in Figure 4.15, which forces you to start thinking about the roles involved with a process or set of processes. Although this diagram will not be correct for many systems, it can serve as a good thought-provoker when initially considering a set of stakeholders.

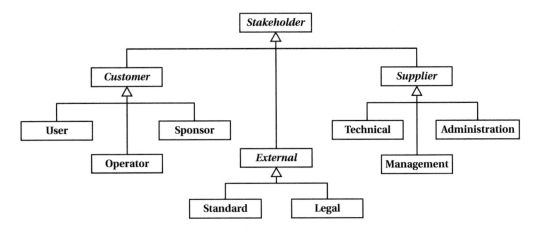

Figure 4.15 *Generic stakeholder view*

There are three main types of 'Stakeholder' in Figure 4.15: 'Customer', 'External' and 'Supplier'. This three-way split is typical for many systems and can be a very good place to start thinking.

Three main 'Customer' stakeholder roles are identified here:

- 'User', which represents all the end users of a system. In the case of a transport system, this role would represent the passengers and, hence, there may be millions of names associated with this role. Likewise, in a healthcare system, this role would represent the actual patients who are receiving treatment.
- 'Operator', which represents the people who will be configuring, controlling and operating the system. In the case of the transport system, this role would cover a range of roles from ticket sales, to driving the vehicles, to controlling the position of vehicles, route planning, and so on. In the case of the healthcare system, this role would again cover a number of other roles including doctors, nurses, surgeons, administrators, and so on.
- 'Sponsor', which represents whoever is providing the financial backing for the system. In the case of the transport system, this may be government related, private or some combination of the two. Similarly, the healthcare system may have a number of different names associated with it.

Two main 'External' roles are identified here:

- 'Standard', which represents standards and standards bodies that may constrain the development and operations of a system in some way. This may relate to safety standards, security, and so on.
- 'Legal', which relates to legal roles that may impact the system in some way, for example, data protection laws, health and safety legislation.

Three main 'Supplier' roles are identified here:

- 'Technical', which represents technical roles such as engineers, scientists and technicians.
- 'Management', which includes all management-related roles, such as project managers, risk managers and configuration managers.
- 'Administration', which includes all administrative or support roles, such as secretaries, administrators, accountants and personnel staff.

There is also a natural link here to traditional organizational charts that, although not within the scope of this book, can form a valuable input for the stakeholders and a good source for validation of the roles that have been identified.

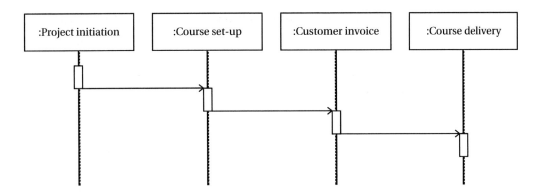

FIGURE 4.16 *Process instance view*

The process instance view

The process instance view comprises a set of diagrams that provides the main validation for the process model. It is the process instance view that relates the actual processes that are specified back to the source requirements and validates that each requirement has been met. The basic elements of the process instance view are executions of (or instances of) individual processes. For each requirement from the requirements view, it should be possible to execute a number of processes in a particular sequence in order to validate that requirement.

The process instance view is realized by a sequence diagram in the UML, with the main elements being executions of processes, represented in UML by life lines. Each life line represents a single, or group of, instances of a UML class or actor. Each life line has a dashed line below it that represents time, on which can be drawn one or more 'focus of control' that shows when the life line is active (i.e. doing something).

Figure 4.16 shows a simple sequence diagram. The life lines that go across the top of the diagram represent executions of individual instances of processes. The lines between show the flow of control between processes and can also be used to show any information flow of message passing. The process instance view allows different scenarios to be explored for each requirement from the requirements view. A scenario allows the exploration of different outcomes for a particular requirement in the form of 'what if' type considerations.

This completes the discussion on the seven views of the process meta-model. The remainder of the chapter focuses on how to use the process meta-model effectively.

CONSISTENCY BETWEEN VIEWS

Consistency is the key to a good model – a model without consistency is simply a collection of drawings. It is impossible to have any degree of confidence in a process model that is inconsistent, as it is important that all the different views of the process model match with one another and, with the aid of the process meta-model, this is very straightforward. There are two main types of consistency checks to apply: structural checks and mechanical checks.

Structural checks may be applied based on the structure or pattern of the meta-model, particularly with respect to their relationships. Many of these checks can be identified based on the relationships in the meta-model.

Table 4.1 shows the specific structural consistency checks that should be applied that are based on the main associations in the process meta-model.

Mechanical checks involve selecting an element from the actual process model, identifying its corresponding class on the meta-model, and then looking for other occurrences of this class name on the meta-model. For example, consider the case where you need to apply consistency checks to stakeholders in the stakeholder view. First of all, look to the meta-model and find the class named 'Stakeholder' in the 'Stakeholder view'. The diagram indicates that the 'Stakeholder' in the 'Stakeholder view' is realized by a <<class>> in UML. Now, it is simply a matter of looking for other occurrences of stakeholder on the meta-model, which can be seen to be in the 'Process content view', where a 'Stakeholder' is realized by a <<Life line>>, and in the 'Requirements view', where a 'Stakeholder' is realized by an <<Actor>> in UML.

TABLE 4.1   *Structural consistency checks*

Check description	Meta-model reference
View check. Do all the views exist?	All classes that describe diagrams, for example: 'Information view' is realized by a <<class diagram>>
Process behaviour check. Does each process in the process content view have its behaviour defined?	'Process behaviour view' defines behaviour of each 'Process'
Is each requirement validated? Does each requirement have at least one scenario defined to ensure that the requirement is met?	'Process instance view' validates each 'Requirement'

Table 4.2 shows the specific mechanical checks that should be applied, based on the common elements within the process meta-model. In order to use this table, select two views that need to be made consistent, for example those in Figures 4.11 and 4.13, which define the process content view and the process behaviour view for the 'Meeting logistics' process. In order to check the consistency of these two views, use Table 4.2 to look at

TABLE 4.2   *Mechanical consistency checks*

Concept	View	Realized in UML by
Stakeholder	Requirements view	<<actor>>
	Process behaviour view	<<swim lane>>
	Stakeholder view	<<class>>
Activity	Process structure view	<<class>>
	Process content view	<<operation>>
	Process behaviour view	<<activity invocation>>
Artefact	Process structure view	<<class>>
	Process behaviour view	<<object>>
	Process content view	<<attribute>>
	Information view	<<class>>
Process	Process structure view	<<class>>
	Process content view	<<class>>
	Process instance view	<<life line>>

the different elements of the diagram and how they relate to elements on its corresponding view. In this example, Figure 4.11, which is a class diagram, and Figure 4.13, which is an activity diagram, share the two terms 'Artefact' and 'Activity' from the meta-model. By looking these two terms up in Table 4.2 we can see that an 'Artefact' is an 'Object' in the process behaviour view and an 'Attribute' in the process content view. The same approach applies to the activity. By applying these simple mechanical checks, it becomes immediately apparent that the two views are actually inconsistent – something that needs to be remedied as soon as possible.

USING THE META-MODEL

Now that the meta-model has been defined, there are a number of ways that it can be used to add value to any process modelling exercise. This section introduces several different scenarios that explain how the process meta-model may be used and then discusses the advantages of its use for each scenario. This is not intended to be an exhaustive list of possible scenarios, but presents a good spread that illustrates the flexibility of the meta-model itself.

Analysing existing processes

In many cases, it is desirable to look at and analyse an existing process model. Some possible reasons for wanting to do this include:

- **As part of a process improvement exercise:** a process model is a living entity and, as such, it needs to be constantly monitored and, where necessary, changed and improved. This is such an important topic, that it has been given its own section heading.

- **To identify the causes of failure in the process:** it is relatively easy to simply define a process, but rather more difficult to ensure that it is an accurate reflection of real life and that it is effective. Therefore, these modelling techniques can be used to capture and analyse existing processes. This is particularly effective when trying to understand why something has gone wrong and can be a very powerful tool for examining the causes of failures and disasters. A key part of this is identifying which process has failed in some way, resulting in the system failure. Once the process causing the problem has been identified, it is then possible to look closer at the causes of the failure. It may be, for example, that the process itself is at fault and contains logical errors. A very common error is to miss off a feedback loop after a decision branch, such as after a review or similar activity. It may also be the case that the definition of the artefacts is inadequate and has led to the system failure. For example, perhaps not enough information has been recorded in an artefact or the wrong type of information has been recorded. Of course, another option is that the single process itself is not to blame, but that the process has not been executed properly or effectively, in which case the exercise could lead to the identification of another process, perhaps related to checking or monitoring that would prevent this type of failure recurring.
- **To gain an appreciation of an undocumented or complex process model:** in many cases, processes are represented as text descriptions, which can be very long and verbose. In such cases, it is desirable to have a simplified version of the process description so that an appreciation of how the process fits together and works can be gained. This is particularly powerful for looking at standards, processes and procedures that are out of the control of the actual organization, such as mandated standards and government initiatives.
- **As part of an audit or assessment:** when carrying out any sort of process-based audit or assessment, it is crucial to have an under standing of both the process under review and the standard to which the process is being audited or assessed. This is actually a powerful combination of the first two points in this section – the standard being audited must be modelled to gain an appreciation and the standard being audited against must also be modelled. Of course, once these source standards have been modelled once, they can be reused as often as desired and mapped onto other standards, which increases the added value of the modelling many times.

In terms of how the meta-model would be used for the previous points, Figure 4.17 shows an example scenario that represents the order of

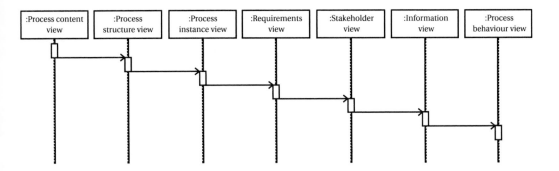

FIGURE 4.17   *Example scenario: Analysing existing processes*

creation of the seven views when analysing an existing process model. The first view that is created is the process content view as, in cases where a process model exists and is well documented, this is often the easiest view to construct first. The process content view may then be used as a basis for abstracting the process structure view, as the structure can be most easily extracted from existing content. The next view to be created is the process instance view as, in many cases, examples of scenarios are given as part of the process description. From the process content view for the process model and the process instance view it is then possible to abstract right back up to the top-level requirements view. A natural progression from the requirements view and the process instance view is the stakeholder view, as many of the stakeholders will have been identified between each of these two views. The artefacts of the process model that have been identified from the process content view, and the information flow in the process instance view can now form the basis of the information view. Finally, the process behaviour views may be extracted from the low-level process descriptions.

Creating a new process document from scratch

In some cases, such as the start of a new business or perhaps the creation of a brand new process description for an impending audit or assessment, it is desirable to start a process description from scratch with, in effect, a blank sheet of paper. Although this situation does not occur very often in real-life industry, it is a very good exercise to get the feel for process modelling, whether it is to understand the how the modelling works or, indeed, to understand process models in the first place.

The generation of information in the situation of creating a process document from scratch can be summarized by creating a simple scenario, with the nodes on the diagram representing instances of the key views from the meta-model.

Figure 4.18 shows a sample scenario that represents creating a process document from scratch. As with all the situations, or scenarios, described in this section, the order of generation of the views is by no means carved

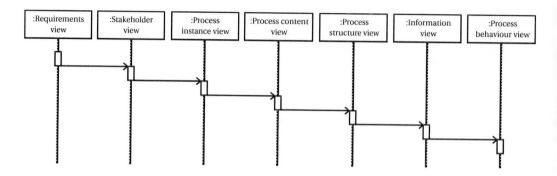

FIGURE 4.18   *Process instance view for creating a process model from scratch*

in stone, but gives an idea of how the meta-model may be used in different ways.

In a situation like this, a good first step is to think about the requirements of the processes themselves. For example, the main requirement for a process may be to 'protect human life' in the case of a safety standard, or to 'process' applications in the case of a patient admission system. This highest-level requirement can then be broken down into lower-level requirements that can relate directly to processes. Also, it is usual for the highest-level requirements to have a number of constraints associated with them, for example meeting another standard, working in a particular environment or context, or even working with an existing system. It is also usual to start thinking about the stakeholders that interact with the processes at this point both by identifying actors in the requirements view and by generating an initial stakeholder view.

Once the requirements have been established, it is then possible to think about how these requirements could possibly be realized by identifying a number of scenarios. The key element of a scenario is that each node, or block, in the diagram represents the execution of a process. In this way, it is possible to create a list of processes that are needed together with the dependencies between them. Once the processes have been identified, there are a number of possible routes, such as defining the process content view, process structure view or even the information view.

Abstracting tacit process knowledge for a new system

It is often the case that the process knowledge required in order to create the process meta-model only exists inside people's heads. In such a situation, it is necessary not only to observe the process in action, but also to talk to the relevant stakeholders to try to gain any complex knowledge that may not be immediately perceived when observing. For example, consider once again the example of the magician performing a card trick. It is actually very simple to observe, capture and record the steps involved in the card-trick process. The problems arise when the process is replicated, as it is only in the execution of the process that you realize that there is far more to the process than meets the eye. It is easy to repeat the steps that are observed when a magician performs, but it is impossible to accurately reproduce the effects of a trick simply by following the steps involved. The whole art of magic is concerned with what is not perceived, deception, misdirection and downright lies! Although these are staple techniques employed deliberately by magicians, they are also techniques that are accidentally employed by many people when carrying out a process. An incomplete and inaccurate process description is often more harmful than no description at all.

It should be stressed here that there are many reasons why these techniques of deception are employed, such as:

- **Deliberate misdirection:** this often occurs in a working environment where the staff are unhappy – perhaps they don't take their job seriously, are worried about being replaced, or are simply mischievous. In such cases, it is important to know what questions to ask the relevant stakeholders and to compare the answers with other answers from the same stakeholder or maybe from other stakeholders. The process meta-model provides the information required to know which questions to ask which person at what time.
- **Misdirection by assumption:** assumption, as the old adage goes, is the mother of all foul-ups and the basic problem here is that the activities carried out by the stakeholder seem so obvious, that they are never mentioned. For example, when it comes to testing a TV set, before any tests can be carried out the TV set must have the power switched on. It is this type of obvious information that is often omitted as people simply *assume* that it is known or done.
- **Misdirection by ignorance:** it may be that the stakeholder who is describing the process does not fully understand the process in the first place. In such situations, it is unlikely that an accurate process description will be provided.

Figure 4.19 shows the order in which the seven views are created to deal with this situation. The first view that is generated is the stakeholder view, as this identifies which roles exist and provides a basis for knowing who to talk to concerning the process behaviours. Therefore, the second view to be generated is the process behaviour view, which consists of a number of diagrams – one for each process with activities. Once the process behaviours have been created, it is then possible to abstract the process content view from them and, from there, the process instance view. From the process instance view and the process content view, it is then possible to create the requirements view and the information view. Finally, the process structure view is abstracted.

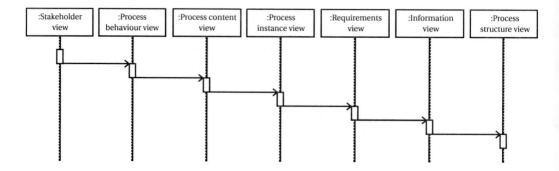

FIGURE 4.19 *Process instance for abstracting tacit process knowledge for a new system*

Abstracting tacit process knowledge for an existing system

This situation is similar to the previous one except, in this case, there is some recorded process information already in existence. Therefore, the class of 'Process knowledge' from Figure 4.1 may be realized by written information, standards and existing process models.

Figure 4.20 shows the order of creation of the seven views for the situation for abstracting tacit process knowledge for an existing system. In this case, the process structure view is created first, based on the limited process knowledge available. It is then possible to generate the process content view and, from this, the information view. The stakeholder view is generated next which, again, is abstracted from existing documentation. Now that the stakeholders and the processes have been identified, it is possible to put them together into scenarios and to generate the process instance view. As the process instance view and the process content view have been identified, the requirements view can be abstracted. Finally, the detailed process behaviour view may be generated.

Process improvement for existing processes

This situation occurs when there is an existing process model that has been well defined and well documented. As part of the continuous

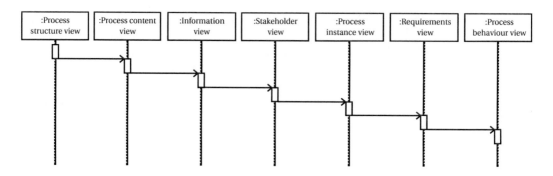

FIGURE 4.20 *Process instance for abstracting tacit process knowledge for an existing system*

process improvement exercise, a basic review is carried out every six months and, rather than a full process model analysis as shown in Figure 4.17, this time a partial analysis is carried out.

Figure 4.21 shows the situation for process improvement. The first view that is generated here is the requirements view. This is done to check that the original requirements for the process model have not changed in any way. Once the requirements have been checked and any new requirements added, the process structure view is generated to check that the basic framework of the process model is unchanged. The main part of this exercise is then to look at the process content view to identify all the existing processes. Finally, the process instance view is created to validate the requirements view.

The example shown here does not need to include all seven views, as everything has gone according to plan in the process improvement exercise – there are no changes to be made.

Consider now what would happen if the process instance view has been used as a basis for a gap analysis to ensure that the existing processes meet the requirements. Where gaps are found, the new processes must be added to the process content view. This would then entail creating the remainder of the seven views, as there has been a major change to the process model and, hence, all views must be revisited.

General notes

It should be stressed that the examples discussed here are just that – examples. Do not feel constrained by the scenarios provided here, as each one could be changed; there just needs to be some rationale behind the order that is specified in the process instance.

In terms of the order of creation of the views, it should be clear by now that there is no strict order that is carved in stone, as the actual order will

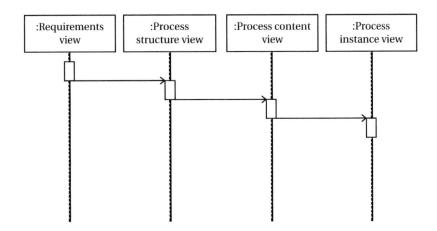

FIGURE 4.21   *Process instance for process improvement*

depend on the situation at hand. There are, however, a few common patterns in the various process instance views shown here, which is only natural, as they are based on the structural consistency checks described in Table 4.1. The structural checks are based on the associations in the process meta-model, therefore, if the process content view and the requirements view are known, then the process instance view is an obvious place to go next. Likewise, if the process instance view and the stakeholder view are known, the requirements view might be a good next move.

Keep in mind that the more that the process meta-model is understood and becomes ingrained as a natural part of process modelling, then the more natural these scenarios will become, and the more robust the final process models will be.

EXTENDING THE PROCESS META-MODEL

The process meta-model is a very powerful tool, but its application does not stop at process analysis, definition, mapping and visualization; it may be extended to include a number of process-related applications. As an example of the flexibility of the process meta-model and its potential use in an organization, consider a very important issue, that of project schedules. The idea of extending the meta-model to include other aspects of the business is explored more fully in Chapter 7 that covers enterprise architecture.

Process modelling for life cycle management

Any project requires an element of project planning and the generation of some sort of project schedule. A project schedule is usually realized in some sort of Gantt chart or Pert chart which are, themselves, a form of visual modelling. However, such schedules are often wildly inaccurate when it comes to representing the actual activities that are carried out by the workers involved with the project and are often regarded as a work of fiction by the people doing the work. Consider the horrific examples concerning project overruns in the field of, for example, IT systems. It is possible to pick up any newspaper in any given week of the year and find examples of projects that have been absolute disasters. For detailed examples of these see (Flowers, 1996).

Such cost and time overruns are quite common but, in many cases, this is not necessarily a fault of the people carrying out the work but more a case of the project not meeting the initial expectations of the project schedule. One indicator of the expectations of the project can be found in the project schedule which, if very unrealistic, will by its very nature result in time and hence cost overruns. Therefore, where does the fault lie – with the people carrying out the work to the best of their ability, or in the unrealistic expectations of the project managers who set unrealizable goals?

These inaccurate estimates of times, costs and resources are inexcusable, and mostly avoidable, when a full knowledge of the processes in an

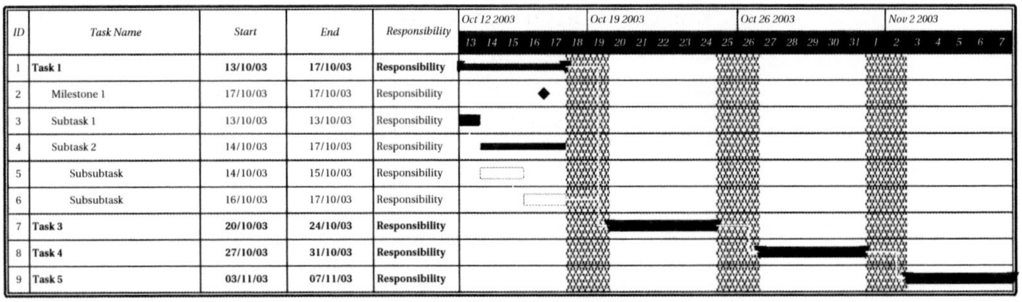

ID	Task Name	Start	End	Responsibility	Oct 12 2003						Oct 19 2003							Oct 26 2003							Nov 2 2003						
					13	14	15	16	17	18	19	20	21	22	23	24	25	26	27	28	29	30	31	1	2	3	4	5	6	7
1	Task 1	13/10/03	17/10/03	**Responsibility**																										
2	Milestone 1	17/10/03	17/10/03	Responsibility																										
3	Subtask 1	13/10/03	13/10/03	Responsibility																										
4	Subtask 2	14/10/03	17/10/03	Responsibility																										
5	Subsubtask	14/10/03	15/10/03	Responsibility																										
6	Subsubtask	16/10/03	17/10/03	Responsibility																										
7	Task 3	20/10/03	24/10/03	**Responsibility**																										
8	Task 4	27/10/03	31/10/03	**Responsibility**																										
9	Task 5	03/11/03	07/11/03	**Responsibility**																										

FIGURE 4.22   *Typical generic Gantt chart*

organization are known. On one level, all that a Gantt chart represents is the execution of processes during the course of a project. If these processes are well defined and have been carried out before, then there is no reason why realistic estimates cannot be put on the process activities at the lowest level, such as in the process behavioural view, and then aggregated up into realistic timing estimations. Of course, in real life there will be timing constraints imposed on a project from day 1, but it is possible to provide an accurate estimation of the time required to execute the relevant processes and then see if they meet the original project constraints.

As an example of this, consider a typical Gantt chart, such as the one in Figure 4.22, where the project tasks are broken down into three levels of detail:

- the major task level, represented by the thick black line that shows the highest grouping of project activity;
- the subtask level, which is a decomposition of the task level and shows a more detailed view of what project activity is occurring;
- the subsubtask level, which is a decomposition of the subtask level and shows a more detailed view of what project activity is occurring.

Also, other information, such as key milestones, dates and resources, may be indicated on the chart. All of this information can be derived directly from the process meta-model and, if this application is to be used extensively, it is possible to extend the process meta-model to include project management information, as shown in Figures 4.23 and 4.24. Remembering that the original meta-model contains a conceptual and realization aspect, then Figures 4.23 and 4.24 should be viewed as extensions to the existing meta-model.

Figure 4.23 shows the additional information required to make the process meta-model concept view usable for project scheduling purposes. In this case, project management concepts are captured in the form of a class diagram. Of course, this extension will differ depending on the approach taken to project management within the organization. Like all the information in the meta-model, this must be tailored, but the

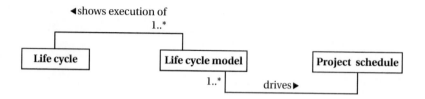

FIGURE 4.23   *Extension to meta-model conceptual view*

tailoring here has the potential to be far more significant than the changes required for the standard meta-model, simply due to the numbers of different approaches that are possible for project management.

Figure 4.23 shows the enhancement to the process concept view for the process meta-model. The new concepts that have been introduced here are:

- 'Life cycle', which identifies the stages in the project, but does not imply any sort of order.
- 'Life cycle model', which defines how the stages in the life cycle are executed. The life cycle is a structural view, whereas the life cycle model is a behavioural view.
- 'Project schedule', which defines how the overall project will be executed and includes time, cost and resource information.

The key point shown on the diagram is the set of associations between the new concepts, as this will form the basis for mapping onto the existing process meta-model. The relationships between these new concepts and the existing process meta-model can now be explored by looking at these concepts in more detail and also by defining how each concept will be realized using modelling.

Once these concepts have been captured, their realization must be defined in order to make the meta-model usable.

Figure 4.24 shows the process meta-model realization view for the project management extension to the meta-model. In this case, the target visualization for the schedule information is not UML but the Gantt chart. Therefore, the stereotypes that indicate how the concepts are realized relate to Gantt chart terminology, rather than UML terminology. Of course, there is no reason why this realization should be limited to Gantt charts as, providing that the language and notation is understood, then any form of visualization, such as Pert charts or even a proprietary notation may be adopted. See chapter 8 for more discussion on different notations.

This process realization view may now be mapped onto the existing one to provide an extended process meta-model. The way that the two views are related will be in terms of relationships between the main concepts and then by identifying common concepts. For example, a relationship will be added, such as, 'Life cycle' uses the 'Process model'. This forms the main link back to the original process model. The next mapping can be

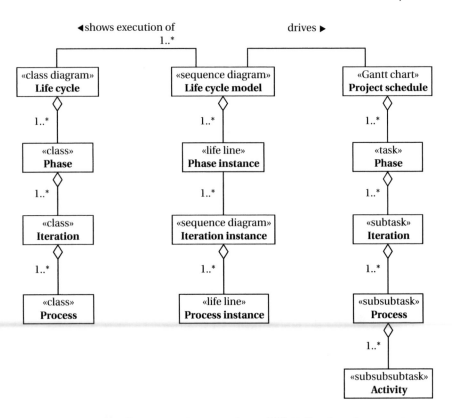

FIGURE 4.24 *Extension to meta-model realization view*

achieved by looking at common terms used between the old view and the new view. Therefore, the following relationships will exist:

- 'Process', which exists as part of an iteration and is represented by a <<class>>, is the same as the concept of a 'Process' in Figure 4.3.
- 'Process instance', which exists as part of an iteration instance and is represented by a <<life line>>, is the same as the concept of a 'Process instance' in Figure 4.3.
- 'Process', which exists as an iteration, again, but is represented by a <<subsubtask>> (part of the Gantt chart terminology), is the same as the concept of the 'Process' in Figure 4.3.

These basic mappings will also form consistency checks that apply to the extended meta-model.

The extension to the meta-model shown here is simply an example and, as with all aspects of process modelling, must be tailored for a particular situation and organization. The intention here is to show the potential for the use of the meta-model, but this need not be limited to project schedules – consider the following applications that may be catered for by an extended process meta-model:

- **Capability determination:** what capabilities can a company offer as part of their service or product to customers? By looking at the processes that the organization can offer, it is possible to abstract a number of capabilities that can then be 'sold' to potential clients. Capabilities and processes should not be confused, as the process represents the core activities, whereas the capability reflects more the application.

- **Tender application:** evaluating and applying for tenders should be based on the capabilities that the organization can offer and, hence, the processes. If a request for proposals can be represented as a requirements view, then the processes in the organization can be mapped onto these requirements to demonstrate that the project requirements can be met. Of course, this will also identify any gaps in the existing process model that need to be filled before the work can be carried out.

- **Skillset identification for recruitment:** each stakeholder represents a role that will have a number of required skills and, if this is built into the meta-model, it can then be used as a basis for recruitment activities. This will be touched upon in the case study in Chapter 6.

The point here is to try not to be limited in using the meta-model, but to look at other areas in which it may be used. After all, processes are fundamental to everything that we do, therefore, the meta-model has many applications.

CONCLUSIONS

This chapter discussed the process meta-model in more detail, in terms of the concepts and how they are realized. This realization takes the form of the seven views that comprise the process meta-model. In order to fully specify a process, all seven views are essential. Each of these views is realized using the UML and a number of consistency checks have been defined based on the structure of the meta-model. Although the description of the meta-model formed the main part of the chapter, the application of the meta-model will provide the tangible benefits to businesses. Therefore, several scenarios were described detailing different applications of the meta-model. Finally, the chapter demonstrated how the meta-model can be extended for different applications, in particular, here, project schedules.

The meta-model should be tailored for particular organizations, as terms and practices will differ, but the pattern of the meta-model will, in most cases, remain very similar.

5 Process Mapping and Metrics

'I'm no good at judging the size of crowds, Ted, but I'd say there's about seventeen million of them out there'

Father Dougal McGuire, *Father Ted*, Channel 4

INTRODUCTION

The benefits of having a well-defined process are many, and one of these is to give people confidence in the way that you do things. For example, a customer may want some degree of confidence in a capability offered by your organization. There are several ways to demonstrate this confidence, and one of these is to demonstrate that the approach adopted is a valid and accepted one.

The way that an approach is demonstrated is usually carried out in one of two ways: through an assessment or through an audit. The process model that is being audited or assessed against (usually a standard) is referred to as the *source process*, whereas the process model under review is referred to as the *target process*. In both audits and assessments, there are three aspects of the process model that are being examined:

- **Source standard compliance:** whether or not there is a basic mapping between the source standard and the target process.
- **Process implementation:** whether or not the target process is being implemented on real projects. Examples of the use of processes being used on projects or process instances, as they are known, are sought and then these are either audited or assessed.
- **Process effectiveness:** whether or not the process is effective. Are any metrics being taken and is the process then being improved as time goes on? Are the requirements for the process correct and up to date?

Although both assessments and audits share the same basic aims, they are executed in very different ways:

- **Audit:** an audit tends to be more formal than an assessment. An audit is usually carried out by a third-party, an independent body, to enforce the source standard. This source standard, for example ISO 9001 (2000), must be well understood and the audit will often make use of specific 'checklists' that enable each part of the standard to be checked against the target process. For an audit, a documented process model must exist, otherwise the full audit cannot take place.

The output of an audit is typically a straight 'pass' or 'fail' result with an indication of which specific parts of the source process were not met – or 'non-compliances' as they are often known.

- **Assessment:** an assessment tends to be more informal than an audit and may be carried out either by independent third-parties or by suitably-qualified people inside the organization. Examples of assessment standards include ISO 15504 (ISO/IEC, 2004) and CMMI (Carnegie Mellon Software Engineering Institute, 2002). An assessment starts out with a blank sheet of paper, the target process is then abstracted and the results of this abstraction are then assessed. This means that the target process may be well documented, in which case the abstraction is relatively simple, or there may be no documentation whatsoever (the process exists purely in someone's head) in which case the abstraction is not so straightforward. Of course, one advantage of this is that *any* target process may be effectively assessed, even if it is not formally documented. The output of an assessment is typically a profile, rather than a simple 'pass' or 'fail', that provides effective feedback about how mature each process is. There is usually a scale of five or so levels that indicates the maturity – a low number indicating an immature and uncontrolled process and a high number indicating a mature and controlled process.

A common aspect of both approaches is being able to demonstrate basic compliance between the source standard and the target process, and this is where, initially, process mapping comes in.

There are several inherent problems associated with process mapping:

- **Terminology differences:** perhaps the most common problem between different standards or process models is one of communication – the actual terminology is very different. For example, consider the different words that may be employed to indicate the activities (using the terminology adopted in this book) within a process – words such as: 'task', 'step', 'practice', 'action'. Although these seem like minor differences, what about the situation where the same word is used, such as 'process', but with different definitions in each process. It is essential, therefore, that these differences in language can be identified and clarified.
- **Volume of data:** in many cases, it is desirable to map, not just between two processes, but between many. It is not uncommon to find a list of relevant standards, either in a requirements specification or in a project contract that forms a formal obligation for the project. Bear in mind, however, that realistically if there are 50 standards listed, this means, potentially, 50 audits or assessments must be carried out. The sheer volume of data involved here, not to mention the time and effort involved, would be phenomenal.

- **Meaningful metrics:** there is an old adage that anything that can't be measured, can't be controlled, therefore it is important that measurements and, hence, metrics can be applied to the process mapping in order to demonstrate how effective the mapping is. However, coming up with meaningful metrics is often difficult, so any effective process mapping should be capable of being measured in some way.

The remainder of this chapter defines an example of a process for process mapping that meets all of the requirements laid out above. Of course, this process is merely an example and is not the only approach that can be taken to perform process mapping, but it is one that has proven to be simple yet effective for real-life situations.

A PROCESS FOR PROCESS MAPPING

This section describes a process for process mapping. Of course, this process is described in UML, so it is an excellent example of how the modelling can be used to specify a process. The process is expressed in terms of the process meta-model and each of the views is presented here.

As each view is presented, the complexity of each diagram will also be discussed, together with any consistency checks that are applied between the various views. One point to bear in mind here is that complexity can occur on any view, which is why it is so important to look at all the views from the process meta-model.

The process structure view

The process structure view is the same as the one already defined (see Chapter 4) and will not be replicated here. This uses all the same terminology as has been used throughout this book.

The requirements view

The first view that we will consider is the requirements view, which explains why we are defining the process mapping process in the first place. This is realized in the use case diagram in Figure 5.1.

Figure 5.1 shows a simple requirements view for a mapping process. At the moment, this is modelled at a high level of abstraction and will be described in more detail later in this section. Note that the main requirement is stated quite simply as 'develop process mapping process', which has three actors associated with it: the 'Process engineer', which represents the person or group of people who will be developing the process; the 'Source process', which represents the model to be mapped against; and, finally, the 'Reviewer'. There is one single constraint on this requirement, which is to 'inspire confidence' and is related to the 'Sponsor' and the 'Standard enforcer'. In this case, the exercise is being

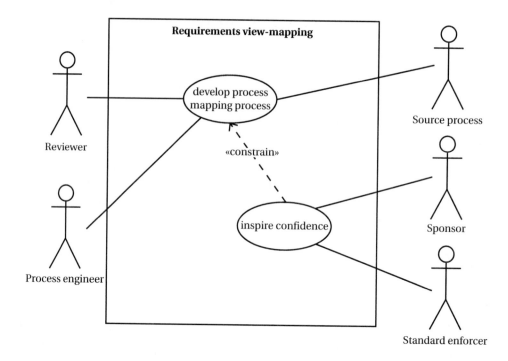

FIGURE 5.1   *Simple requirements view*

carried out at the request of sponsors, who require some confidence that their processes map onto the relevant standards. The standards enforcer is involved as any mapping that is produced and any compliance issues will need to be approved by the appropriate authority.

The stakeholder view

The stakeholder view can be abstracted from the actors that were identified in the requirements view, and then arranged into a classification hierarchy.

Figure 5.2 identifies the stakeholder roles that are relevant to the project. These stakeholders are consistent with the actors on the stakeholder view and also the names that govern each swim lane in the process behaviour view. The roles that have been identified are as follows:

- 'Sponsor': the person or organization who is paying for the process mapping exercise, maybe as part of an audit or assessment.
- 'Standard enforcer': the people who will be carrying out the audit or assessment. In the case of an audit, these people are independent of the target organization or, in the case of an assessment, they may be either internal or external to the target organization.

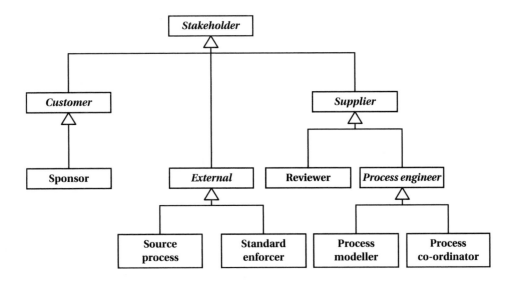

FIGURE 5.2   *Stakeholder view*

- 'Process engineer': the person or people who are defining the process mapping approach. In this case, there are two roles defined as types of 'Process engineer' which are the 'Process modeller', who performs all modelling activities and the 'Process co-ordinator' who manages and controls the exercise.
- 'Source process': this role represents the source standard. It may seem a little odd to have a process model as a stakeholder, but it meets all the requirements of being one – it is outside the boundary of the system and has an interest in the project.

Now that the requirements and the stakeholders have been identified, it is time to look at the actual processes that need to be defined in order to meet these requirements.

The process content view

The process content view, for the process mapping application, consists initially of three processes as shown in Figure 5.3.

Figure 5.3 shows the process content view that identifies the processes that have been created along with their relevant artefacts (represented by attributes) and activities (represented by operations). In this case, three processes have been identified as being necessary to meet the requirements shown in Figure 5.1. All of these processes could have been shown as a single process, but consider the number of attributes and operations for that single class and imagine how the complexity would increase.

The three processes that have been identified are described as follows:

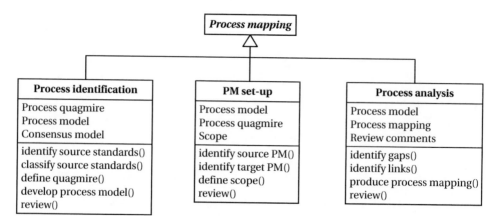

FIGURE 5.3   *Process content view*

- 'Process identification': the aim of this process is to identify all the relevant source processes that are applicable to the mapping exercise. One of the main outputs here is the 'Process quagmire', which is a variation of the information view and is realized by a class diagram where each class represents a different source process. In the situation where only a single source standard is being used, this quagmire is quite simple (more of a puddle than a quagmire), however, as soon as more than one source process is used, the complexity increases and the quagmire becomes deeper and deeper.
- 'PM set-up': the main aim of this process is to define the scope of the assessment or audit (which processes in the target process will be evaluated) and then to identify the relevant parts of each source process.
- 'Process analysis': the aim of this process is to actually perform the mapping between the source processes and the target process. This involves looking for links between them as well as gaps.

In terms of the way that these processes are executed, they are quite 'tightly coupled'. This means that the relationships between the processes are actually dependencies and, hence, does not allow for much freedom in terms of variation of execution. This can be seen more clearly in the slightly extended diagram in Figure 5.4.

Figure 5.4 shows dependencies between the three processes, which highlights the high degree of coupling between them. In reality, this translates as restricting the order of execution of the processes. This can be illustrated by looking at the process instance view.

The process instance view

The processes that were identified in the process content view can now be executed in order to meet the original requirements. Bearing in mind that

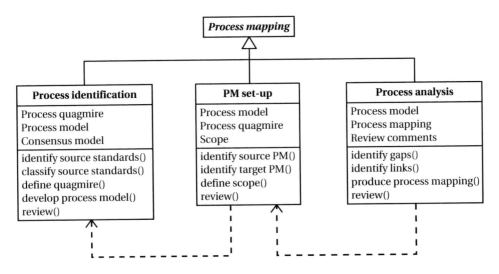

FIGURE 5.4   *Extended process content view*

there were dependencies identified between these processes, this constrains the number of different scenarios that can be applied.

Figure 5.5 shows a single scenario for executing the processes defined in the process content view. In this case, this is because of the limitations imposed by the dependencies defined in Figure 5.4. The order of execution for the processes has been defined, but not the execution of each individual process, which will be defined in the process behaviour view.

The process behaviour view

A process behaviour view is defined for each of the processes defined in Figure 5.3.

Figure 5.6 shows *how* the 'Process identification' process behaves over time. Each of the activity invocations (represented by the sausage shapes) is checked for consistency against the operations from the parent class. The information flow is represented by simple text statements that

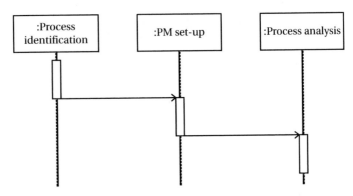

FIGURE 5.5   *Process instance view for the mapping exercise*

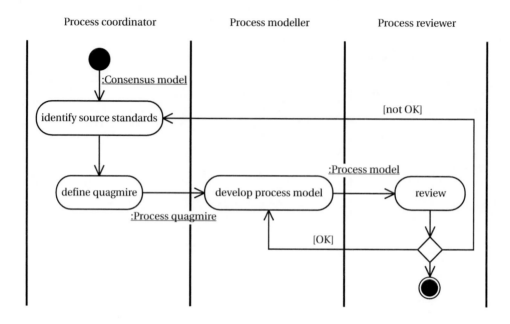

FIGURE 5.6   *Process behaviour view for the 'Process identification' process*

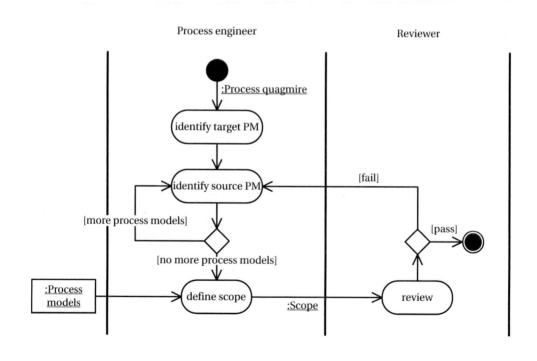

FIGURE 5.7   *Process behaviour view for the 'PM set-up' process*

are associated with the flows between the activity invocations. This information is a set of instances of the attributes from the parent class. The final piece of information that is specified here is the responsibility for each activity invocation that is grouped by using swim lanes (represented by the parallel vertical lines). Any activity invocation that lies within the boundaries of a swim lane is defined as being the responsibility of the stakeholder role that is specified at the top of each swim lane.

Figure 5.7 shows the process behaviour view for the 'PM set-up' process. Note the two representations of UML objects being used here to represent the process artefacts. The short form is to use simple text and a colon, as in ':Process quagmire' which works well when there is a sequential information flow throughout the process. However, in some situations, information is coming in from outside the process part-way through its execution. In such cases, it is more usual to see the artefact represented in a rectangle, as in 'Process model'.

Figure 5.8 shows the process behaviour view for the 'Process analysis' process. Note the use of UML control splits and joins here to show that there is no specific order to the execution of the activities 'identify gaps' and 'identify links'. Although the concurrent operation shown here is

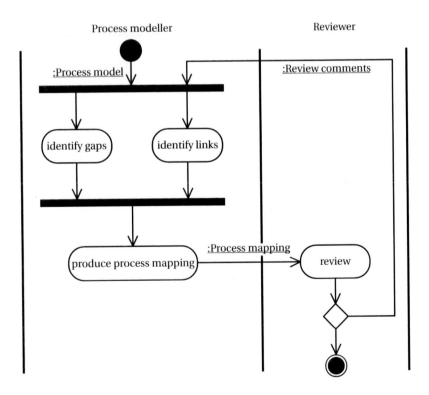

FIGURE 5.8 *Process behaviour view for the 'Process analysis' process*

meaningful, it is very easy to fall into the trap of making all activities concurrent, which results in a flat structure in the pattern of the model. When such flat structures occur, it is usually a sign of a poorly thought-out process behaviour and can often lead to management problems when the process is executed, as there is no semblance of order to the activity invocations.

The information view

The information view for the process mapping processes relates all the artefacts together, and can be seen in Figure 5.9. From the diagram, it can be seen that there is a 'Consensus model' representing a set of requirements that provides the background information needed for all the process models (the 'Process model' class) to be identified. There are two types of 'Process model': the single 'Target process' and the one or more 'Source process'. A 'Process quagmire' is produced that identifies the relationships between all the process models that have been identified. The 'Scope' defines a subset of the 'Target process' identifying a subset of processes in the target process that will form the basis of the assessment. The mapping between the source standards and the single target process is captured in the 'Process mapping', and this is commented upon and the results captured in the 'Review comments'.

This completes the process description for the process mapping processes.

PROCESS MAPPING METRICS

So far, the processes that have been defined have been concerned with the actual process mapping itself and do not include any form of measurement nor the application of metrics.

Metrics can take many shapes and sizes, and it is important to have a process defined for their application. The process that will be defined here

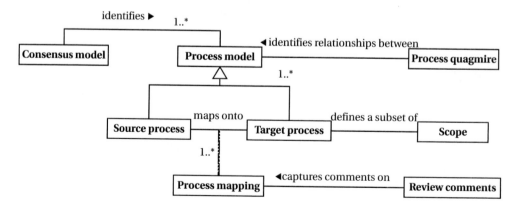

FIGURE 5.9 *Information view for process mapping*

is concerned with calculating the number of mappings (relationships) between two process models and involves some very simple measurements (mainly counting), and calculating some simple metrics based on these measurements.

In order to define the metrics process, the process model defined so far must have a number of its views extended, in particular: the process content view, the process behaviour view and the information view.

The extended process content view

The process content view is extended by introducing a new process. Figure 5.10 shows the new process, 'Metric application', that must be added to the process content view. Note the interesting use of multiplicity here on the attributes of the class. Although this is by no means compulsory, it is often useful to show that an attribute will manifest itself more than once. In this case, several of the attributes have a multiplicity of one-to-many, indicated as [1..*].

The extended information view

The key to the metrics application process lies in the extension to the information view, as the process itself is very much dependent on the measurements that are being taken. These measurements and subsequent metrics are defined more clearly in the information view.

Figure 5.11 shows the extended information view that relates the measurements and metrics to the process structure view. Note that only a

Metric application
Target process[1]
Source process[1..*]
Process group ratio[1..*]
Process group index[1..*]
Process ratio[1..*]
Process index[1..*]
Artefact ratio[1..*]
Artefact index[1..*]
Process model index[1]
identify target process model()
measure PGR()
measure PR()
measure artefact ratio()
measure activity ratio()
calculate PI()
calculate PGI()
calculate PMI()
review()

FIGURE 5.10 *New process for the process content view*

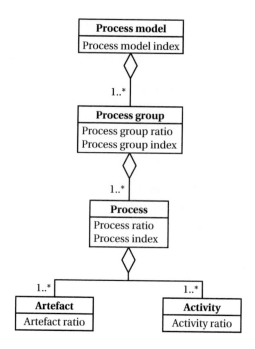

FIGURE 5.11 *Extended information view*

subset of the process structure view is shown here – just the parts that have measurements or metrics applied to them. Therefore, it can be seen from Figure 5.11 that:

- The 'Process model' has a single metric, identified as the 'Process model index'.
- The 'Process group' has a single metric, 'Process group index' and a single measurement, 'Process group ratio'.
- The 'Process' has a single metric, 'Process index' and a single measurement, 'Process ratio'.
- The 'Artefact' has a single measurement, 'Artefact ratio'.
- The 'Activity' has a single measurement, 'Activity ratio'.

Now that the simple metrics and measurements have been defined and applied to the existing structure, it is time to look at how they are actually generated, by considering the process behaviour view for the 'Metric application' process.

Figure 5.12 shows the behavioural view for the 'Metric application' process. This process is immediately more complex than any of the process mapping processes. There is far more iteration in this process, which results in a higher level of complexity and the amount of information is also far higher.

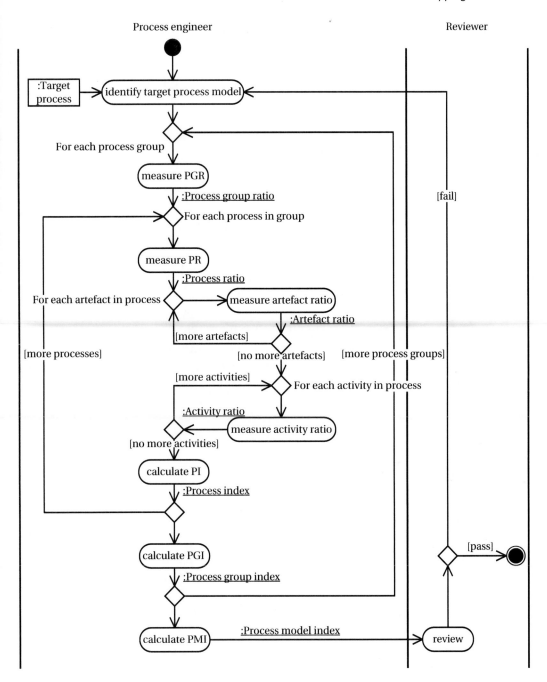

FIGURE 5.12   *Process behaviour view for the 'Metric application' process*

Each of the activities in the process must be described in more detail. This can be done using more activity diagrams or using text descriptions. At some point in the process modelling exercise, each element will have a text description associated with it. The activity descriptions are as follows:

- 'identify target process model': this activity just confirms the inputs to the process.
- 'measure PGR': the PGR, or process group ratio, is the ratio between the number of process groups (or equivalent terms) for both standards.
- 'measure PR': for each process group, there will be a certain number of processes contained therein. The PR, or process ratio, is the ratio between the number of processes in each process group. Therefore, there will be a PR measurement for each process group.
- 'measure artefact ratio': for each process, there will be a number of artefacts and the artefact ratio is the ratio between each artefact in the target process and the source process. Therefore, there will be an artefact ratio for each artefact in the process.
- 'measure activity ratio': similar to the artefact ratio, but this time based on the number of activities, rather than artefacts.
- 'calculate PI': the PI, or process index, provides a measure of mapping between the processes. The process index is calculated by counting the number of artefacts and activities that have a non-zero ratio (for example, 2:0, is a zero ratio, whereas 4:3 is a non-zero ratio) for their artefact and activity ratios and then dividing this by the total number of artefacts and activities. Therefore, a process that has artefacts and activities that map completely to the source process has a PI of 1, whereas any incomplete ratios result in a PI of less than 1.
- 'calculate PGI': the PGI, or process group index, is calculated by adding each PI for the processes in the process group and dividing by the number of processes in that group. Again, a complete mapping will result in a PGI of 1.
- 'calculate PMI': the PMI, or process model index, is calculated by adding each PGI for the process group in the process model and then dividing by the total number of process groups. Again, a complete process mapping will result in a PMI of 1.
- 'review': a review of the artefacts and the content of each artefact for this process.

These descriptions are used in the next section when the process is implemented.

APPLICATION OF METRICS

The processes associated with process mapping and metrics have been defined, but these processes have not yet been executed. This section, therefore, is concerned with applying these processes.

The processes defined in this chapter are applied in the order defined in the process instance view in Figure 5.5, that is:

1. process identification;
2. PM set-up;
3. process analysis.

The 'Process identification' process

The 'identify source standards' activity

The source standards will be: ISO/IEC 15504, *Software Process Assessment* (2004), ISO 15288, *Systems engineering: Systems life cycle processes* (2002), ISO 9001, *Model for quality assurance in design, development, production, installation and servicing* (2000), ISO 12207, *Information technology: Software life cycle processes* (2004) and CMMI (Carnegie Mellon Software Engineering Institute, 2002). These were chosen based on the 'Consensus' model, which is simply a statement of requirements for the exercise. In some cases this will be recorded in a specification report, while in other cases it may be abstracted from talking to people, conducting interviews, surveys, and so on.

The 'define quagmire' activity

The quagmire identifies any related standards or processes that may have an influence on the process mapping exercise. Figure 5.13 shows a process quagmire for the exercise, where 'ISO 15288' is related to 'ISO 12207', which is related to 'ISO 9001'. Also, 'ISO 15288' is related to 'ISO 15504' which is related to 'CMM'.

This diagram is still relatively simple, but for an excellent example of how complex such diagrams can be, see The Frameworks Quagmire at www.software.org/quagmire.

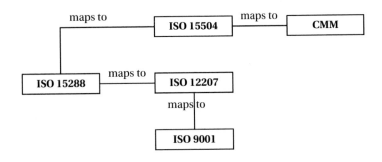

FIGURE 5.13 *Process quagmire*

If this exercise was taken further, it would be possible to provide a full mapping between all of these standards based on the relationships between them in the quagmire.

The 'develop process model' activity

In this activity, any necessary process models will be produced. The two main views that will be used as a basis for the basic process mapping are the process structure view and the process content view.

Figure 5.14 shows the process structure view for both the source and target processes. On the left is the structure of ISO 15288, which is the target process, and on the right is ISO 15504, which is the source process. There is an immediate similarity between the two structures, in fact the pattern is identical. Note, however, the difference in terminology that is being used here. Therefore, there is an immediate benefit from putting these two views side-by-side as straightaway a mapping between terms has been established.

The next level down in the process structure view looks at the grouping level for each standard.

Figure 5.15 shows a lower-level aspect of the process structure view for both standards, but this time the emphasis is on the grouping level. By looking at these two views side-by-side, the patterns are not immediately obvious, but, upon closer inspection, it will be demonstrated that there is indeed a mapping between them.

When looking for where a mapping exists between two process models, it is important to look at the different levels of abstraction in the models. For example, in Figure 5.15 it is tempting to map at the highest levels ('Process group' to 'Process category') and then to drop down to the next

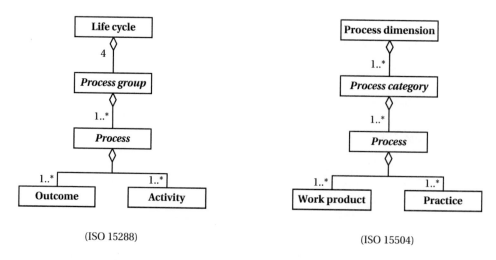

(ISO 15288)   (ISO 15504)

FIGURE 5.14   *Process structure views for ISO 15288 and 15504*

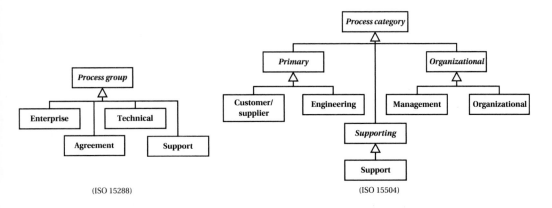

FIGURE 5.15 *Process structure views, with an emphasis on the grouping level, for the standards*

level and map across. This would result in a second-level mapping of 'Enterprise', 'Agreement', 'Technical' and 'Support' directly to 'Primary', 'Supporting' and 'Organizational'. This would leave the third level for ISO 15504 with no mapping. In this situation, this is incorrect, as the second level of the ISO 15504 process model ('Primary', 'Supporting' and 'Organizational') is simply another level of classification, and the correct mapping is between 'Enterprise', 'Agreement', 'Technical' and 'Support' in ISO 15288, and 'Customer/supplier', 'Engineering', Support', 'Management' and 'Organizational' in ISO 15504.

Therefore, it is important to think about each mapping rather than just assuming that all levels will map exactly.

Figure 5.16 shows the process content view for both standards. This is not the entire process content view but is the subset of the target process model that will defined by the scope. Again, the basic patterns look quite different, but this will be explored during the 'Process analysis' process.

The 'review' activity

At this point, there would be a review of the artefacts that have been produced so far in the process. Once this review has been completed satisfactorily, the next process can be invoked.

The 'PM set-up' process

The 'identify target PM' activity

Based on the process quagmire, the target process model has been identified as ISO 15288.

The 'identify source PM' activity

Based on the process quagmire, the source process model has been identified as ISO 15504.

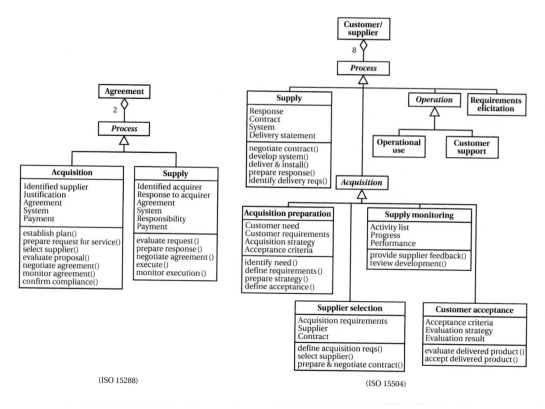

FIGURE 5.16 *Process content views for the standards*

The 'define scope' activity

The next step is to look at the target process model and to identify which processes are to be involved in the mapping exercise. For the sake of brevity for this example, the processes chosen are the ones in the 'Agreement' process group in ISO 15288.

The 'review' activity

As with many processes, there is a review activity at the end of the process that must be passed before progress can be made to the next process from the process instance view.

The 'Process analysis' process

The 'identify gaps' activity

This activity uses the information in Figures 5.14, 5.15 and 5.16 to try to identify any gaps in the mapping between the two standards. Therefore, the question that will be asked is: 'Are there any features of the target process model that do not map onto the source process model?'

The 'identify links' activity

This activity uses the information in Figure 5.14, Figure 5.15 and Figure 5.16 to try to identify any links in the mapping between the two standards. Therefore, the question that will be asked is: 'For each feature of the target process model, which features of the source process model map onto it?'

The 'produce process mapping' activity

This is the activity where the actual results of the previous two activities are recorded. This can be done using any appropriate mechanism and simple tables will be used here to capture the results. This mapping will occur at different levels.

Table 5.1 shows the basic mapping between the two views shown in Figure 5.14. This highlights the differences in the basic language used in both standards. At this level there is a one-to-one mapping for each term, which makes the whole exercise simpler. Once this has been mapped, it is then possible to drop down a level of detail and look at the grouping level.

Table 5.2 shows the mapping between the two views shown in Figure 5.15. This establishes the mapping between the terms used for the process groups and categories. Notice here the first occurrence of a one-to-many mapping between the grouping terms. In ISO 15288, the term 'Project' maps to both 'Support' and 'Management' in ISO 15504.

Table 5.3 shows the mapping between the process terms that are being used in the two standards. Again, there is a one-to-many mapping here where a single term in ISO 15288 ('Acquisition') maps to four terms in ISO 15504.

TABLE 5.1 *Basic terminology mapping*

ISO 15288	ISO 15504
Process group	Process category
Process	Process
Outcome	Work product
Activity	Practice

TABLE 5.2 *Process grouping terminology mapping*

ISO 15288		ISO 15504	
Process group	Enterprise	Process category	Organizational
	Agreement		Customer/supplier
	Technical		Engineering
	Project		Management
			Support

TABLE 5.3 *Process terminology mapping*

ISO 15288		ISO 15504	
Agreement	Acquisition	Customer/supplier	Acquisition preparation
			Supplier selection
			Supplier monitoring
			Customer acceptance
	Supply		Supply

TABLE 5.4 *Process feature mapping*

ISO 15288		ISO 15504	
Acquisition (outcome)	Identified supplier	Supplier selection	Supplier
	Justification	Supplier selection	Acquisition requirements
	Agreement	Supplier selection	Contract
	System		
	Payment		
Acquisition (activity)	Establish plan	Acquisition preparation	Prepare strategy
	Prepare request for service	Acquisition preparation	Identify needs
			Define requirements
	Select supplier	Supplier selection	Select supplier
	Evaluate proposal	Supplier selection	Select supplier
	Negotiate agreement	Supplier selection	Prepare and negotiate contract
	Monitor agreement	Supplier monitoring	Review development
			Provide supplier feedback
	Confirm compliance	Customer acceptance	Evaluate delivered product
			Accept delivered product
Supply (outcome)	Identified acquirer		
	Response to acquirer	Supply	Response
	Agreement	Supply	Contract
	System	Supply	System
	Responsibility		
	Payment		
Supply (activity)	Evaluate request		
	Prepare response	Supply	Prepare response
	Negotiate agreement	Supply	Negotiate contract
	Execute	Supply	Develop system
			Deliver and install
	Monitor execution		

Table 5.4 shows the mapping between the terms used for the features of the processes – the outcomes and activities of the processes in ISO 15288 to the work products and practices in ISO 15504.

The 'review' activity

Once more, there is a review activity before the process is completed.

The 'Metrics application' process

The 'identify target process' activity

The target process is confirmed as being ISO 15288.

The 'measure PGR' activity

The PGR is calculated by:

(number of target process groups)/(number of source process groups)

In this case, this is 4:5.

The 'measure PR' activity

The process ratio (PR) is calculated by:

(number of processes in target process group)/(number of processes in source process group)

In this case, as there is only a single process group, Agreement, selected in the scope, the process ratio is: 2:8.

The 'measure artefact ratio' activity

The artefact ratio is defined as:

(artefact in target process)/(number of equivalent artefacts in source process)

In this case, the artefact ratios are:

Acquisition	Identified supplier	1:1
	Justification	1:1
	Agreement	1:1
	System	1:0
	Payment	1:0
Supply	Identified acquirer	1:0
	Response to acquirer	1:1
	Agreement	1:1
	System	1:1
	Responsibility	1:0
	Payment	1:0

All these figures are taken from Table 5.4.

The 'measure activity ratio' activity

The activity ratio is defined as:

(activity in target process)/(number of equivalent activities in source process)

In this case, the activity ratios are:

Acquisition	Establish plan	1:1
	Prepare request for service	1:2
	Select supplier	1:1
	Evaluate proposal	1:1
	Negotiate agreement	1:1
	Monitor agreement	1:2
	Confirm compliance	1:2
Supply	Evaluate request	1:0
	Prepare response	1:1
	Negotiate agreement	1:1
	Execute	1:2
	Monitor execution	1:0

All these figures are taken from Table 5.4.

The 'calculate PI' activity

The PI is calculated by:

(number of non-zero artefact ratios + number non-zero activity ratios)/(number artefacts + number activities)

In this case, these are calculated as:

Acquisition PI $\quad (3 + 7)/(5 + 7) = 10/12 = 0.83$
Supply PI $\quad\quad\; (3 + 3)/(6 + 5) = 6/11 = 0.82$

These calculations are based on the figures from the previous section.

The 'calculate PGI' activity

The process group index is calculated as:

(Sum of PI for each process in process group)/(number of processes in process group)

This is calculated as:

Agreement PGI $\quad (0.83 + 0.82)/2 = 0.825$

These calculations are based on figures from the previous section.

The 'calculate PMI' activity

The process model index is defined as:

(Sum of all PGI)/(total number of PG in the scope)

This is calculated as:
Total PMI $(0.825)/(1) = 0.825$

The figures used here are taken from the previous section

The 'review' activity

The final activity in this process is another review, which will evaluate the results of the measurements and metrics applied during this process.

INTERPRETING THE RESULTS

Any metric is useless unless it can be interpreted in some way. The metrics applied in the previous section produced a set of results that can be interpreted according to a set of heuristics, or rules of thumb:

- **PMI of 1:** this means that there is a complete mapping between the target process and the source process. A PMI of 1 does not warrant any further investigation, as the entire process model has a complete mapping. It should be noted that the PMI refers to a mapping in a single direction. Or, to put it another way, a process model index of 1 from target to source does not imply a process model index of 1 from source to target.
- **PMI of under 1:** this implies that there is not a complete mapping between the two process models – the lower the number, the more incomplete the mapping. Therefore this situation needs to be investigated further by looking at the process group indices.
- **PGI of 1:** when each of the process group indices is looked at, any with a value of 1 indicates a complete mapping for that process group and can therefore be ignored for investigation purposes.
- **PGI of under 1:** a process group index of under 1 indicates an incomplete mapping – the lower the number, the more incomplete the mapping. Therefore, any process group with a PGI under 1 should be investigated further by looking at the process indices that went into the calculation.
- **PI of 1:** any processes with a process index of 1 can be ignored for investigation purposes, as this indicates a complete mapping.

- **PI of under 1:** any process that has a process index of under 1 indicates an incomplete mapping for that process. This applies to the artefact ratios and activity ratios that went into the process index calculation. Any artefact ratio or activity ratio that is non-zero will yield the source of the overall mapping incompleteness.

This is by no means an exhaustive list of interpretation of the metrics, but should provide an idea of the sort of use that these metrics can be put to.

CONCLUSIONS

This chapter introduced the concept of process mapping and defined a number of example processes that can be used for such purposes. The processes have been defined according to the process meta-model already introduced in this book. In addition to the mapping processes, an example of a metrics process was defined that used the results of the process mapping processes.

These processes were then illustrated by applying them to a set of standards and identifying a narrow scope of two standards for the example exercise. The processes were executed and the results recorded.

It should be stressed that the processes presented in this chapter are purely for example and should not be taken as the *only* approach to process mapping (although this is a real approach that has been demonstrated on a number of real-life projects). The main purpose here is to illustrate how the process models produced by using the process meta-model can be used as a basis for audit or assessment and any subsequent measurement or metrics exercise.

6 Case Study

'Tiffany Case – definitely distinctive'

James Bond, *Diamonds Are Forever*, UA/Eon/Danjaq

INTRODUCTION

This chapter provides a case study, based on a real organization, where a number of processes are identified and defined according to the meta-model introduced in this book. Particular notice is taken of examples already provided in the book, and some of the approaches taken during the process modelling exercise are discussed.

For reasons of brevity, the case study looks at just a few of the processes in the organization rather than the complete set – a complete process model would probably double the page count of the book. The case study also provides the opportunity for a series of exercises that you can work through at your discretion.

BACKGROUND

The organization under scrutiny is a medium-sized enterprise with approximately 150 employees, and whose main business is the development and support of new products and services for a number of different industries.

The company itself was started as a small enterprise with only five employees. It then grew in size to about 30 members of staff, before being bought out and amalgamated into a larger organization, which is the situation today. This evolution of the organization has resulted in a number of concerns and issues with regards to the processes carried out in the organization, such as:

- The work carried out by the original, small company is mainly concerned with training and support of the products that are developed by the rest of the company. Because the company started out as a few like-minded individuals, there were very few, if any, processes defined, as everyone had a good appreciation (or so they thought) of the work carried out by all other employees. Although this worked out fine when there were only a few people, as the company grew, the communication issues between the various members of staff increased enormously and it was only when the takeover occurred that the truth of the lack of process truly struck home.

- The main work carried out by the larger arm of the organization was split into two main camps – the technical camp and the sales camp. The technical camp was made up of engineers, scientists and support technicians who worked on the conception and development of new products. The ideas for new developments came directly from the sales and marketing staff who were, on the whole, non-technical people who had a terrible habit of promising the world to customers without understanding whether the promised goods and services were feasible either in terms of technology or the timescales involved. Also, the semantic gap between the technical and non-technical staff often resulted in the wrong system being delivered to the customer.

- On top of all these problems, some customers started to insist on something called 'quality', which was a new concept to the organization. Therefore, a quality team was hastily put together comprising project managers, who were then assigned the task of bringing the company's quality up-to-scratch, as quickly as possible and with limited resources. Indeed, several large customers from both the medical and transport industries decided that independent auditors would be brought in to ensure that the products and services offered met particular industry and international standards.

These are not insignificant problems. However, they are also very real problems that occur within many organizations, large, medium or small, and represent a typical set of problems.

The initial reaction to ensuring quality was to get an independent auditor in to carry out a pre-audit to see at what stage the company was, in terms of maturity of processes. This resulted in an anti-climax, as the formal auditor simply declared that as no processes were formally documented, it was impossible to carry out a proper pre-audit. The auditor advised the company to save their money and not bother with a full, formal audit until things had changed significantly.

At this point, when the perception was that all was lost, somebody made the point that the company must actually have processes that were executed successfully, otherwise the organization would not produce anything and would have no customers. The conclusion was, therefore, that the processes must be hidden and that they needed to be captured and then documented, which would keep the auditors happy.

The resulting action, therefore, was to apply process modelling to see how it could help the organization.

THE APPROACH

As has been stated already, there are many starting points for process modelling and deciding what to do first is often the most difficult part of the whole approach. Remember that the overall intention is to generate a complete process description based on the process meta-model and this process model has seven views. Therefore there are seven different start points to choose from, depending on what information is already known to the modeller. A good piece of advice is always to start where you have some information or, better still, an understanding of some aspect of the process. Each of the seven view points is discussed in turn below, with a few possible reasons why each particular view may be chosen as the start point.

- **Process content view:** this is a good starting point when there is some evidence of a documented process in the organization. Processes can be identified, their artefacts and activities captured and then this information used to drive the rest of the project. This is often the starting point when conducting an audit or assessment against some sort of standard.

- **Process structure view:** similarly, the process structure view can be a good start point where there is an existing, or partial, process model.

- **Process behaviour view:** the process behaviour view is a popular view to begin with where there are hidden processes that have been carried out by individuals over a period of time, yet there is no documentation. If you ask someone how they do something, the usual response is to describe a series of simple steps that equate to the process behaviour view. This is often the start point when talking with the people who actually carry out the processes, rather than managers of the process. This view can also be useful for gaining a consensus of opinion between different people who work on either the same process or on two processes that interact in some way.

- **Stakeholder view:** often, especially when dealing with managers, people will start to describe either the people or (more correctly) the roles of people in the organization and then use this as a starting point to find out who is responsible for what sort of activities.

- **Information view:** this is a good place to start when there is very little process description yet there is evidence of artefacts being produced, such as design specifications, minutes from meetings, test results, and so on. It is possible to start to identify processes based on the information that has been produced on a particular project or from a particular section of the work force.

- **Requirements view:** very often people want to forget about the actual processes and concentrate on what it is that they are trying to achieve by the process modelling exercise. In such circumstances, the requirements view can be a very good place to start the process modelling.

- **Process instance view:** the process instance, although not a common start point, can be used to generate the rest of the model when someone is describing an overall life cycle of a project. Very often, rather than talking about real stages of projects, people will often (confusingly and incorrectly) be talking about processes. In such situations, then the process instance view is a good start point for the generation of the whole process model.

Bear in mind also that it is possible to have more than one starting point. Consider the organization in the case study, where the single enterprise has grown from two separate sources. In this case, the information known about the processes will fall into two distinct camps.

Once a process model has a starting point, it is possible to see which other views are related to it in some way and, hence, the whole of the meta-model can then be navigated, captured and populated. The consistency checks that were presented in Chapter 4 are a very good means of understanding where to go next with the process modelling.

INTERPRETING THE PROCESS MODEL

When considering the process model, it is important to be able to read and understand the processes that are being described. This may seem obvious from the whole tone of this book, but there are far more benefits that may be obtained by thinking again about the content of the process model, for example:

- **Identifying complexity:** it has already been established that complexity is one of the three 'evils of life' (see Chapter 4) and that it is important to be able to identify and, hence, control it, but the reason why complexity exists can be very useful. Suppose a process behaviour view is created that is very complex; it is easy to see that complexity exists – the diagram will be messy and difficult to understand. However, it is worth finding out what the original source information for the diagram was – was it legacy information, or information that was created from scratch? If the answer is that the process has been started from scratch with a blank sheet of paper, then the process *must* be redefined, as the complexity has crept in through the fault of the person designing the process. This is what Brooks refers to as *accidental* complexity that can be avoided (Brooks, 1995). The other option, of course, is that the process model is based on an existing process, in which case the answer is not as simple, as it may not be possible to change the nature of the processes themselves. In such cases, the complexity is not the fault of the process modeller, as the complexity is inherent in the system. This is what Brooks refers to as *essential* complexity as it is in the essence of the system (Brooks, 1995).

- **Sanity checking:** it is possible to use the process model as a sanity check to ensure that the whole model fits together and, at the end of the day, that it makes sense. It is perfectly possible to have a well-defined process model but one that makes no logical sense to any of the users. The key view to consider here is the requirements view, which is setting the scene for the whole process model and will form the basic sense of the system.

- **Business analysis:** once the model exists, all sorts of analysis techniques may be applied. For example, the process model may be examined for efficiency, usually by looking at the behavioural aspect of the process model. For example, individual processes may be analysed for complexity by considering the process behaviour view, whereas the overall efficiency may be examined by considering the process instance view.

This is by no means an exhaustive list, but gives a general idea about the different ways that the process model may be considered and used.

The process model for the case study is introduced in the next section and, as each view is considered, some of these interpretation issues will be used as discussion points.

THE CASE STUDY PROCESS MODEL

The process model for the case study consists of the seven views from the process meta-model. The views are presented here in no particular order.

Process structure view

The process structure view for the case study is shown in Figure 6.1 and defines the basic structure and terminology to be used in the process model.

The diagram in Figure 6.1 shows the process structure view which includes the basic structure of the process model and the types of process group that have been identified. The basic terms that are used to define a process are:

- **Artefact:** describes any input or output of a process. Artefacts may include: reports, documents, minutes, components of the system, the system, specifications, and so on. The actual artefacts themselves are described in the information view.

- **Activity:** describes the steps involved in the process or the things that must be done in order to execute the process correctly. Activities produce and consume artefacts.

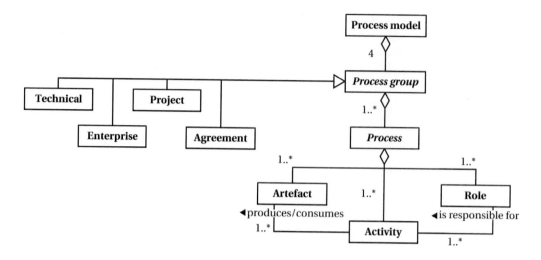

FIGURE 6.1   *Process structure view*

- **Role:** describes the stakeholder role that is responsible for the various activities. All activities must have an associated role.

All processes are categorized according to four process groups, which have been identified as:

- **Agreement:** describes all processes that relate to the customer-supplier relationship with the organization.
- **Project:** describes all processes associated with management and support within the organization.
- **Technical:** describes all processes associated with development and engineering activities within the organization.
- **Enterprise:** describes all the processes that apply across the whole of the organization.

The actual processes within each group are identified and described by the process content view for each of the process categories.

The process structure view also forms the basis for the high-level mapping to any source standards or process models that may be relevant to the organization.

Process content view

The process content view describes the actual processes that are contained within each of the process groups identified in the process structure view. As is often the case in real-life process models, this amounts to a number of processes and, therefore, it is usual to split the view into several lower-level views. An obvious choice for partitioning this split is to base each of the lower-level views on one of the process groups. Therefore, in this case there will be at least four basic views that make up the entire process content view. It is possible, and likely, that there will eventually be more than four views as, in some cases, there may be a lot of processes within a single view, particularly when it comes to describing the core capability of the organization by its processes. For example, an organization that is predominately concerned with managing projects is likely to have a complex process content view for the 'Project' process group, whereas an organization more focused on, say, product development, will have a more complex process content view for the 'technical' process group.

In some cases, it is common for one or more of the process groups to be further divided into lower-level groups. In the example in this case study, the 'Project' process group has been subdivided into two other groups: 'Management' and 'Support', as shown in Figure 6.2. Although this is fine in theory, caution must be exercised that too many levels are not introduced, which will lead to an increase in the complexity of the model. As a simple rule-of-thumb, it is a good idea to minimize the number of levels of process group to two or three nested levels, in other words, no more than in the example shown in Figure 6.2.

Now that the process groups have been subdivided, it is possible to look inside each one and see what processes exist and what associated artefacts and activities (using the terminology here) exist for each process.

Figure 6.3 shows the first of the process content views, for the 'Enterprise' process group. Remember that these processes are ones that will apply across the whole of the organization and are, therefore, applicable to everyone within the company.

Figure 6.3 shows the processes that have been identified for the 'Enterprise' process category and the first thing that springs to mind is

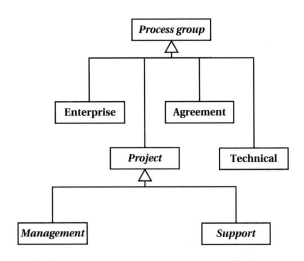

FIGURE 6.2 *Further breakdown of the 'Project' process group*

that there are not many processes in this group. This could be for a number of reasons:

- Bear in mind that the company in question has grown from two small companies into a single larger company. In situations like this it is not uncommon for there to be a lack of enterprise-level processes. In a small organization, there tends to be more emphasis on the technical and management-related processes than on higher-level processes that apply to the core business. Conversely, some large organizations have many more of these high-level processes defined and fewer technical and management ones. This can often reflect the distribution of roles in the organization – too many levels of management often result in a top-heavy process model that leans towards enterprise-level processes.

- As the process modelling initiative has only just started, there are no processes in place that actually relate to process modelling or process improvement. This is to be expected in such a scenario but, if the process content view was to be examined in, say,

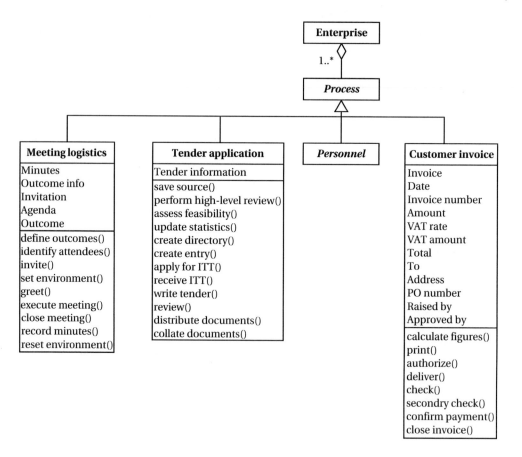

FIGURE 6.3   *Process content view for the 'Enterprise' process group*

six months' time, you would certainly expect to see more high-level processes relating to process modelling and/or process improvement.

- The company itself is still relatively small. Perhaps it does not have a dedicated personnel department, hence the lack of employment-related processes. In fact, the only process that relates directly to employees here is the 'Personnel' process, which is broken down in Figure 6.4.

Although four 'Personnel' processes have been identified in Figure 6.4, none of them has any artefacts or activities defined. In this situation, it so happened that the area of 'Personnel' processes was identified as being very weak, therefore a set of processes was identified, but not fully. This can serve two useful purposes. The first is that it demonstrates to a third party that, although no processes exist at the moment, the whole area has not been overlooked but is waiting for attention. The other purpose is to remind the process modellers that the model is still incomplete. It is possible that if these empty processes did not exist, someone would assume that the process model was complete, as all processes that exist have been populated.

Note the use of the '{incomplete}' constraint here to indicate that there are more processes on the same level as 'Personnel' not shown here.

As with all views in the process meta-model, it is important to look not just at what processes are present, but also which processes are missing from the process model. When carrying out business-related analysis exercises, the lack of processes is often as revealing as the presence of processes and can give a good indication of the focus of the organization and where areas of knowledge exist.

The next group to be examined is the 'Technical' process group.

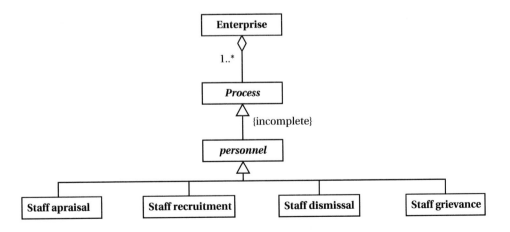

Figure 6.4 *Process content view for 'Enterprise' with an emphasis on 'Personnel'*

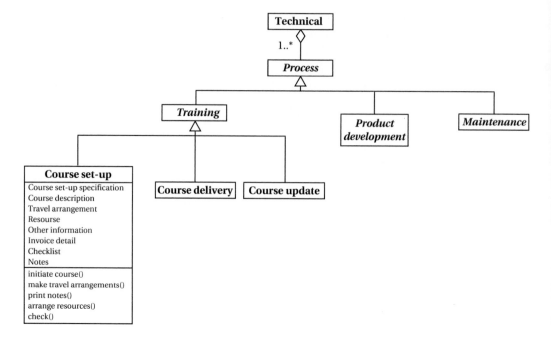

FIGURE 6.5   *Process content view for the 'Technical' process group, with an emphasis on the 'Training' processes*

Figure 6.5 shows the process content view for the 'Technical' process group but, as much of the emphasis of this organization is on product development and training, the process group has been split into three main subdivisions, which are:

- **Training:** describes processes related to training activities. These processes are based on the original, small company that was purely devoted to training.
- **Product development:** focuses on the development of new products. This has originated from the parent organization that bought out the smaller company.
- **Maintenance:** focuses on the maintenance of products that are in the market place and, again, was originated from the parent organization.

It should be clear from this summary of the subdivisions that there is a potential for problems in integrating these processes that have originated from two different sources.

There are three processes that have been identified that are associated with training, each with different levels of detail defined. These are:

- **Course set-up:** describes the activities involved in making sure that all the preparations have been made to run a successful course.

- **Course delivery:** describes how the course itself must be delivered. This includes not only course delivery, but also monitoring of the course and how the tutor must behave towards attendees (greeting, introductions, and so on).
- **Course update:** allows feedback to be taken from the course and then used as a basis for improvements and enhancements to future courses. It also allows for any mistakes or ambiguities that were highlighted during the course delivery to be fed back into the system.

Figure 6.6 emphasizes the technical processes associated with product development and the first impression is one of surprise at how many process there are. This is clearly indicative of an organization with a strong history of product development and one that has quite a level of understanding of the processes involved. There are two interesting things to notice about this view:

- The processes identified reflect the typical processes described by many technical life cycle models. The processes that relate

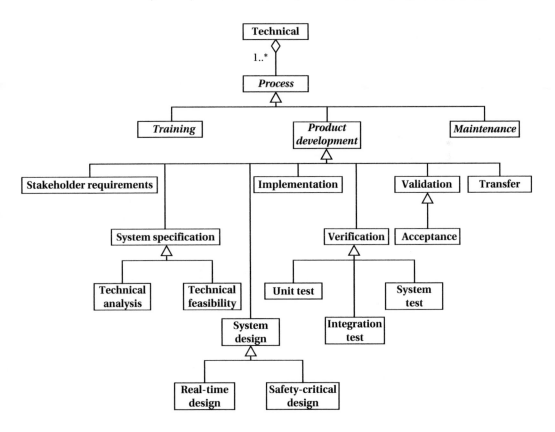

FIGURE 6.6 *Process content view for the 'Technical' process group, with an emphasis on 'Product development'*

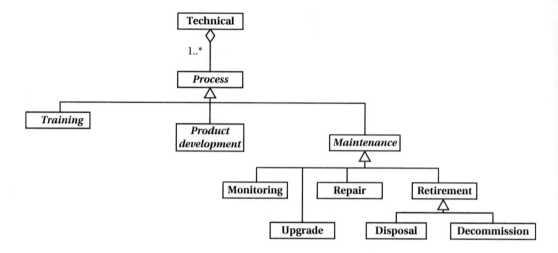

FIGURE 6.7 *Process content view for the 'Technical' process group, with an emphasis on 'Maintenance' processes*

to requirements, specification and design will be familiar to many engineers and will form the backbone of any sort of development.

- Several of the processes have been tailored for slightly different approaches to meet the same process. For example, the 'Design' process, the 'System specification' process and the 'Verification' process.

Figure 6.7 shows the technical processes once again, but this time emphasizes the maintenance processes within the organization. There are two aspects of this view that are of interest:

- There is a focus on the operations of the product and, hence, any error reporting activities that need to be executed.
- There is also a focus on the eventual retirement of the system. This is often indicative of the organization taking a responsible view towards its products. Indeed, many organizations do not even consider what happens to their products once they have reached the end of their life cycle. In this example, there is not one, but two options for retiring the system:
- The 'Decommission' process, which describes how to take a system out of action. It may then be left in existence or, indeed, disposed of, as described by the next process.
- The 'Disposal' process, which describes how to get rid of the product in a responsible way. In fact, as the world becomes more and more environmentally aware of the fact that something must happen when systems 'die', this is an encouraging sign within an organization.

By considering these processes, think about what sort of products this company may be involved in producing. If any harmful substances were involved, then one would expect to see far more processes identified for disposal. There is no mention of recycling here, so this may mean that there is little opportunity for recycling or, in a worse scenario, that the organization has not considered recycling for the products.

Figures 6.8 and 6.9 concentrate on the 'Project' process group and look at the various processes that are used within the organization.

Figure 6.8 shows the process content view for the 'Project' process group (which has two main types: 'Management' and 'Support') and this diagram concentrates on the 'Management' processes.

There are three management-related processes that have been identified:

- **Project scheduling:** describes the process for generating the initial project schedule and project plan.
- **Project monitoring:** describes the process for monitoring the project once it has started and that continues until completion.
- **Project review:** describes a review process that may be invoked periodically throughout the project to ensure that, for example, project gates can be passed effectively.

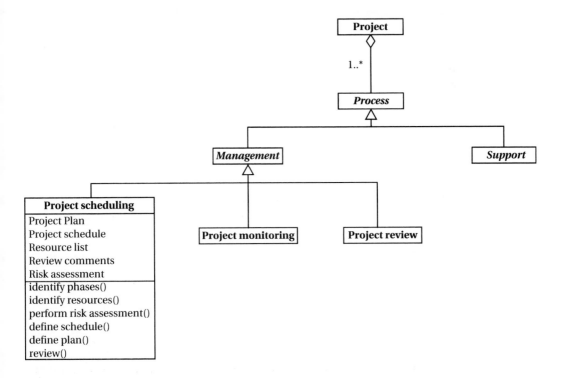

FIGURE 6.8 *Process content view for the 'Project' process group, with an emphasis on 'Management'*

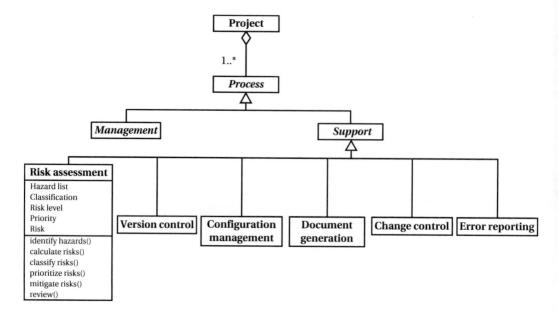

FIGURE 6.9   *Process content view for the 'Project' process group, with an emphasis on 'Support'*

On the whole, you might consider this part of the process content view to be fairly lightweight, as three is not a huge number. Again, rather than simply reading the diagram, it is worth looking beneath the surface of the model and considering why there are few processes for project management.

Figure 6.9 shows the same process content view but, this time, with an emphasis on the 'Support' processes. There are six support processes identified:

- **Risk assessment:** potential hazards are identified and the risk classified, prioritized and mitigated against.
- **Version control:** the mechanisms for identifying all artefacts in a unique way is defined.
- **Configuration management:** covers how the different versions of artefacts are managed and controlled, including build control.
- **Document generation:** covers how documents must be created and describes any templates or structures that must be used in the documents themselves.
- **Change control:** defines the identification and execution of changes.
- **Error reporting:** covers the mechanisms for identifying, reporting and resolving errors that may occur at any point in the process.

Again, these processes have been identified but not yet defined, which shows that, although the definitions are missing, the organization is aware of this omission. When such omissions occur, it is worth trying to understand why they occur in the first place. There could be several reasons for a pattern in the process model like this to occur in the management area, such as:

- **Engineers as project managers:** in a company that has evolved from a small group of engineers, such as this one, it is common to find out that all the project management roles are being carried out by engineers who are also working on the development of the project. This can often result in an emphasis on the engineering activities, rather than the management activities, as is the case here.
- **Small or short-term projects:** very often, small projects or projects with a short timeframe exhibit a lack of management processes. This may be because the perception is that there is not enough time for management, or perhaps more informal, agile management techniques are being implemented.
- **Small project teams:** in some cases, it may be that the number of people working on a project is very small, or is in fact just a single person. In such situations, management practices are often nonexistent, as the communication tends to be, or is perceived to be, very strong. However, when these projects increase in size and more people are assigned, this lack of management processes becomes very apparent. Although an informal approach to management may seem adequate when few people are involved, it falls apart when the project is scaled up.
- **Slackness or arrogance:** of course, the most obvious reason why there are few management processes could simply be due to slackness or arrogance on behalf of the project personnel. If the project staff have no real motivation, this can result in slackness, whereas if the project team have an inflated opinion of their abilities, this can result in arrogance. Another cause of arrogance is when someone (it is usually a single person) views themselves as a 'project champion' who can turn a bad or failing project around through their own project prowess, immortality and general greatness of being. Unfortunately, these causes are nowhere near as uncommon as they should be.

These are not all of the reasons for a dearth of management processes, but it provides an indication that the patterns manifested in the process model should be thought about, rather than just read and accepted.

Figure 6.10 shows the process content view for the 'Agreement' process group, which has four processes identified:

- **Project initiation:** concerned with making the initial contact with the customer, defining the initial requirements for the project and coming up with the original agreement or contract.
- **Project monitoring:** once a problem is up and running, it should be continuously monitored to ensure that it is both on schedule and still meeting its original requirements.

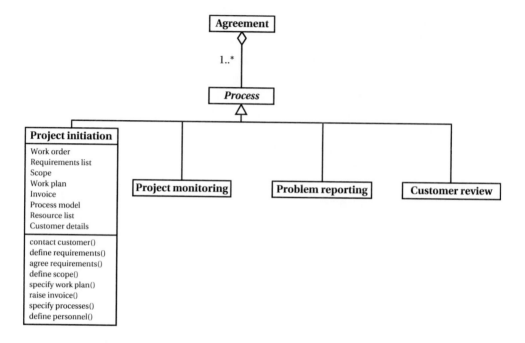

FIGURE 6.10   *Process content view for the 'Agreement' process group*

- **Problem reporting:** when problems do occur, which is inevitable, then it is important that they can be picked up and dealt with effectively.
- **Customer review:** it is important that not only the project team thinks that they have executed a successful project, but also that the customer does as well. These reviews may be periodical throughout the course of the project (particularly where long projects are concerned) and also at the end of the project as part of the final acceptance.

This completes the process content view, which can often turn out to be one of the largest views in the project.

Stakeholder view

The stakeholder view is concerned with identifying all the roles in the organization. If the process behaviour view or the requirements view already exist, then they can be a good source for identifying stakeholders.

The stakeholder view itself is shown in the Figures 6.11, 6.12 and 6.13.

Figure 6.11 shows the stakeholder view with an emphasis on 'Customer'. These stakeholders are described as follows:

- **Sponsor:** describes the role of the person or organization who will, ultimately, be funding any work.

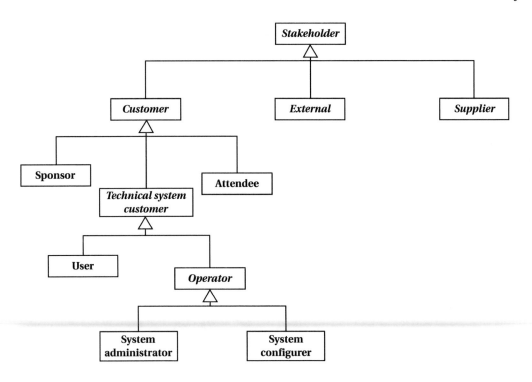

FIGURE 6.11 *Stakeholder view with an emphasis on 'Customer'*

- **Technical system customer:** an abstract role that serves as a simple grouping.
- **User:** Represents the role of the end-users of the system being produced.
- **Operator:** another abstract role, which groups together all types of people who will operate the system.
- **System administrator:** represents the role of the people who will be responsible for controlling the final system.
- **System configurer:** represents the role of the people who will be responsible for the installation and set-up of the final system.

Figure 6.12 identifies the stakeholder roles associated with 'External'. The roles are described in more detail as follows:

- **Standards:** represents a grouping of all roles relating to standards.
- **Standard provider:** represents the role of the organizations who produce standards, such as the BSI, ISO, and so on.
- **Standard enforcer:** represents the role of all those involved with independent audits and assessments.
- **Safety enforcer:** represents the role of all those involved with safety assurance for the products.

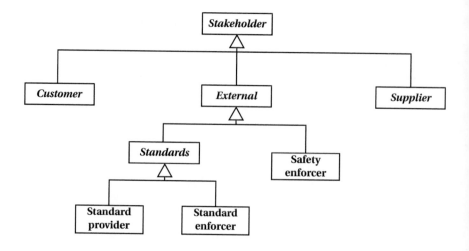

FIGURE 6.12   *Stakeholder view with an emphasis on 'External'*

Figure 6.13 shows all the roles associated with the 'Supplier' class. Rather than go into detail about all these roles, as there are many, we will discuss the diagram from the point of view of looking at the patterns in the diagram and comparing them to previous ones.

This first thing that stands out with Figure 6.13 is that it is far more complex than Figures 6.11 or 6.12. This is only to be expected as there are usually far more roles that can be identified within an organization than outside it. This is because people will usually have a better understanding of their own organization than of others.

There are two main groupings here: 'Technical' and 'Management'. Notice the difference between the number of technical roles that

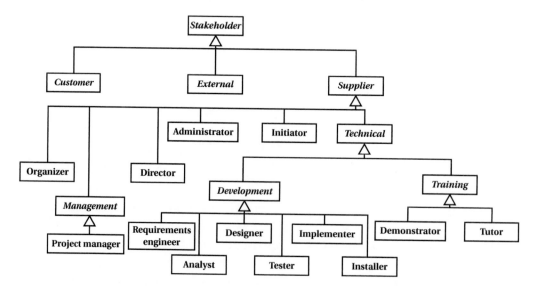

FIGURE 6.13   *Stakeholder view with an emphasis on 'Supplier'*

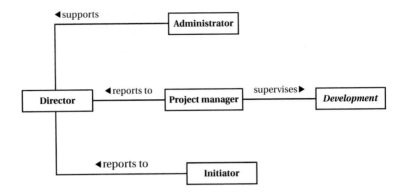

FIGURE 6.14 *Enhancing stakeholders with additional relationships*

have been identified (in fact, this is divided into two further groups) compared to the management roles (a single role – 'Project manager'). This can be explained by the background of the company having originally few employees and most of those with a technical background.

Further investigation of the 'Technical' role reveals that it is split between 'Training' and 'Development', which mirrors the main capabilities of the original companies.

The roles that do not fall into either of these categories also bear consideration. It is tempting to put all of these roles into another grouping but caution must be exercised as some of these roles are not similar enough to be grouped together. The other temptation is to create a generic grouping called something like 'Other roles' to serve as a general catch-all. Although this seems quite sensible, it can often lead to people being lazy and simply putting any role that has not been thought about into the same category.

Extending the stakeholder view

The stakeholder view can be extended to add extra value to the process model in three different ways, as follows:

- Tie it into a more traditional organizational chart. It is possible, for example, to start to add relationships between the various roles that can form the basis for an organizational chart. Figure 6.14 shows how the stakeholder view may be extended by considering the relationship between the various roles, rather than just the classification of roles. This can be used as a driver for, or indeed part of the analysis of, an organizational chart. Typical relationships that can be shown on such an extended view include: 'reports to', 'supports' and 'supervises'.

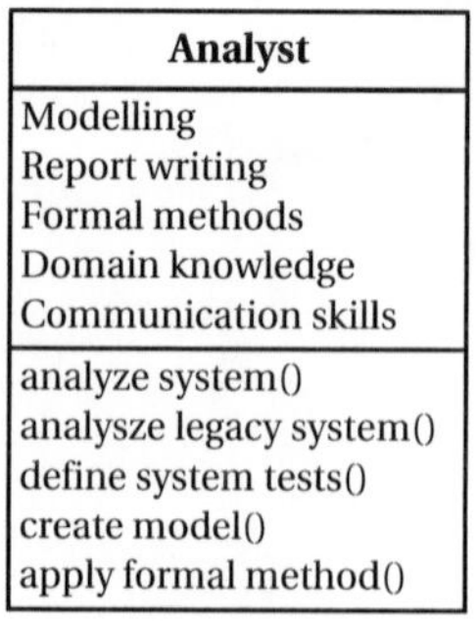

Analyst
Modelling
Report writing
Formal methods
Domain knowledge
Communication skills
analyze system()
analysze legacy system()
define system tests()
create model()
apply formal method()

FIGURE 6.15   *Defining skills and responsibilities for stakeholders*

- Consider the skills associated with each role. This is important for areas like recruitment activities or staff appraisals. It is important to understand the skills required by each stakeholder and can be a powerful way to ensure that the stakeholder name is an appropriate one. In terms of representing this information on the model, this is quite straightforward, as skills may be thought of as a list of features that the role must exhibit, which means that they can be represented on the stakeholder class by simply populating the class attributes for the stakeholder.
- Associate responsibilities for each role. Providing that the process behaviour view exists, then this is a simple step as it is simply a matter of identifying all processes with a particular role as a swim lane name, and then abstracting the activities that it is responsible for. This can also be represented very simply on the model by creating a list of class operations for each stakeholder.

Figure 6.15 shows an example of how the skills and responsibilities of a stakeholder may be represented visually on the model as attributes and operations respectively.

Requirements view

The requirements view captures the driving needs behind the processes. There will be several diagrams that comprise the requirements view depending on the nature of the organization. Potentially, there may be more than one requirements view for each process, as each process will be viewed differently by each stakeholder. In order to minimize the number of diagrams in the requirements view, while still capturing enough business knowledge, it is important to consider each diagram carefully.

For this case study, we consider two main areas of work – training and invoicing. First, we consider the company's training-related processes.

Training

Figure 6.5 identified a number of processes related to the company training capability, which were identified as: 'Course set-up', 'Course delivery'

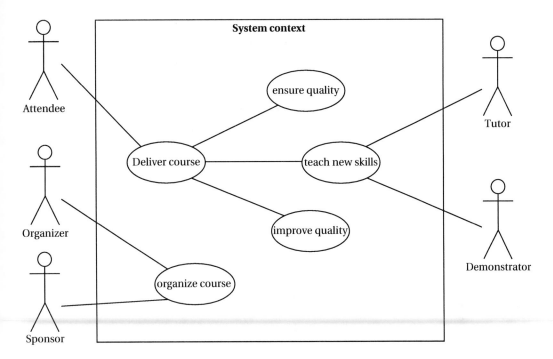

FIGURE 6.16   *Simple context for training-related processes*

and 'Course update', but the question to be answered here is 'why?' The company requirements for the training capability need to be identified, as shown in Figure 6.16.

Figure 6.16 shows a simple context for training-related processes. There are two main requirements shown here: 'Deliver course' and 'organize course'. 'Deliver course' is related in some way to three other requirements: 'ensure quality', 'teach new skills' and 'improve quality'. Notice that this diagram has not been fully populated in terms of the relationship as, at the moment, these are all represented as simple lines, rather than the more meaningful relationships discussed in Chapter 2.

It is quite common to consider one of these high-level requirements in more detail by decomposing it into lower-level requirements on another diagram, as shown in Figure 6.17, which shows a decomposition of the 'organize course' requirement. Notice how this diagram is more meaningful as the relationships are more explicit between the various requirements.

There is one main requirement identified here, 'organize course', which has three included requirements: 'set up', 'publicize' and 'support'. The '<<include>>' relationship implies that these three requirements are always part of the main requirement. There is also an extension to the 'publicize' requirement that has been identified as 'cancel course'.

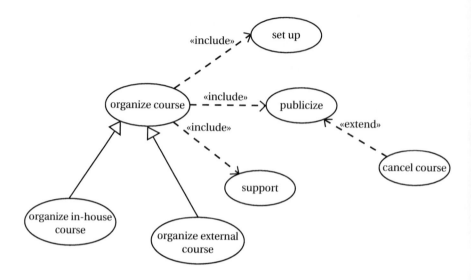

FIGURE 6.17   *Breakdown of the 'organize course' requirement*

The '<<extend>>' relationship implies that the 'cancel course' requirement is only sometimes part of the 'publicize' requirement.

The other interesting mechanism here is the use of the specialization relationship, as 'organize course' has two types: 'organize in-house course' and 'organize external course'. What is interesting here is that both of these specializations inherit the structure from their parent requirement. Therefore, both 'organize in-house course' and 'organize external course' include: 'set up', 'publicize' and 'support'.

Invoicing

As our second example of a requirements view, consider Figure 6.18, which shows the requirements view for invoice-related processes. Note here that the main requirement, 'Ensure payment' has four included requirements: 'Raise invoice', 'Check', 'Deliver invoice' and 'Monitor invoice'. Also note here that the main requirement has two constraints upon it: 'Ensure timeliness' and 'Maintain accountancy records'.

The validation of these requirements by the processes from the process content are demonstrated in the process instance view.

Information view

The information view shows the artefacts that are present in the process model and, just as importantly, it also shows the relationships between them. The information model may be split over different levels of abstraction. It is quite common to have an overall information model that shows the high-level artefacts and the conceptual relationships between them, but then to also break down each artefact into more detail and to describe the exact content and structure of each one. Figure 6.19 focuses on the artefacts for a single process – the 'Course set-up' process.

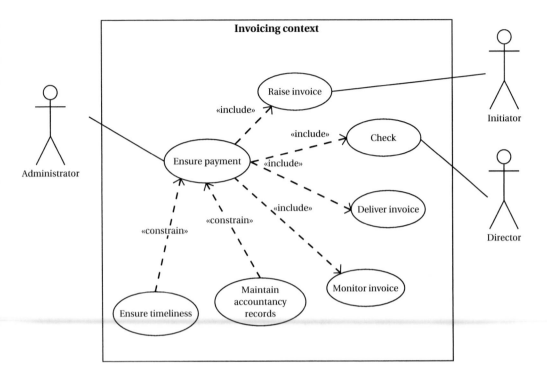

FIGURE 6.18 *Requirements view for invoice-related processes*

Figure 6.19 shows the main artefact for the 'Course set-up' process discussed previously. This diagram is particularly interesting, as there is only a single main artefact, 'Course set-up specification'. Although the artefact itself is relatively complex, all the information generated as part of the artefact is gathered into a single entity, in this case it is actually realized by a document. Different parts of the document are generated by different stakeholders (the exact nature of which will be discussed in the process behaviour view for this process) and they all come together in a single document.

This is quite a contrast to the next example of an information view, which is shown in Figure 6.20.

Figure 6.20 shows the main artefact for the 'Customer invoice' process artefacts. Again, there is a single artefact but, this time, the actual structure of the information is quite simple – just a list of attributes representing information to be recorded in the artefact.

In this example, the dependency relationship has been used to show instances, or real-life examples, of the process artefact. This has been shown explicitly on the information, as for each invoice generated, there must be three copies printed out: the 'Customer copy' sent to the customer for payment; the 'Accountant copy', initially retained and then sent to the accountants as required; and, finally, the 'Company copy', retained for the company's internal book-keeping records. The use of

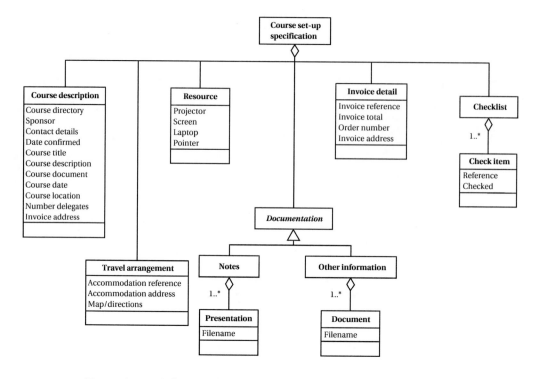

FIGURE 6.19 *Information view for the 'Course set-up' process artefacts*

instances is quite common in areas such as accountancy where multiple copies of artefacts are required to maintain audit trails.

The two examples shown so far are actually related. Note that the course set-up artefact has a section named 'Invoice' that captures some of the invoice details, which is, quite obviously related to the invoice artefact itself. Indeed, the 'Invoice' artefact is related to a number of other

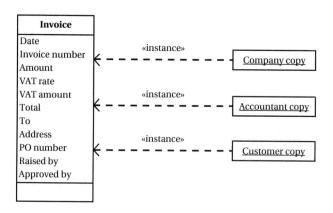

FIGURE 6.20 *Information view for the 'Customer invoice' process artefacts*

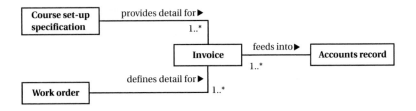

FIGURE 6.21 *Information view relating artefacts*

artefacts from other processes that must be identified in order to ensure that the process model is consistent and that the processes will work together when executed (this is further explored in the discussion of the process instance view). Figure 6.21 illustrates this.

Figure 6.21 shows how higher-level artefacts from different processes can be related together in the information view. It is these higher-level relationships that verify that the processes will work with one another, in terms of their inputs, outputs and general information consistency. The artefacts shown here are from the following processes: 'Course set-up', 'Customer invoice', 'Project initiation' and an, as-yet undefined, accounts-related process. Clearly, this forms the basis for traceability checking for all artefacts.

Process instance view

The process instance view forms the heart of the validation of the processes that are defined in the process model. As has already been discussed, the requirements for a set of processes are likely to change as time goes on, therefore it is essential that there is a mechanism for validating each requirement. The basic mechanism of the process instance view is to validate a particular requirement, or set of require-ments, by executing a number of processes that have been identified in the process content view and seeing whether they meet the desired capability of the requirements.

In the following two examples, the 'Ensure payment' requirement from Figure 6.18 will be chosen as the requirement to be validated. For any requirement, there are always a number of ways that the requirement can be met that manifest themselves into a sequence of processes; in other words, a number of scenarios may be defined for each requirement. The following two diagrams show two different scenarios for the same requirement that allow the requirements to be validated by executing a number of different processes.

Figure 6.22 shows the process instance view that represent a scenario for normal operation of a project and invoicing. In this example, the first process to be instantiated, or executed, is that of 'Project initiation'.

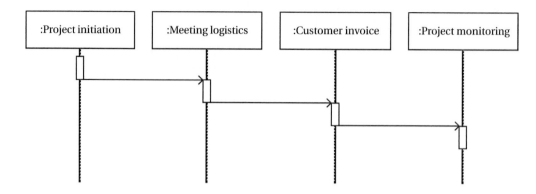

Figure 6.22 *Process instance view for the 'Ensure payment' requirement for a normal project scenario*

This then invokes the 'Meeting logistics' process, which in turn invokes the 'Customer invoice' process and, finally, the 'Project monitoring' process. The execution of these processes in this particular sequence represents how a normal project is run and also validates that the 'Customer invoice' process is correctly executed during the course of a normal project. There are, however, a number of other scenarios in which the 'Customer invoice' process may be required, another of which is described in the scenario below. Note how processes from different process groups are used together here to make a variety of scenarios.

Figure 6.23 again shows a scenario for the 'Ensure payment' requirement but, in this instance, the scenario represents how a course is set up, delivered and invoiced. As can be seen from the diagram, the order of process execution is: (i) 'Project initiation' as in the previous scenario; (ii) 'Course set up'; (iii) 'Customer invoice'; and (iv) 'Course delivery'.

Another option with the process instance view that can greatly help with validating the stakeholders is to include instances of these stakeholders on the diagram.

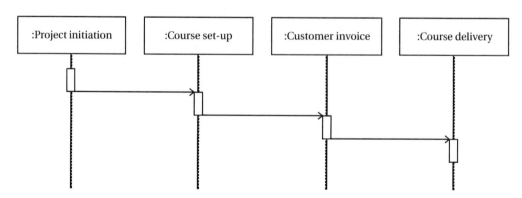

Figure 6.23 *Process instance view for the 'Ensure payment' requirement for the scenario of running a course*

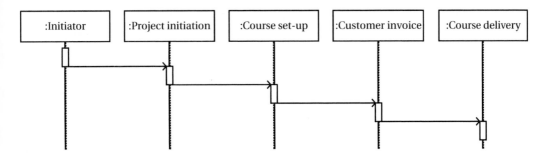

FIGURE 6.24   *Process instance view including stakeholder instance*

Figure 6.24 shows the same scenario as in Figure 6.23, but this time an instance of a stakeholder has been identified and included as a life line.

The number of scenarios required by a single requirement is potentially infinite, as there are countless possibilities. Creating scenarios is analogous to testing in that there is no limit to the amount of testing that can be carried out. It is important to execute enough scenarios that provide sufficient coverage for the requirements while providing a level of confidence that the processes will work effectively.

Process behaviour view

The process behaviour view describes how each process is executed in terms of its activities, artefacts and responsibilities. The process behaviour view can often be the start point of a process modelling exercise, particularly where information is to be extracted from inside someone's head and reproduced on paper. The process behaviour view has very strong links to the process content view and for each process identified, there must exist a process behaviour view. The process behaviour view is realized using an activity diagram that will be a 'comfortable' view to many people as it looks like, and indeed has its origins in, a flowchart diagram.

Figure 6.25 shows how the 'Customer invoice' process is executed in terms of the order of execution of the activities and the production and consumption of artefacts by each activity. Also, note how responsibility for each activity has been allocated using swim lanes that are themselves related to stakeholders from the stakeholder view.

Figure 6.26 shows the process behaviour view for the 'Course set-up' process. Of interest in this diagram is the use of UML signals, represented graphically by an irregular pentagon, to indicate that a message is being sent to another part of the model. In this case, the signals are showing messages that start off other processes. The first signal, 'raise invoice', is sent once the course has been initiated and it kicks off the 'Customer invoice' process. This is a good way to show the relationships between processes that are tightly coupled.

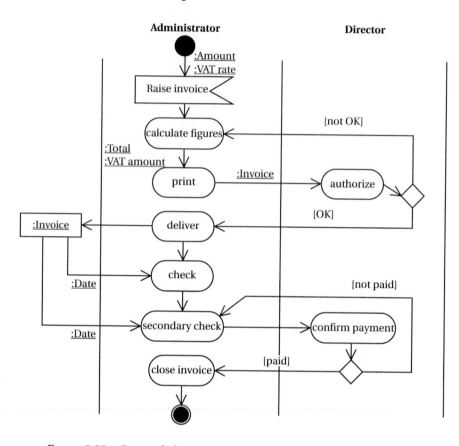

FIGURE 6.25   *Process behaviour view for the 'Customer invoice' process*

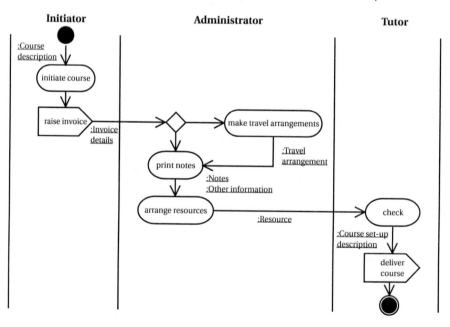

FIGURE 6.26   *Process behaviour view for the 'Course set-up' process*

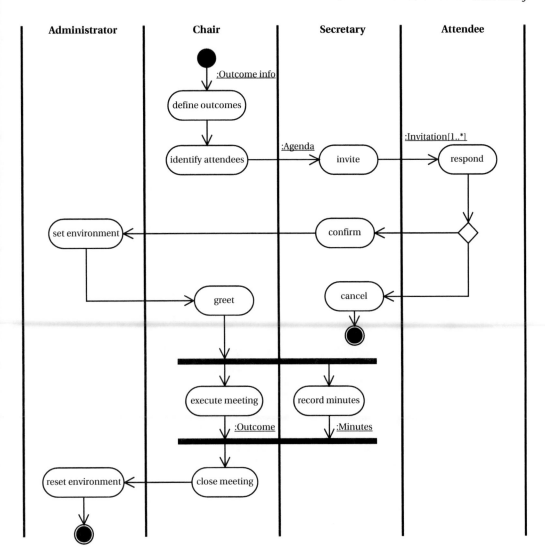

FIGURE 6.27   *Process behaviour view for the 'Meeting logistics' process*

Figure 6.27 shows the process behaviour view for the 'Meeting logistics' process. Of interest here is a control split and join, but notice this time how the responsibility for each of the concurrent activities is controlled by different swim lanes.

PROCESS MAPPING

The process model that has been generated so far, as was stated in the introduction, will be used ultimately as the source for various standard assessments. To give a broad idea of how this model maps onto source

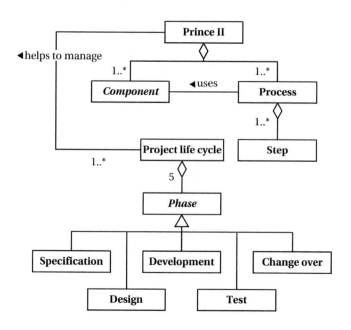

FIGURE 6.28   *Process structure view for Prince II*

standards, we take two standards as a simple example of basic process mapping. These two standards are:

- **ISO 15288:** a generic systems standard for systems life cycle management that can be applied to almost any project. Although ISO 15288 covers all process areas, it is particularly strong in the technical areas (ISO, 2002).
- **Prince II:** for projects in a controlled environment. This is a process model that is used extensively on UK government projects and that is focused primarily on management issues (Bentley, 2001).

Figure 6.28 shows the process structure view for Prince II, which provides a good overview of the whole standard. It can be seen that

TABLE 6.1   *Initial mapping between ISO 15288 and Prince II*

ISO 15288	Prince II
Life cycle	Project life cycle
Process group	
Conception	Specification
Development	Design
Construction	Development
	Test
Transition	Change over
Operations	
Retirement	

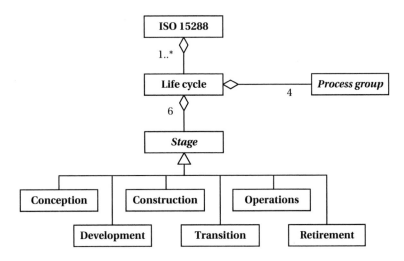

FIGURE 6.29 *Process structure view for ISO 15288*

there are two main elements that go to make up the Prince II process model – 'Component' and 'Process'. The Prince II process model helps to manage a 'Project life cycle' that is made up of five types of 'Phase', which are: 'Specification', 'Design', 'Development', 'Test' and 'Change over'.

Figure 6.29 shows a similar-looking process structure for ISO 15288. If an initial mapping between the two process models is considered, the mappings listed in Table 6.1 emerge. In some cases, the mapping is quite obvious, as the terminology used is very similar. For example, 'Life cycle' and 'Project life cycle' are similar terms and they do indeed map. Caution must be exercised, however, as some terms, although they appear similar, or the same, actually represent different concepts. As an example of this, consider the term 'Development' that is used in both process models to describe a particular type of phase. At first glance, this appears to be a straightforward mapping, but when taken in the context of the other mappings, it is clear that they are fundamentally different. In ISO 15288, the development stage is concerned with analysing the problem and producing an optimum design, whereas in Prince II, the development phase is more concerned with constructing the system, with all the analysis and design activities having been carried out in the design phase.

Figures 6.30 and 6.31 show the next level down in the models and are used as a basis for one of the exercises at the end of the chapter, hence they are not described in any detail.

Figure 6.30 shows another process structure view, this time with the emphasis on the 'Component' element in the process model.

Figure 6.31 shows the process structure view for ISO 15288, with an emphasis on 'Process group'.

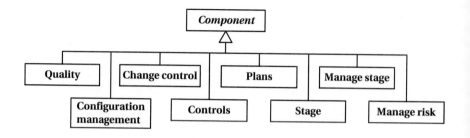

FIGURE 6.30   *Process structure view for Prince II, with an emphasis on 'Component'*

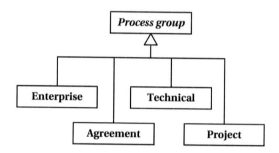

FIGURE 6.31   *Process structure view for ISO 15288, with an emphasis on 'Process group'*

CONCLUSIONS

This final chapter presented a case study that uses all of the techniques described in this book. The main aim has been to demonstrate how a complete process model may be developed. Although not fully populated, enough of the model has been completed to illustrate all the main concepts and ideas presented in the book. Also, the areas that have not been fully covered in this case study form the basis for a number of exercises in the next section.

EXERCISES

The following set of exercises have been specially designed to apply all the techniques employed in this book. There are two reasons for this. The obvious one is to enable you to test your knowledge and understanding of this book. The second reason is a bit more subtle, as carrying out these exercises will increase your confidence in both the approach and your own abilities before employing them 'in anger' in the real world.

1. Extend the process structure view to include the concepts of skills and responsibilities introduced in Figure 6.15.
2. Check the consistency between the process behaviour view in Figure 6.27 and the process content view in Figure 6.3.
3. Extend the mapping exercise to include the elements in Figures 6.30 and 6.31.
4. Update the requirements view in Figure 6.16 to include more detailed relationships between the requirements.
5. Add the following roles to the stakeholder view: 'Sales person', 'Marketer' and 'Sales manager'. In which grouping will they appear?
6. Increase the number of artefacts in the information view in Figure 6.21.
7. Populate some of the existing processes in the process content views shown in Figures 6.3 to 6.10.
8. Add some new processes to the process content view to reflect marketing-related processes.
9. Add some new instances of stakeholders to the process information views in Figures 6.22 and 6.23. Ensure consistency with the original requirements view.
10. Create a new process instance view diagram for any of the requirements in Figures 6.16 or 6.18.
11. Modify the process realization view of the existing process meta-model to include instances of stakeholders under the process instance view.
12. Create a process behaviour view for any of the processes in the process content views in Figures 6.3 to 6.10.
13. Define a process quagmire for the two process models introduced in Figures 6.28 and 6.29. Add some new source processes to the quagmire.
14. Consider the requirements view in Figure 6.17. What are the implications of moving the '<<extend>>' relationship, which currently exists between 'Cancel course' and 'Publicize', to between 'Cancel course' and 'Organize course'?

Some sample answers to these exercises are provided in Chapter 11.

7 The Bigger Picture – Enterprise Architecture

'Learn from yesterday, live for today, hope for tomorrow.'

Albert Einstein

INTRODUCTION

The aim of this book is to help people to understand, analyse and define processes of all types through effective modelling techniques. However, it is also important to understand how the process model for the organization fits in with the rest of the business. Exactly what the rest of the business is will depend on its nature, its size, and so on. Some of the aspects of the business that must be considered include, for example, process models, process descriptions, competencies, standards, methodologies, tools, people and business goals.

It is important not only that these different aspects of the business are understood, but also that they are both *consistent* and *congruent* with one another. By 'consistent' here, we mean in terms of modelling as has been discussed throughout this book. By 'congruency', we mean that the intentions and meanings of all aspects are consistent with one another. For example, given any model of a business, it is important that each diagram is consistent with all the others – this consistency is what gives us a model rather than a group of pictures. However, it is important that each aspect of the business also meets the business goals, or business requirements, of the enterprise. It is this congruency that makes the model an enterprise architecture, rather than just an expanded process model.

When all this business knowledge is gathered together into a consistent model and all aspects of the model are congruent with the aims of the business, it is referred to as an *enterprise architecture.*

Identifying and understanding an enterprise architecture is crucial to the success of any business and a good process model forms the heart of any enterprise architecture.

An enterprise architecture is a living entity that will evolve over time. Time is crucial to its effectiveness, as there are usually three periods of time when it is used: the present, the immediate future and the far future. These are often referred to as 'current', 'immediate' and 'visionary', or other similar terms. An effective enterprise architecture is used to help predict future business changes, in order to take steps as early as possible to meet any perceived or actual problems.

ENTERPRISE ARCHITECTURE

In order to understand the nature of an enterprise architecture, a meta-model has been created to identify the key elements that must be present in any enterprise architecture or architecture framework. The basic meta-model is shown in Figure 7.1 (in which 'EA-SE' stands for 'enterprise architecture systems engineering').

The meta-model itself is composed of a number of elements that can be grouped together into three main areas: the organizational process, the requirements and the structure. The structure refers to the viewpoints and views that are the fundamental building blocks of any enterprise architecture. The requirements capture the needs of the enterprise architecture at all of its levels of abstraction. Finally, the organizational process refers to the processes that form part of the enterprise architecture, in terms of the company process model.

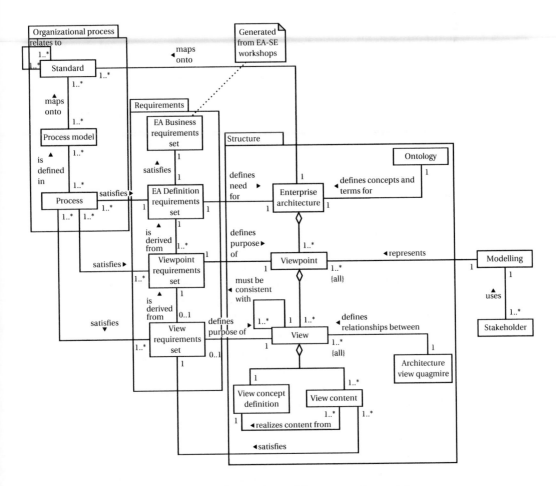

FIGURE 7.1 *Enterprise architecture meta-model*

ENTERPRISE ARCHITECTURE STRUCTURE

If one were to look at a number of existing enterprise architectures and try to abstract what they have in common, then the results would be very interesting. Although there are many frameworks out in the real world (which are all used to good effect) the simple truth is that as soon as a framework starts to dictate exactly what views and viewpoints must exist, then it constrains the way that the business can be modelled. What can be said, however, and what holds true for all enterprise architectures, is that any given enterprise architecture will be made up of *viewpoints* and *views*. In order to discuss this, consider what is meant by a 'view'. It may be thought of as any information concerning a business that is looked at in a particular way, or from a particular point of view. Imagine now, just for the sake of the discussion, that this information is to be realized using modelling and that each view is, in this example, represented by a single diagram: basically a diagram of a small part of the business from a particular point of view. These views form the basic building blocks of any enterprise architecture.

In almost all cases, these views will have common themes and be grouped into 'viewpoints'. A viewpoint is defined, therefore as a collection of views.

An enterprise architecture, however, is not just a collection of views that are brought together; this is a misunderstanding that is all too common in the real world. In order for these views to become an effective enterprise architecture, and not just pictures, there is more to consider: consistency of the views, the definition of an effective ontology and a view quagmire, and an understanding of the nature of the view itself.

Consistency of the views turns the pictures into a model – a point that has been made any number of times already in this book and one that will not be dwelt upon (yet again!) here.

Any enterprise architecture must use a defined terminology and have each term related to all the others. This is more than a simple glossary, where each term is given a description; it is the relationships between these terms that turn the glossary into an ontology. In fact, this ontology is a higher-level process structure view that relates to the whole enterprise, rather than just the processes and the process model.

Each of the views in the enterprise architecture must also relate to other views, and it is important to look at the complexity of these relationships. This is done by defining a *view quagmire* that represents each view as a simple class and then identifies the relationships between these. This always turns out to be very complex, but, as discussed later in the book, this is an important part of the reason why this diagram is created in the first place.

It is also important to understand the nature of each view. It is very easy to create any number of views and thus create what may be perceived as an enterprise architecture. There is more to enterprise architecture than defining a number of views, and concepts such as consistency and the ontology are very important. However, it is also very important to consider the nature of each view in terms of its definition, its requirements and its population.

When many people create a view, they simply think of some information and draw a diagram. Although this approach may work to a certain extent, it is far from ideal and will not necessarily lead to an enterprise architecture. Fundamental to any view is an understanding of why the view is necessary, or, to put it another way, the requirements for each view must be considered.

In order to meet these requirements it is necessary that information from the enterprise is used in some way. This is made possible because of the enterprise architecture ontology. Any view in the enterprise architecture must be a more detailed description of some subset of the ontology.

Once the requirements for each view have been described and the relevant parts of the ontology have been identified and described in more detail, it is then possible to populate each view. This is achieved by effectively instantiating each element in the view definition, which, it must be remembered, is a subset of the ontology.

All of this information may be summarized as in Figure 7.2.

REQUIREMENTS FOR ENTERPRISE ARCHITECTURE

In several sections of this book the importance of identifying and understanding requirements has been discussed. When considering enterprise architecture the same holds true. All enterprise architectures have the potential to be unique, as every business is potentially unique. Therefore the reason why an enterprise architecture is important will vary depending on the nature of the enterprise. It is possible to consider a generic set of requirements (as shown in Figure 7.2) that may be used as a starting point for any enterprise architecture, but the actual requirements for a specific one will be unique to that organization.

The main requirement for the enterprise architecture is 'Manage business change', which includes three other requirements:

- 'Understand business needs', which is fundamental to any enterprise. It is important to understand what the requirements for the business are, what the capabilities of the company are, if there are any gaps, and so on. Unfortunately, many organizations do not have a clear idea of these. This is one of the many benefits that an effective enterprise architecture will bring to an organization.
- 'Understand change', which means to understand the nature of the change in the business. There could be any number of reasons for business change, such as new technology, new markets, expansion,

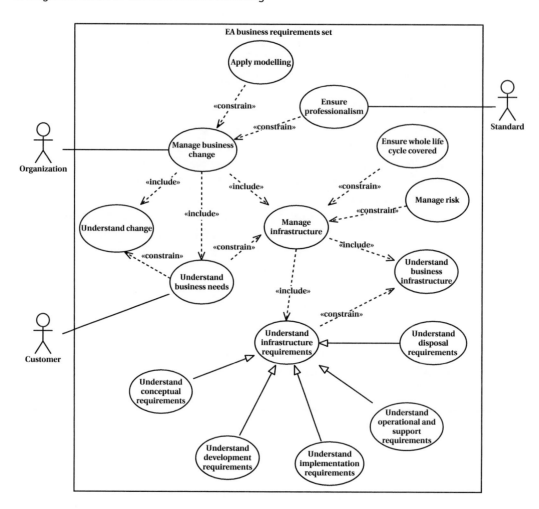

FIGURE 7.2   *Generic requirements view for enterprise architecture*

or recession. The main point here is to understand what these reasons are and how they will impact on the business in either a positive or a negative way. This requirement is constrained by the 'Understand business needs' requirement, since, if there is no understanding of the business needs, it is impossible to identify business drivers, reasons for change, and so on.

- 'Manage infrastructure', which relates to the infrastructure of the business itself. This will include 'Understand business infrastructure'; infrastructure itself could include all buildings, facilities, IT equipment, staff, and any other assets. It is important that all of these assets are identified and their attributes recorded (for example, cost, purchase date, stage in their life cycle, and so on). This requirement will also include understanding the requirements for the infrastructure across a typical product life cycle. Again, this will be constrained by the 'Understand business needs' requirement and also by 'Ensure whole life cycle covered' and 'Manage risk'. One of the reasons why it is important to understand the infrastructure is to enable the risk to be managed and controlled as much as possible, which cannot be done without this full understanding.

There are two major constraints that will have an impact on everything that is done in order to 'Manage business change', and they are:

- 'Apply modelling'. This constraint should not really have to be explained at this point in the book. If it is unclear, please return to Chapter 1 and start reading the book again (a bit more slowly this time).
- 'Ensure professionalism'. This relates to the two main issues of establishing and maintaining appropriate levels of capability and competency in the organization. Capability here refers to the ability of the organization (or a part of it), which is demonstrated through having effective processes in place. Competency here refers to the ability of the individual and is demonstrated through using established competency frameworks.

This set of requirements is not intended to be exhaustive, but they form a good starting point when beginning to think about why you need an enterprise architecture, and they should certainly be considered.

EXISTING SOURCES

Many examples of enterprise architectures, and variations thereof, exist. Many of them embody different ideas about what views should or should not be in the enterprise architecture, and what they should be used for. The point that this book is trying to make is that there is no single enterprise architecture that will apply to everybody, so it is important to understand why one is needed in the first place and then to be able to define and develop it in such a way as to meet these requirements.

The following list contains descriptions of several of the more popular (or widely used) enterprise architectures, although there are far too many of them in existence for it to be exhaustive. As will be seen from the descriptions, several of these are not actually enterprise architectures, but they are often viewed as such, and they all provide some contribution to establishing one.

- **The Zachman framework™ (Zachman, 2008)**, which was originally conceived by John Zachman in the 1980s for IBM. The Zachman framework asks basic questions concerning the business, such as what, how, where, who and why, and maps these onto different stakeholder groups. Various models that detail the intersections between the questions and the stakeholder groups are then created and refined. This framework is arguably the oldest and one of the most widely-used frameworks in existence and has had extensive implementation in the USA.

- **DoDAF, the Department Of Defense Architectural Framework (DoD, 2007)**, defines a set of views that enable the modelling of an enterprise architecture or systems architecture. A set of views and viewpoints are described and these form the basis of the architectural models. DODAF was generated by, and is used primarily by, the US military.

- **MODAF, the Ministry of Defence Architectural Framework (MODAF, 2008)**. The imaginatively-named MODAF has its roots in both DODAF and Zachman and defines a set of viewpoints and views that are intended to be used as part of an enterprise architecture or systems architecture exercise. MODAF was developed by, and is used primarily by, the UK defence and aerospace industry.

- **TOGAF, the Open Group Architectural Framework (TOGAF, 2009)**, defines a set of processes that can be used to develop an enterprise architecture. TOGAF is used extensively in the public sector for creating enterprise architectures.

- **IEEE 1471, ANSI/IEEE 1471-2000,** *Recommended Practice for Architectural Description of Software-Intensive Systems (IEEE, 2000).* This is the first formal standard for architecture and is aimed at software and systems architectures. Although not strictly an enterprise architecture standard, this has been used as a source for many other enterprise architecture exercises. Also, this standard provides a meta-model of the standard using the UML notation.

The list goes on and on, but the notes above should provide an indication of some of the existing source information that is readily available.

MODELLING AN ENTERPRISE ARCHITECTURE

The discussion so far in this chapter has been concerned with the main concepts involved with enterprise architecture and some of the challenges that face those trying to understand it. One thing that should be quite clear from this is that enterprise architecture exhibits the three evils of life (see Chapter 4) and, therefore, is a prime candidate for modelling. Indeed, it is almost impossible to realize any practical enterprise architecture without applying modelling techniques.

Modelling enterprise architectures versus process modelling

There are some interesting parallels between the two worlds of modelling processes and modelling enterprise architectures. Some of these parallels are more obvious than others; this section discusses some of the key similarities.

The approach taken in this book for process modelling is equally applicable to the world of modelling enterprise architectures – in particular:

- The whole approach to process modelling in this book relies on the definition of a meta-model (in particular the process meta-model conceptual view) that defines the main concepts involved with process modelling.

- The process meta-model conceptual view gives rise to the process meta-model realization view, which identifies a number of views and how they relate to one another. This is analogous to the view quagmire from the enterprise architecture meta-model.

- One of the essential views for process modelling is the process structure view. In this view the key terminology and concepts are defined in the form of a single diagram. This is analogous to the ontology in the world of enterprise architecture. In fact, the process structure view and the ontology are conceptually the same, with the main difference being that the scope of the process structure view is far narrower than the scope of the ontology, since the ontology covers the entire enterprise. Indeed, the process structure view will be a true subset of the ontology when the two are compared.

- One of the other essential views is the requirements view. The theory behind this is that it is impossible to realize a process without understanding why the process is needed. This is the same as the various levels of requirements that are necessary in the enterprise architecture meta-model.

A summary of these similarities is shown in Table 7.1.

In fact, it is possible to apply exactly the same approach to enterprise architecture modelling as has been applied to process modelling in this book. Modelling enterprise architectures is conceptually the same as process modelling, but on a larger scale.

Example ontology

The ontology is arguably the single most important view to get right when it comes to enterprise architecture. Not only does the ontology define all

TABLE 7.1 *Comparison of terms between process modelling and enterprise architecture*

Process modelling	Enterprise architecture modelling
Meta-model conceptual view	Enterprise architecture meta-model
Meta-model realization view	View quagmire
Process structure view	Ontology
Requirements view	All requirements views
Other views	Other views

of the terminology and concepts for the entire enterprise, but it forms the basis for every view in the enterprise architecture and the cornerstone of all consistency checks for the model.

Figure 7.3 shows an example ontology for a particular enterprise. For the sake of this discussion, take as a starting point the centre of the diagram – in particular, the class 'Process model'. The diagram states that the 'Process model' is made up of one or more 'Process' and each 'Process' is made up of one or more 'Stakeholder role', one or more 'Activity' and one or more 'Artefact'. Notice that this is the same as a basic process structure view. It is now possible to see how the process model fits in with the rest of the organizational concepts. There is the concept of 'Capability' in the enterprise, which is realized by one or more 'Process'. It can also be seen that there are several types of 'Capability'. These capabilities also trace back to the 'Customer', which is in itself a type of 'Stakeholder role'. The capabilities also realize one or more 'Business goal', which themselves relate to the 'Supplier' stakeholder role (that relates to the organization itself). This realization of business goals is achieved via one or more 'Project', each of which is part of a larger 'Programme' and each of which has a 'Life cycle'.

Moving our attention back to the process, it can be seen that each 'Process' utilizes one or more 'Asset', which form the 'Infrastructure' of the business; these have several types: 'Person', 'Technical asset' and 'Data'. Each 'Asset' has an 'Asset life cycle' defined, and a 'Location'. Each 'Person' is defined by a 'Position', which is itself defined by a number of stakeholder roles. Each 'Stakeholder role' has one or more 'Competency' associated with it, and these are defined via the 'Competency profile'. These competencies are themselves related back to activities within

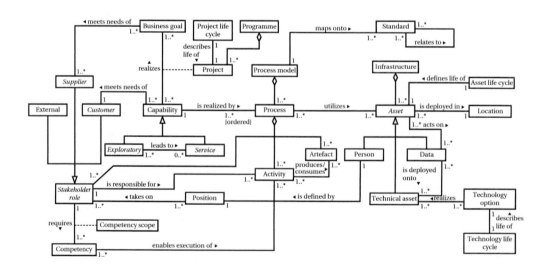

FIGURE 7.3   *Example ontology*

the process, and hence the competencies are based on the process. As for the 'Technical asset', each has its own 'Technology option', which in turn has a 'Technology Life Cycle'.

The ontology shown here presents a high-level view of all of the key concepts of the enterprise and how they relate to one another. This ontology may now be used in a number of ways:

- It allows traceability from any part of the business to another. For example, how do the technical assets, such as PCs, software applications, communications equipment, and so on, help the business to realize its business goals? The answer is found by looking for the paths between these two concepts. It can be seen that the assets relate directly to the process and that the process is what realizes the capability of the business. This capability is what allows the company to meet its business goals. Therefore, we have traceability between the two.

- The ontology forms the basis of every view in the enterprise architecture. Any view in the enterprise architecture is created by taking a subset of the ontology and then realizing it. For example, it may be desirable to have a competency view that defines what competencies are required for each stakeholder role, so that competencies for any position and, hence, person may be defined. In this case, imagine drawing an ellipse around the areas of interest on the ontology, as shown in Figure 7.4.

Figure 7.4 shows that the area of interest for the competency view encompasses the 'Stakeholder role', 'Competency' and 'Competency scope'. According to the enterprise architecture meta-model, any view needs a

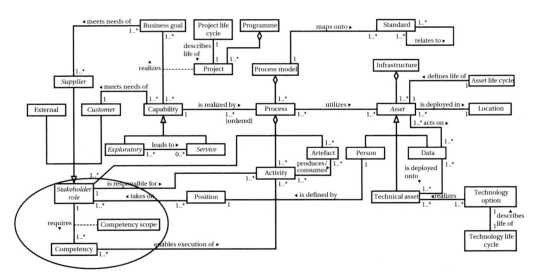

FIGURE 7.4 *Ontology with area of interest for a competency view shown*

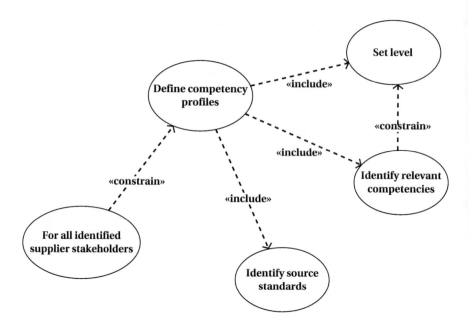

Figure 7.5 *Simple requirements view for a competency view*

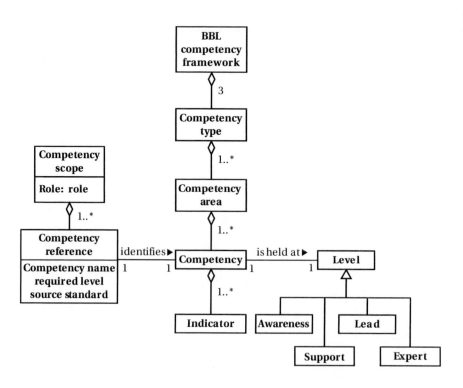

Figure 7.6 *Example viewpoint definition showing an expansion of the 'Competency scope' element from the ontology*

set of requirements (the 'View requirements set'), a breakdown of the information to be captured in this view (the 'View concept definition'), and the actual view itself (one or more 'View Content').

The 'View requirements set' is exactly the same as the requirements view that has been discussed previously in this book, an example of which can be seen in Figure 7.5.

Figure 7.5 shows a simple set of requirements for the competency view. It is important that users of the enterprise architecture can understand why the view is necessary, and this is what this view provides. On the basis of these requirements, it is now possible to identify which areas of the enterprise architecture ontology are appropriate for inclusion in the view, as shown in Figure 7.5. These elements then form the basis of the 'View content definition', which is a breakdown, in more detail, of a small subset of the ontology.

Figure 7.6 shows a breakdown of the key concepts that were abstracted from the ontology. It can be seen that this diagram is simply a more detailed breakdown of the ontology, and it would be possible to include all of this information directly in the ontology itself. In this case, the element named 'Competency scope' is taken and looked at in more detail.

CONCLUSIONS

An enterprise architecture is a very powerful tool indeed when it comes to running an effective and efficient business. Key to defining an enterprise architecture is the application of modelling and the use of processes. It has been shown here how process modelling is actually a natural part of a larger-scale enterprise architecture. Indeed, the modelling techniques that form the basis of this book are equally applicable to the world of enterprise architecture, and the same approach is taken there. Fundamental to this approach is the identification and definition of the meta-model and its associated views.

8 Presentation

'The limits of my language means the limits of my world.'
Tractatus Logico-Philosophicus, Ludwig Wittgenstein

INTRODUCTION

Perhaps one of the biggest areas of concern for many people when it comes to process modelling is the question of how to present the results of the process modelling exercise. The initial conceptual view of the process meta-model indicated that there were three main areas that must be considered for process modelling: the source, the understanding and the presentation. The source represents where the information for the process model originates. The understanding represents the process model itself, and, hence, the main focus of this book lies here. Indeed, the process meta-model realization view is concerned solely with the understanding portion of the meta-model conceptual view. This chapter takes a step outside the realization view and focuses on the right-hand side of the conceptual model – the presentation.

PRESENTATION ISSUES

Different notations

It has been mentioned previously in this book that many notations exist for visualizing processes. This book just happens to use the UML for process modelling, but, as has been indicated previously, any notation that is rich enough to allow one to realize each of the seven views is perfectly adequate.

A problem arises, however, when a client wants the output of the process modelling exercise to be in a different format. For example, just imagine that the notation to be used for process modelling has been decided upon, and, for the sake of the example, that this is the UML. Then imagine that the client wants the final output in a different format, for example flowcharts, text, or even an ad hoc notation. The assumption that many people will make is that the UML cannot be used at all, since it does not match the presentation notation choice. This is, however, a total fallacy! Just because the UML is not being used for the final output, this does not mean that it cannot be used as the notation for the understanding. In fact, one powerful aspect of using the UML for the meta-model is that it allows the identification and definition of different notations to be related to different parts of the meta-model, by using its 'stereotype' construction.

Text versus diagrammatical techniques

It is quite usual for someone to request that the final presentation of the process model is represented in text, especially when the final output is some sort of document, such as a standard or a work instruction. There are two very important points to make here:

- There is nothing whatsoever wrong with using text as the final presentation.
- The text, however, must be based directly on the model and not the other way around.

In fact, the best approach for using text, or any other notation for that matter, is to do one of two things:

- Change the stereotypes on the meta-model realization view to match the chosen notation. This is the focus in this chapter.
- Define one or more new views and add them to the realization view. This approach is identical to the one described in Chapter 4 concerning Gantt charts, and so is not dwelt upon in this chapter.

In order to provide a mapping to a different notation, it is essential that a good understanding of that notation exists. One way to achieve this understanding is to create a model of the language or notation. In this chapter three notations are looked at briefly as part of the discussion – the Business process modelling notation (BPMN), UML and flowcharts.

EXAMPLE MAPPINGS TO DIFFERENT NOTATIONS

This section looks at two of the most popular other (non-UML) notations to see how they may be used in conjunction with the process modelling meta-model. The two notations chosen are:

- The BPMN, which is a widely adopted and widely used notation for process modelling. This has been chosen because it is often seen as UML's main 'competition', and vice versa. However, the point of this book is to understand views and how to use the meta-model, so it does not present a full, formal comparison between the two techniques. (For a full exploration and comparison of the two techniques, see Perry (2006)). It does, however, give a demonstration of where the BPMN can be used effectively as part of the meta-model.
- Flowcharts. Flowcharts, love them or hate them, are everywhere; this is probably the most widely recognized notation in the world today. The term 'flowcharting' has entered the English language and, although in most cases people do not actually use nor

understand flowcharts properly, just about everyone thinks that they know what a flowchart is.

Each of these notations will be modelled at a high level and then used as part of the discussion.

BPMN

Background

The business process modelling notation is a standardized graphical notation for visualizing processes within a business. The BPMN was created as part of the business process modelling initiative (BPMI) and the language is currently managed by the Object Management Group. The BPMN is intended to be a common language for identifying and defining processes and their associated workflows within a business – see OMG (2009) for more details and the full technical specification of the language.

The BPMN consists of a single diagram, known as the process diagram, that may be used to describe the behaviour of a process at a number of different levels of abstraction.

Modelling the language

The first step in trying to understand something is to generate a model for it. A simple meta-model for the BPMN has been created, in exactly the same way that a meta-model for UML can be created.

Figure 8.1 shows the process structure view for the BPMN. It can be seen from the left-hand side of this figure that any BPMN diagram is

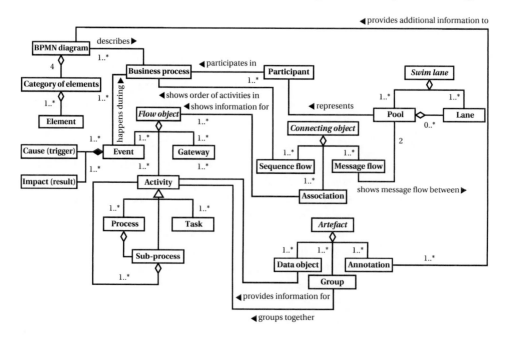

FIGURE 8.1   *Process structure view for the BPMN language*

made up of four 'Category of elements', each of which is made up of one or more 'Element'. One or more BPMN diagrams describe a single business process. In this way, the language is flexible enough to allow a number of different descriptions for each business process that has been identified. These categories of elements are further described by the actual elements that exist in a BPMN process diagram.

The BPMN concepts also include the notion of a 'Participant' who participates in a business process. This participant maps neatly onto the concept of a stakeholder role that is used elsewhere throughout this book.

Figure 8.2 shows (in no particular order) the graphical notation that is available for the 'Category of elements' and their associated set of 'Element', the core modelling elements of the BPMN. There are many more detailed elements that may also be used in BPMN but, for most applications, the notation shown here is sufficient. For a full definition of the BPMN notation, see OMG (2009).

The elements themselves are described in terms of their 'Category of elements' and the elements that make it up. There is a 'Category of elements' named 'Flow object', which is made up of the following elements:

- 'Event', which is something that happens during the course of a process. An event will typically have a 'Cause', some sort of trigger, and an 'Impact', some sort of result. Events can occur at any point during a process and there are three types of event to reflect this: start events, which occur at the start of a process; end events, which occur at the end of a process; and intermediate events, which occur anywhere between a start and an end event.

- 'Activity', which reflects any sort of work that is carried out during a business process. This has three specialist types. The first is a 'Task', which represents an atomic level of behaviour. The term 'atomic' here means that a task cannot be broken down into further diagrams. The second is a 'Process', which is non-atomic (it *can* be broken down), and is made up of the third type of task, which is the 'Sub-process'. A 'Sub-process' is also non-atomic and it can also

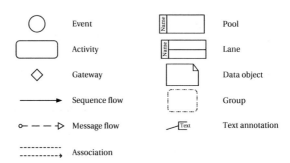

FIGURE 8.2 *Graphical representation of core modelling elements in BPMN*

be made up of any of the three types of activity. This means that the language will allow a nested hierarchy of activities that form the process structure. Any number of these activities may be collected into a 'Group'.

- 'Gateway', which describes how to control flows. A gateway allows flows to be converged and diverged and hence can be used for branching (including conditional branches), forking, merging and joining. It is also possible, when considering different branches from, say, a decision, to define the default exit flow. In this case, the sequence flow is enhanced by showing a short diagonal line that crosses the flow.

The next type of 'Category of elements' is the 'Connecting object', which is made up of three elements:

- 'Sequence flow', which shows the order in which activities in a business process are to be executed. Typical uses for sequence flows are to connect the different types of flow objects. For example, a start event may be connected to an activity via a sequence flow, which in turn may be connected to other activities or gateways via more sequence flows.
- 'Association', which shows the information associated with an activity. For example, it may be desirable to link some text with a flow object, which can be achieved using an association. Indeed, any type of artefact may be linked with a flow object using the association notation.
- 'Message flow', which shows the flow of information between pools from the 'Swim lane' 'Category of elements'. As pools represent participants in a business process, the message flow actually represents the flow of information between two participants.

The next type of 'Category of elements' is the 'Swim lane', which is made up of two elements:

- 'Pool', which represents a participant in a business process. Any activities that are encapsulated by the pool are deemed to be the responsibility of that participant.
- 'Lane', which is a partition within a pool. This represents other participants and may be used to further categorize the activities within the pool. A lane extends for the whole length of the pool.

The final type of 'Category of elements' is the 'Artefact', which is made up of three elements:

- 'Data object', which provides information about one or more activities. This can be used to describe any of the three types of activity. A data object does not affect the execution of activities, but they provide information about what information is produced or consumed by each activity, where appropriate.

- 'Group', which groups activities together. This grouping does not affect the order of execution of activities, and a group may even include activities from several pools and lanes. This may be used for a variety of purposes, such as grouping together activities for documentation, or providing a logical grouping of activities for analysis purposes.
- 'Annotation', which is a less formal artefact that can be used to show additional information concerning the BPMN diagram.

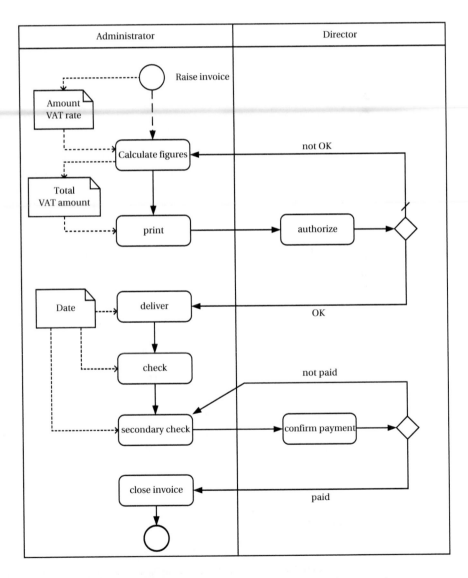

FIGURE 8.3 *BPMN notation showing a process behaviour view*

An annotation may be added to any information within the diagram or, indeed, to the diagram itself.

As can be seen from this description, the notation is rich and flexible for describing the behaviour of a process. Indeed, this notation can be used to realize two of the views from the meta-model, as shown in Figures 8.3 and 8.4.

The diagram in Figure 8.3 shows the equivalent of Figure 6.25 from Chapter 6. The diagrams actually look very similar, although the notation itself is different. The BPMN notation is being used at the same level of abstraction as the activity diagram from UML.

The diagram in Figure 8.4 shows the same BPMN notation being used, but this time at a slightly higher level of abstraction – that of the process instance view. The BPMN notation looks closer visually to the UML activity diagram than it does to the UML sequence diagram, so, although the parallels are clear here, the notation is not quite as similar as in Figure 8.3. The inclusion of the plus ('+') symbol in a small box here indicates that the task may be broken down into subprocesses and, hence, may be used for indicating that this task represents a process, rather than an activity.

It should also be pointed out here that the use of the BPMN notation has been restricted to the core notation, where possible, to keep the diagrams simple. It is possible that different notation could be used to make the diagrams closer to reality, but the core notation is more than powerful enough to show this information and it makes the comparisons later in this chapter slightly simpler.

Populating the meta-model

It is now possible to look at the BPMN meta-model and use that information to populate the process modelling meta-model so that BPMN, rather than UML, notation may be used for realizing the views where appropriate. However, there are no explicit structural mechanisms in the BPMN, which means that it is unsuitable for realizing the structural views of the process meta-model. This can be seen more clearly on the diagram in Figure 8.5.

Figure 8.5 shows which of the seven views of the process meta-model can be realized using the BPMN. It can be seen here that the notation is more than up to the job of visualizing two of the behavioural views but, unfortunately, cannot be used to visualize any of the

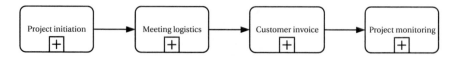

FIGURE 8.4   *BPMN notation showing a process instance view*

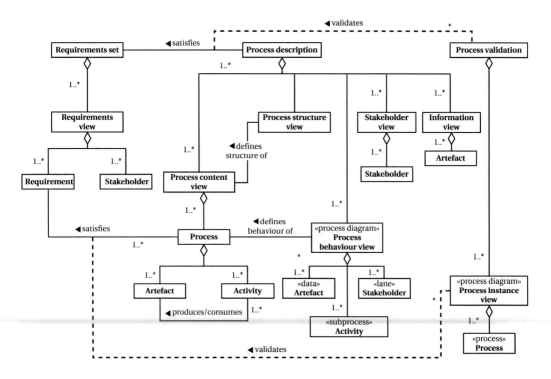

FIGURE 8.5   *Process meta-model realization view with BPMN notation shown as stereotypes*

structural views. This is not necessarily a problem as long as some other notation is used for modelling the structural views. This could be an established notation or it could be an extension of the existing mechanisms.

Flowcharts

Background

The use of flowcharts for process modelling, or predecessors of them, can be traced back to the 1920s. In the 1940s they were also rediscovered by the likes of Jon von Neumann at Princeton University, where they were used for software algorithms and problem solving (Goldstine, 1972). Is it any wonder, then, that they are so widely recognized in the world today?

Flowcharts have been used extensively in just about every industry, and there are myriad tools that either use them or are based directly on them.

Modelling the language

The flowchart notation consists of a single behavioural view that can be applied at various levels of abstraction. Its basic syntax can be seen in Figure 8.6.

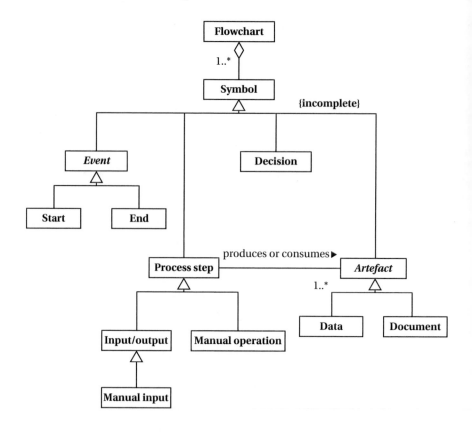

FIGURE 8.6   *Process structure view for the flowchart notation*

The graphical notation for each of these symbols is shown in Figure 8.7.

Figures 8.6 and 8.7 show only a subset of the symbols available for flowchart modelling, and herein lies one of the main problems with the whole flowchart notation – there are many 'definitive' versions of flowcharts. These range from slightly different symbols in various textbooks, to formal 'standardized' definitions of flowchart symbols such as the ISO standard (ISO, 1985). The symbols in Figure 8.7 are:

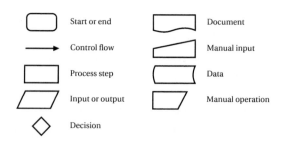

FIGURE 8.7   *Symbol legend for the flowchart notation*

- 'Start' or 'End', which are events that signify the beginning or end of a process, and are represented graphically by a soft box. A flowchart should always start and end with one or more of each of these.
- 'Control flow', which allows control of the process to pass from one process step (or other symbol) to another. The control flows represent the basic paths between the various elements in the diagram, and are represented graphically by directed lines. They represent a true control flow, and, as such, do not imply any sort of data flow.
- 'Process step', which represents basic execution of functionality within a flowchart. A process step may represent the execution of code in the case of software, or the execution of any sort of activity in the case of process modelling.
- 'Input' or 'Output', which show incoming or outgoing data, and are in themselves process steps. This is also expanded by having a 'Manual input' symbol, which allows the process to represent a user entering data, or hitting particular keys.
- 'Manual operation', which allows the process to represent human-based activity. This is actually a special type of process step.
- 'Decision', which represents making any sort of choice, and which is represented graphically by a diamond symbol.
- 'Document', which represents (unsurprisingly) some sort of document, and which is actually a specific type of input or output.
- 'Data', which allows data flows within the process to be shown. This is a special type of an artefact of the process.

As can be seen from this description, the notation is rich and flexible for describing the behaviour of a process. Indeed, this notation can be used to realize only one of the views from the meta-model, as shown in Figure 8.8.

The information contained in Figure 8.8 may now be used as a basis for changing the stereotypes on the process modelling meta-model.

Inclusion in the meta-model

The process meta-model realization view may now be populated with the information gathered from the flowchart notation process structure view shown in Figure 8.6.

As can be seen in Figure 8.9, the information from the flowchart notation can now be used as a basis for the stereotypes in the process modelling meta-model. However, it can be clearly seen that there are only a few classes in the diagram where the flowchart notation is of any use. In fact, there is really only a single view where the flowchart notation is rich enough to support the requirements of the meta-model. This means that the flowchart notation is certainly suitable for the process behaviour view,

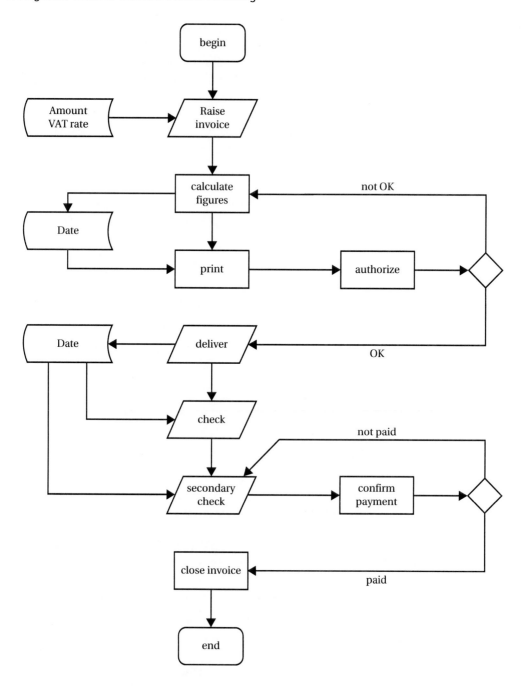

Figure 8.8 *Flowchart notation showing a process behaviour view*

but may need to be tailored or, more likely, used in conjunction with other notations, to fully realize the seven views.

Quite significantly, there is no mechanism for allowing the inclusion of stakeholders in the flowchart notation, which is a serious omission.

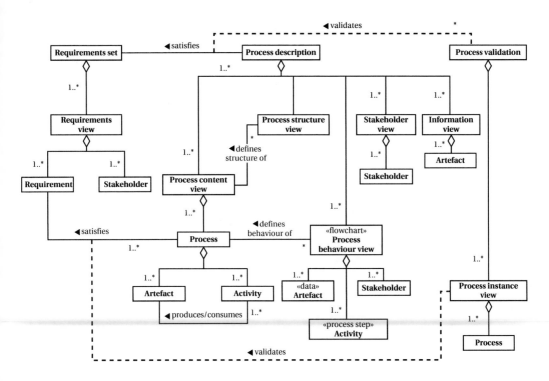

FIGURE 8.9 *Process meta-model realization view with flowchart notation stereotypes*

Comparison of three notations

This section looks at a comparison of the three notations that have been discussed so far in this book – the UML, BPMN and flowcharts. In comparing these three, one thing should leap out immediately: they all look very similar indeed!

There are some very good reasons for this. One is that most behavioural notations will, at some point, be traceable back to flowcharts if one looks hard enough, so it is hardly surprising that the notations look similar.

A more fundamental reason, however, is that all of these notations are attempts to visualize the same concepts, and they are, therefore, the same at a conceptual level.

This will also hold true for any other notation, whether it is a formally recognized notation (such as the three discussed above) or some proprietary notation associated with a particular tool. At the end of the day, it is important to consider the concepts required for process modelling. Also, the fact that there is only a finite number of basic shapes makes it again hardly surprising that there is more than a little similarity between the notations.

All of these notations, and in particular the BPMN process diagram and the UML activity diagrams, have a very rich notation that will allow for all kinds of detailed modelling. This is where some of the notation starts to look a little unusual, as the limited choice of basic shapes has been reached and, therefore, the authors of the notations have been forced to come up with composite shapes and symbols, which can be a little unusual, to say the least. As with all the modelling presented in this book, it is advisable to concentrate on understanding the concepts and then to choose an appropriate notation, rather than being caught up in the details.

CONCLUSIONS

The approach taken here, that of understanding (modelling) any notation and then using this knowledge to create stereotypes and including them in the meta-model, may be used for any notation whatsoever. Again, it must be stressed that the purpose of this book is to make the point that views are necessary, that modelling is important and that consistency is the key to both.

The simple fact is that *any* notation, or combination of notations, may be used for process modelling. As to how effective any technique is, this is really up to the process modeller to decide. However, a good way to compare and contrast notations and to decide which is the best for you is to use the meta-model approach: identify and define the relevant views for the meta-model, identify and model the chosen notation or notations, and see how many of the relevant views in the meta-model may be realized using the selected notation. If the selected notation allows all views to be realized, then all is well and good and the notation is entirely appropriate for the job. If, however, not all views may be realized using the selected notation, then there are a few options available:

- Decide that the notation is not suitable and choose another. This, of course, could be very costly in terms of time and effort and, hence, is often not a feasible solution for some, even if common sense dictates that it should be.
- Decide that the notation is not suitable and use another in conjunction with the selected one. This is often a halfway-house solution, and, although it can be very powerful and work very effectively, caution must be exercised to ensure that the use of too many notations does not lead to unmanaged and uncontrolled complexity in the system.
- Decide to continue using the selected notation, while being aware of its shortfalls. This is an approach that is often taken, but one that people often follow blindly. Again, this can work very well but caution must be exercised.
- Blunder on regardless with no regard for different views. Sadly, this is not as uncommon as one would hope. It is to be discouraged.

9 Teaching Guide

'We called him Tortoise because he taught us.'
The Mock Turtle, *Alice's Adventures in Wonderland*, Lewis Carroll

INTRODUCTION

One of the main topic areas that arise when presenting information regarding process modelling is that of how to teach or train people to carry it out. There is no single correct way to do this, so this chapter provides a discussion on communicating process modelling to people using various teaching and training techniques. The information presented here is intended for guidance only and is based on the author's years of experience in teaching at both undergraduate and postgraduate levels as well as of developing and delivering professional training courses for major industries.

Different types of teaching

There is no definitive way to teach process modelling, so this chapter provides a few examples of how teaching may be approached, depending on the audience. One key part of any teaching or training is to know and understand the audience, and by this what we really mean is understanding the stakeholders' requirements. The point here is that the teaching requirements will differ depending on who the target audience is, and this will be discussed in some detail.

The diagram in Figure 9.1 shows a generic set of teaching requirements that will be used as a basis for discussion. It should be borne in mind, however, that this set of requirements will need to be tailored, or even started again from scratch, to fit the reader's needs. It is strongly recommended, if you are interested in teaching or training, that you carry out this short requirements exercise, as it will really improve your own understanding of the teaching and help to ensure that the course that is developed actually meets these requirements. This will clearly result in a better course and, hopefully, a better learning experience for the teaching subjects.

Figure 9.1 shows the generic system context for delivering training or teaching courses. The requirements are described in more detail below, along with a few suggestions for each as to how this basic set may be tailored.

- 'Deliver course': this is the overall requirement that sets the scene for the context. This could be tailored by adding different 'types of'

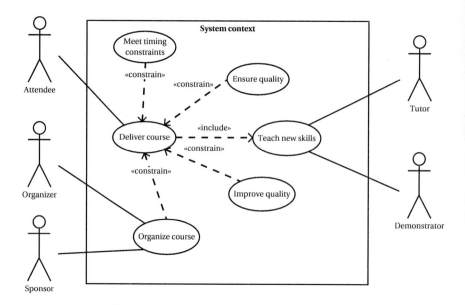

FIGURE 9.1 *Generic teaching or training context*

(specialization) relationships to the diagram, to show requirements for different types of courses.

- 'Teach new skills': note that this is the only inclusion in the overall requirement of 'Deliver course', and hence it will form the basis of the course. This could be expanded upon by adding in more included requirements. For example, it could be a requirement to provide examples or to set course work – these could be added in as new requirements.

- 'Organize course': this requirement could mean almost anything, depending on the nature of the course being taught. For example, it could be as simple as making sure that a room is booked, or something as complex as making travel arrangements, renting facilities, hiring equipment, and so on.

- 'Ensure quality': this is a constraint on delivering the course and may include issues such as making sure that the course material is printed out and bound nicely, making sure that the facilities for the course measure up, and so on. This may also be extended to include other concerns, such as making sure that the presenters wear suits and have a wash before the course, or whatever else is deemed important.

- 'Improve quality': it is always important to continuously improve everything that we do in our work, and, therefore, this should be a requirement that is always present in the context. It could include collecting feedback from the course, making notes of any corrections or enhancements that could be made to the course afterwards, and so on.

- 'Meet timing constraints': this is very important, as it will limit what can be delivered and when. Understanding the timing constraints can often be the difference between a successful and an unsuccessful course, and its importance cannot be stressed strongly enough. For example, if a course is to be taught for ten sessions, each of an hour's duration, then it will have a different structure from that of a course that will be taught over eight hours on a single day.

Due to the space limitations of this book, and commercial constraints, the emphasis of the examples provided in this chapter will be mainly on providing a course as part of a university syllabus.

The stakeholders that are shown on the diagram will differ significantly depending on the type of teaching or training, and will be discussed in more detail in the following two sections.

PROFESSIONAL TRAINING

Teaching requirements

When considering a professional training course, the core requirements are as shown in Figure 9.1. With regard to the stakeholder roles that have been identified, the following is a typical list of names that may be associated with each of them:

- 'Attendee': this stakeholder role represents the actual delegates on a training course. It may be useful in the case of professional courses to record information about them, such as name, organization, position, contact details, and so on.
- 'Organizer': this may be the training company or the client company, depending on how the training is set up. This is a very important role to consider, as the possible scenarios for the two will differ significantly.
- 'Tutor': this will be the actual primary trainer for the course.
- 'Demonstrator': this will be the demonstrator or secondary trainer on the course. In some cases, the role of the tutor and the demonstrator may be taken on by a single person.
- 'Sponsor': this is the role of whoever is paying the bill at the end of the day, which may be a company or a number of individuals, depending on the nature of the course.

In terms of the requirements for the course, there are some specific items that must be considered:

- 'Organize course': this requirement can vary massively, depending on who is taking on the role of the organizer, as discussed above. One of the big differences will depend on whether the organizer is part of the training or the client organisation. For example, if the course is being organized by the client company, then the onus on the training provider may simply be to turn up and deliver the course. If the organization of the course, on the other hand, is being managed by the training organisation, then a number of logistical processes will start to be necessary, such as arranging the event venue, refreshments and meals, accommodation, and so on. This is a good example of a project varying enormously depending on the nature of the people or organizations that map onto the generic stakeholder roles from the requirements view.

- 'Teach new skills': this is the main core requirement for any training or teaching. In the case of a professional course, this may be related directly back to staff assessments, competency profiles, or standards of some description.

- 'Ensure quality': when given by a professional training organisation, the quality of the course may be driven by an external source, such as an independent or industry-driven endorsement from a recognized body. Another aspect of quality here relates to mapping the course content to recognized competency frameworks (see, for example, INCOSE (2006)).

- 'Improve quality': this will entail capturing any problems or mistakes in the course notes, capturing and addressing any comments that are made by the attendees of the course, updating course materials, ensuring that best practice is being adhered to with regard to the course content, and so on.

- 'Meet timing constraints': the timing constraints for a professional training course will usually be concerned with making sure that the course is delivered over the duration of perhaps two or three working days. There may also be some client-specific constraints that come into play here. For example, some organizations only allow training on particular days of the week, or it may be desirable to avoid school holidays.

There are a lot of considerations to bear in mind with regard to professional training. Interestingly, depending on which of the above requirements and stakeholders apply to your organization, the diagram itself will change. For example, new stakeholders may be introduced that represent, say, a professional body that accredits trainers.

TEACHING AS PART OF AN UNDERGRADUATE OR POSTGRADUATE COURSE

This section considers the situation where process modelling needs to be taught as part of a university or college course. The generic requirements will be revisited and discussed in more detail within the context of an educational establishment.

Teaching requirements and stakeholders

The generic stakeholders remain the same as those discussed previously, but the following points need to be borne in mind.

- 'Attendee': this stakeholder role represents the actual students who are enrolled in the course.
- 'Organizer': this will be the department that offers the course.
- 'Tutor': this will be the actual lecturer for the course.
- 'Demonstrator': this may be the lecturer, or any assistants who may supervise example classes and laboratory sessions.
- 'Sponsor': this will be whoever pays the university fees for the students.

In terms of the requirements for the course, there are some specific items that must be considered.

- 'Organize course': this will involve ensuring that the rooms are booked, and that they and any necessary resources are available. In the case of a college or university, however, this will also include ensuing that the information regarding the course, such as its time and location, is disseminated to students.
- 'Teach new skills': in the case of a university environment, there may be a specific set of skills that is required to be taught.
- 'Ensure quality': this will involve making sure that the course maps onto any generic teaching requirement. An example is Bloom's taxonomy, which is often used in the UK (Bloom, 1956; Anderson et al., 2001).
- 'Improve quality': this will entail capturing any problems or mistakes in the course notes, capturing and addressing any comments that are made by the students, updating course materials, ensuring that best practice is being adhered to with regard to the course content, and so on. Most universities will have an established means of student feedback that will apply to all courses.
- 'Meet timing constraints': the timing constraints for a university course are very strict and will rely on the number of teaching and access hours with students, the structure of the timetable, holidays, and so on. For example, some courses may be taught in intensive two-week modules, whereas another course may be one hour per week over a 20-week duration.

A generic course structure

It is possible to identify several key elements that should be considered when defining a course structure. The structure provided here is intended as a guide only, and should be used as a starting point for developing a full course and its associated resources. The structure presented here is based primarily on the experience of the author in presenting material to students in a university environment.

The diagram in Figure 9.2 shows a generic structure for a university-type course. Each of the main elements is explained in more detail below.

Introduction

The introduction section of the course contains three main elements, as detailed below.

Background

It is important to put the course into context and get the students to understand where the course has come from and why it is necessary. For example, the course may form part, or the whole, of a module in a larger course. This material could be applied in many different areas, such as a business-related or an IT-focused course, for example.

Aims and objectives

It is important that the teaching aims of the course are identified early on. A good way to think about this is to generate a use case diagram that will have the teaching aims and objectives represented as the use cases and the main stakeholders represented as the actors. One important consideration here is to identify any constraints that may come into play with regard to source standards or information. For example, it may be that the

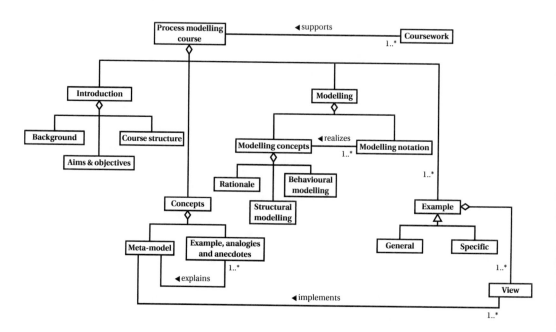

FIGURE 9.2 *Generic course structure for a university-type course*

course needs to map onto the teaching objectives of Bloom, in which case the Bloom taxonomy (Bloom, 1956) would be represented as an actor and there would be an associated use case, named something along the lines of 'meet source standards' or similar.

Of course, the use cases will also reflect the more functional aims and goals. It may be that you want the students to be able to define a process, in which case this would then become a use case. It may be that you require the students to be able to analyse an existing process, or apply metrics to it, or automate the process. In fact there is an almost endless set of aims for a course such as this, but it is crucial to identify what they are and then to ensure that course content addresses these aims.

Course structure

This section is relatively simple, since it just states the major elements of the course and the relationships between them. If it is only using the information in this chapter, then the course structure is simply the diagram in Figure 9.2 along with some explanatory notes.

Concepts

Getting the key concepts across is very important, and the obvious place to start is the meta-model. Rather than just diving straight into showing the meta-model, the course lecturer should consider talking about some examples, anecdotes and analogies. The basic reason for doing this is to try to establish a strong connection between the meta-model, when it is introduced, and the real world. To this end, it is important to communicate to the students using language and material that they can readily associate with. This is where the examples, anecdotes and analogies come into play.

In the case of examples, this is fairly straightforward – for example, it may be desirable to show an example of a process that is good, bad or indifferent. Unfortunately, it is all too common to come across examples of bad processes and many are available in the public domain. If in any doubt, just look at some of the public-domain standards that apply to your particular business or domain! Another excellent source of information is the current news. On any given day, it is possible to look at the daily news and find a report on a project that has gone wrong, overrun, been cancelled, or otherwise failed. This sort of thing provides a superb resource for examples. Not only is the information current and relevant, but it is something that students can understand since it is a *real* example of process failure. It also provides a good foundation for encouraging the students to look for processes in the real world.

In the case of anecdotes, again there are all too many examples. A good anecdote should be based firmly in the real world and should hold some sort of meaning or relevance. A particularly good anecdote will involve people, organizations or projects with which students are already familiar, and that can then form the basis for a good story (while avoiding slander). Also, a good anecdote should inspire a healthy dose of humour, incredulity, or, some cases, horror, about what can happen when processes go wrong or are ignored. One way to ensure that students find anecdotes interesting is to try to find something in your personal life that illustrates the point – from personal experience, the more humiliating for the lecturer, the better it will be received!

At this point, having established a connection with the students and with the real world, it is time to introduce the conceptual view of the meta-model. The conceptual view should form the basis for discussion with the students. This is one slide that does definitely need to be unhurried, and reference should be made back to the examples and anecdotes provided by the lecturer and related to elements in the meta-model. Students should be encouraged to ask questions and give their own point of view at this juncture, along with any examples that they can think of.

Once the concepts have been firmly introduced and discussed, it is time to introduce the realization view of the process meta-model. At this point, it is suggested that the diagram is introduced only very briefly with the promise that each of the views will be discussed in more detail later. Emphasis should be put on the consistency between this view and the conceptual view, stressing that the realization view can be seen as a breakdown of the main elements in the 'understanding' part of the conceptual view.

Modelling

The second major section concerns modelling. When introducing modelling, it is suggested that this is covered initially with no direct reference to process modelling, as this connection will be established gently later on in the course. It is suggested that examples provided here should be simple, understandable to the students, and chosen so as to allow them to focus on the modelling concepts and notation, rather than on the application of the modelling. A good example of this is the use of dogs and cats, as seen in this book.

Modelling concepts

Modelling concepts, like the process model concepts, should be introduced by way of examples, analogies and anecdotes, as discussed previously.

It is important here to stress why modelling is important and to give the four requirements for modelling, as introduced earlier in this book. These requirements for modelling should be referred back to later in the course, not only to emphasise their importance, but also to show how each may be realized using the notation.

Modelling notation

When introducing the modelling notation, it should be stressed that any notation deemed suitable for process modelling may be used here. In the context of this book the notation that is chosen is the UML, for reasons discussed in earlier chapters. It is also worth considering that the notation chosen should not rely on any specific tool or application, and that students should be able to work out as much as possible, in the first instance, by using a PAPS (pen and paper system) tool. This is for very pragmatic reasons. When attending a course, students will potentially be learning about a number of new ideas and concepts simultaneously. For example, they will be learning about processes, modelling, and also the UML (in this case), all for the first time. It is important to try to isolate each of these, initially, when communicating the information to the students, and then to bring them together to form a complete knowledge. If any tool is introduced too early, then students will immediately dive into trying to use the tool, which adds another layer of complexity and shifts the students' focus away from understanding to 'trying to do'.

It is suggested that the actual notation is underplayed; instead, concentrate on examples and emphasise the consistency checks that are contained in the meta-model, rather than the individual parts of the notation. The notation should be correct but should also be kept to a minimum.

The use of summary sheets, such as the ones found in the appendices of this book, is also highly recommended. One approach is to have the two conceptual and realization views on one side of a sheet of paper, with the four notation guides on the reverse. This forms an excellent quick-reference guide for all students.

Examples

Examples are best worked out as a group, rather than just providing detailed case studies. Another approach is to provide partial models and then to get the students to fill in the gaps in the model. This is a good way to emphasise the consistency between the views, and, if used sensibly, can be an excellent way to show how the meta-model may be navigated by asking the right questions at the right time.

The best types of examples are ones that are based either on real-life situations or on situations of which most people would have some knowledge, such as films and books. One excellent source for examples is the film *Jurassic Park*, which is a process modeller's dream come true in terms of the processes, stakeholders and life cycles that it illustrates, and the problems that occur with each of them. This forms the basis for a really good group exercise that can be carried out in either a classroom or a laboratory setting. Not only is this a good example, but students tend to appreciate course work that insists that they watch a film about dinosaurs! See Holt (2007) for an example of this.

Coursework and projects

It is suggested that any course work that is given out should be phrased using the terminology of the meta-model. An example of a generic project description is provided in Figure 9.3.

Project description:

Choose any example project, such as the development of a robot, and produce the following information, in line with the summary sheet:

- **Life cycle:** *a class diagram, showing the structure of the life cycle and including the relationship with iterations and processes.*

- **Life cycle model:** *a sequence diagram, showing the order of execution of the phases that were identified in the previous point. Justify your choice of life cycle model.*

- **Iteration:** *a sequence diagram. Choose a single stage from the life cycle model, and show the iterations within it.*

- **Stakeholder view:** *a class diagram. Develop a stakeholder view and show the types of stakeholders that are involved in the project.*

- **Process content view:** *a class diagram. Show the relevant processes for your project. These should be based on, although not restricted to, the processes defined in the sample process model. Show artefacts and activities as attributes and operations on the classes.*

- **Process behaviour view:** *an activity diagram. Choose one of the processes and show the activity diagram for its internal operation.*

Each diagram should be accompanied by a short textual description, no more than half a page long.

Students are not obliged to use any particular tool or drawing package, but all diagrams should be neat and easy to read.

Please note that marks will only be awarded for the information requested above. Any missing views will lose marks; additional diagrams will not warrant extra marks. Many of the marks will be awarded for consistency of the diagrams, as discussed in the lectures and shown on the summary sheet.

Do not choose a cash-point machine (ATM), any library system (or variations thereof) or a petrol pump.

FIGURE 9.3   *Example project description*

The project description in Figure 9.3 should be treated purely as a guide. For example, it asks for some life cycle information that may or may not be relevant for other courses.

It is worth putting some constraints on the solutions, such as not allowing ATMs or library systems, which are standard examples used in many, many textbooks. If you don't want 30 copies of a petrol pump submitted, then please consider these constraints seriously!

Marking schedules

Due to the rigorous nature of the process meta-model, it is possible to have an equally rigorous marking schedule. The bulk of the marks should be awarded based directly on the meta-model itself, which will include both the views and the relationships between the views and their various elements.

CONCLUSIONS

This chapter has provided a starting point for developing teaching courses and material, whether they are for professional training or university-based teaching. Much about teaching is subjective and the details will depend upon the nature of the teacher, the format of the courses, the type of attendees or students, and so on. The information contained in this chapter is based on many years' experience of teaching and training at many levels, and is offered in order to promote thought, rather than to be prescriptive.

10 Tools and Automation

'a fool with a tool is still a fool'

unknown

INTRODUCTION

One of the key considerations when implementing a process is how to get the information disseminated and used effectively. After all, it is one thing to have perfectly modelled processes and another matter entirely to get people to understand and use these processes. This is where tools enter into the picture.

For the purposes of the discussion in this chapter, tools can be used for a number of purposes – for example, tools for actually modelling the process and tools for automation and dissemination. It should also be stressed that no specific tools are mentioned explicitly in this chapter; only the requirements for selecting a tool are discussed here.

This chapter looks at some of the issues that you should consider when choosing modelling tools. These are presented as general ideas and discussed. It is up to the reader to decide which of them are important and what priority they should have.

GENERAL CAPABILITIES OF A TOOL

Before beginning any sort of evaluation or assessment of tools, it is important to consider two aspects of them: what the tool can do and what it cannot do.

Tools can be very powerful, but it is essential to have a clear and pragmatic understanding of exactly what their capabilities are. In general, a modelling tool will help in three ways:

- **Modelling:** starting with the obvious, a modelling tool should help with modelling. In particular, it should present the user with the full modelling toolkit and have a clear, intuitive interface. In the case of a UML- or BPMN-based modelling tool, the software should be no more difficult to use, in terms of creating a simple model, than an everyday drawing package.
- **Verification:** the importance of consistency has been mentioned on many occasions throughout this book. A set of diagrams that is consistent is a model, whereas a set of diagrams that is not consistent is a bunch of pictures. In order to ensure that we are modelling, as opposed to drawing pictures, it is essential that consistency

checks are performed on the model. Performing these checks can be a long and tedious process, and this is one area where tools should be outstanding.

- **Documentation:** The diagrammatic part of the model shows the simplest views, but it must be remembered that there will be lots of descriptions that support the model, and that every element in the model has, potentially, a description associated with it. Many tools will allow the user to collate these descriptions with the model and output them in a word-processor-friendly format. After all, presentation is key to the successful implementation of the process model.

That gives a very broad idea of how tools may help a user, but it is equally important to understand what tools *cannot* do. They cannot:

- **Guarantee good models:** it is a common and all too frequent mistake to assume that, just because something in a tool looks nice, it is of any value. No tool can guarantee that the output generated is of any quality; this is simply a matter of 'rubbish in means rubbish out'. If the information being modelled, or entered into the model, is of low quality, then it is very likely that the output will be so too. Effective modelling will help to minimize the chance of this happening, but do not assume that something is correct because it has come out of a tool.
- **Teach the approach:** another common mistake is to think that a tool is a replacement for effective training or mentoring. Yes, tools can offer advice on modelling, but they cannot teach how to model effectively, nor how to react to the requirements of the users.

SPECIFIC CAPABILITIES OF A TOOL

This section looks at some specific capabilities that should be considered when looking at modelling tools. The points that are raised here are general points and will apply regardless of the modelling notation that has been adopted. Each of the points here will apply to any number of different modelling notations.

Modelling capabilities

This is a fundamental capability for any visual modelling tool. After all, if there are no diagrams, then there cannot be a model. There are a few main points to consider for the modelling capabilities of any tool: compatibility with the source notation, the ability to draw diagrams, navigation, and checking.

When it comes to compatibility with the source notation, there are good reasons to adopt a notation that is standardized, such as UML or BPMN. In the case of the UML, there is a definitive specification for every version of the language that exists. The UML has gone through several changes and has evolved over time, but there is a single source reference for any particular version. Also, UML is now an ISO standard, which again adds value to its use.

One of the problems with flowcharts is that there are many different definitions of the notation and, hence, it is difficult to find compatibility between tools. It is important, therefore, to choose a tool that supports a particular notation, but then it is also important that the tool is, indeed, compatible with the source notation, since a surprising number of those that are on the market do not fully support their source notations.

Once a tool has been assessed in terms of its compatibility, it is then important to look at how easy the tool is to use. Some of this will be subjective, depending on the user's preference, but a tool should be simple to use and have an intuitive interface. If someone can use a standard drawing package, then it should be possible for that person, after a limited amount of 'playing around' time, to use a good tool effectively.

Assuming that a tool is in place and that there is a model in it, it is then time to consider the navigation capabilities of the tool. The diagrams of a model are interconnected by their behavioural and structural aspects. It should, then, be possible, for example, to create a class diagram that is structural and from one of its classes navigate to the relevant sequence diagrams or activity diagrams representing its behaviour. Process models tend to be large and complex beasts and, therefore, being able to navigate around them with ease is essential.

As a related point, it is desirable that a tool has some sort of checking facilities built in to it. Any tool should take the drudgery out of a task, and checking the model in terms of its consistency is certainly a slow and tedious activity if performed manually. It is also prone to human errors, so this is where the tools should excel. There are two types of check that are desirable: mechanical checks and application-specific checks. Mechanical checks are those that are part of the standard UML notation: an element may appear on more than one diagram, providing a basis for a consistency check. The application-specific checks, in the context of this book, are the checks that relate specifically to process modelling. Some tools come with no checking facilities (in which case they are glorified drawing packages), some come with built-in checking, and others will also allow users to define their own checks.

It is important to consider each of these points when looking into the modelling capabilities of a tool. One way to tackle all of these points is to take part of one of the models from this book and simply enter it into a tool, to see for yourself how well (or badly) the tool performs.

Documentation capabilities

Once a process model has been developed it is important to get as much value from it as possible. One simple way to look at this is to think that the more the model can be used, the more value can be derived from it. One tool capability that can help enormously in this area is that of documentation and report generation.

Before the full potential of report generation can be appreciated, there is a fundamental question that must be considered: where does the corporate knowledge of the process reside? Is it in the documentation, or in the model? Or, to put it another way, where does one have to go in order to get hold of the definitive information regarding the process – the model or the document?

Maybe the answer to this question is that the knowledge resides in the documentation. In this case, report generation is a very effective way to generate the structure of the core documentation. The diagrams can be put directly into the documents, and then each view may be described with text to accompany each diagram. This approach has the following features:

- The core knowledge of the corporate process resides in the documents themselves. The model supports the documents.
- If a change is made to the process knowledge, then a change in the documentation *must* occur. The same change in the process knowledge may also result in a change to the model that supports the documents. Consistency between the model and the documents is a major concern here, and it is important to ensure that they are congruent.

This is a very widely adopted approach to documenting and maintaining a process model, and can be very effective when controlled properly.

The second possible answer to this question is that the knowledge resides in the model rather than the documentation. In this case, the model is created and then each element in the model (such as diagrams, modelling elements, package names, and so on) is accompanied by a text description that forms an inherent part of the model. This approach has the following features:

- The core knowledge resides in the model and *not* the document. This is a very important distinction, as the document is generated entirely from the model.
- Any changes to the core knowledge are made to the original model, and then the whole document is regenerated. Effectively, the original document is discarded and a new version is created from scratch – the document itself is not changed. Consistency between the model and the document is not an issue, as the document may be thought of as simply another view of the model, rather than a separate entity.

Clearly, if the second approach is taken, then documentation and report generation becomes a critical function of the tool, whereas with the first approach report generation is only desirable.

If, however, the second approach is taken and the tool does have sufficiently sophisticated report-generation capabilities, then a whole new world of possibilities opens up. For example, some tools will allow different filters and templates to be applied to the model to generate different reports as output. This means that it becomes possible to produce different documents for different stakeholders. The fact that different stakeholders may have completely different requirements for the process document has already been discussed; by using different filters and templates, production of all the documentation may be automated. Not only this, but the reports that are created are guaranteed to be consistent, since they are generated from the *same* core model.

Answering this question of whether the model supports the document or the document supports the model is a very important one. Once this has been decided, there are a few other, more mundane, questions that must also be answered.

One of the biggest dangers associated with report and document generation is in the process that the tool follows in the transition from the model to the report that is generated. Any errors or ambiguities in this process can lead to enormous problems with the report that is produced, because it may not be consistent with the model as a result. Also, at a more basic level, it is important that the process that is being followed by the tool is actually understood. If the process cannot be understood, then it cannot be verified in any way and this leads to non-determinism in the system.

BUSINESS CONSIDERATIONS

The choice of tools is far more complex than at first appears, and this is not just limited to the functional capabilities of the tool. Buying a tool that meets a set of functional requirements can be achieved relatively easily, but is really only just the beginning, as it is just as important to consider the constraints that the business itself will put on the choice. One of the first factors that must be considered is the way the tool will integrate into the existing toolset within the organization.

Some modelling tools will have support for other packages, such as planning applications, configuration control, and so on. One fundamental question that needs to be answered is whether the tool actually *needs* to integrate into an existing toolset and, if so, to what level. It may be that it is perfectly acceptable to have the modelling tool as a stand-alone application that does not need to integrate in any way with any other tool, in which case there is little problem. However, if it is the case that the modelling tool does need to integrate into an existing suite, then there are a number of other questions that need to be addressed.

Many tools now come as part of a suite of tools from a particular vendor, and the natural assumption to make is that tools that are sold by the same vendor will integrate effectively and seamlessly. The truth, however, can be far from this, since in many cases the tool company may have acquired other tools from different companies that are then integrated into their own toolset. If this is the case, then in many instances caution must be exercised to ensure that the tools do, indeed, work well together.

Many tools now offer output in the form of an extensible markup language (XML)-compliant or similar format. For example, most UML-based tools on the market use an XML implementation of the UML known as the XML modelling interchange (XMI). These XMI-format files may then be used by any other tool that is compliant with XMI, and this provides a degree of interoperability between tools. Also, some tools are geared specifically towards translating between different tool formats, in order to make other tools operate together more easily. Of course, the introduction of yet another tool may lead to problems of its own.

Another key business consideration is to think about how the tool will be used and from where. For example, will everyone who uses the tool require full editing rights, or will many of the users only need to be able to read the output? Some tools will require additional licenses to be purchased for users to view their output files. Other tools, on the other hand, allow their output to be viewed via an internet browser, which is, to all intents and purposes, free.

The type of licensing agreement is also a big factor. It may entail recurring cost over a period of years with full maintenance and support, at the cost of making you more or less obliged to use the tool, regardless of how useful it is. Or it may be a one-off payment, with varying degrees of support, a help line or an email correspondence help desk.

One final business consideration is to look at the vendor's quality of service and pedigree. There are many tools on the market, ranging from free or open-source software to very expensive bespoke packages. It is important to understand exactly what role the vendor is to play in your business. For example, it may be possible to obtain a tool for free or at minimal cost, but what support will the vendor offer? Usually very little! At the other extreme there are very expensive tools whose vendors will tailor them, provide training and even place their own staff within your business to ensure that everything goes smoothly.

AUTOMATION TOOLS

One of the most attractive features of many tools is the ability to automate or animate a process. In some cases, this may be a walk-through that users can access from a terminal, where they can click on different processes or sets of processes and see related views or decompositions of processes. Another very powerful feature is the ability to call up templates, guidelines and other artefacts directly from the tool itself.

This can be very useful when it comes to ensuring that people use the same sets of information to realize the process artefacts.

CONCLUSIONS

Buying tools can be very expensive and it is essential that you understand your own requirements before spending any money. Contrary to popular belief, there is no 'best tool' on the market, since every tool has its own pros and cons and the choice of tool may be highly subjective.

The main point to take away from the discussion in this chapter is that you must understand your own requirements and make an informed decision as to which tool is right for you.

11 Answers to Exercises

'Forty-two'

> Deep Thought, *The Hitchhiker's Guide to the Galaxy*, Douglas Adams

This section presents a set of example answers to the exercises given in Chapter 6. Due to the nature of process modelling, there are always many answers to a single problem, so it should be borne in mind that these are *example* answers to be used for guidance, and should not be taken as the *only* answer to the problems.

1. Extend the process structure view to include the concepts of skills and responsibilities introduced in Figure 6.15.

The key point here is to look at the diagram in Figure 6.15 and abstract a process structure view from it, and then add it to the existing process structure view in Figure 6.1.

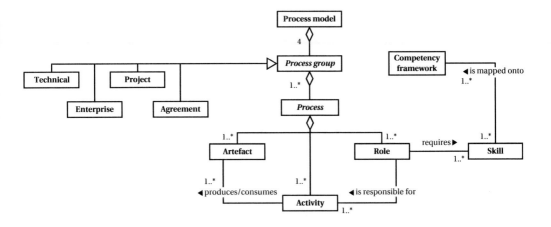

FIGURE 11.1 *Extended process structure view*

The example answer shown in Figure 11.1 has related the new element 'Skill' to the existing element 'Role'. This is consistent with Figure 6.15.

Another new element has also been introduced here, named 'Competency framework', and the diagram shows that all skills should be mapped onto one or more 'Competency framework'.

2. Check the consistency between the process behaviour view in Figure 6.27 and the process content view in Figure 6.3.

A straightforward consistency check may be applied here between the two views. Three basic checks may be done, relating to the process name, the process activities and the process artefacts.

Process name check

The check is that the process name, 'Meeting logistics', maps onto the title of the process behaviour view.

Process activity check

A two-way check needs to be done here, from the process content view (PCV) to the process behaviour view (PBV) and then the other way around. Therefore, first check that every activity (operation) that is shown in Figure 6.3 (PCV) exists as an activity invocation (sausage) in Figure 6.27 (PBV). In this case, the check passes.

Now, check that every activity invocation (sausage) that is shown in Figure 6.27 (PBV) exists as an activity (operation) in Figure 6.3 (PCV). In this case the check fails, as 'respond', 'confirm' and 'cancel' exist in the PBV but not in the PCV.

Process artefact check

A two-way check needs to be carried out, from the PCV to the PBV and then the other way around. Therefore, the first check is that every artefact (attribute) that appears in Figure 6.3 appears as an object in Figure 6.27. In this case, the check passes.

Now, check that every artefact (object on the PBV) appears as an artefact on the PCV (an attribute). In this case the check passes.

Further notes

Care should be taken when checking artefacts, as a situation often occurs where an artefact is broken down into smaller artefacts, all of which are represented on the PCV. In such cases, it is common to see only the higher-level artefacts, rather than all of them. This information can be seen by looking at the information view, which will show the relationships between all the artefacts and will reveal any aggregation ('made up of') relationships between them.

An interesting point here is to question how much consistency checking the modeller should be doing, compared with what the tool does. A good tool will, at a minimum, allow consistency to be enforced between, for example, attributes on a class diagram and classes on an information view, by use of 'typing'. This means that an attribute is allocated a type, which is set to the appropriate class name from the information view.

3. Extend the mapping exercise to include the elements in Figures 6.30 and 6.31.

A not-so-straightforward mapping exercise can be performed here: see Table 11.1. At first, the mapping looks simple, but a problem occurs because the element 'Component' in the Prince II model is not very well defined, since some of the components relate well to processes, in which case they can be mapped, but others relate better to artefacts, in which case they cannot be mapped onto processes.

TABLE 11.1 *Consistency-checking table*

ISO 15288	Prince II
Process group	
Enterprise	Quality
Agreement	
Technical	
Project	Configuration management
	Change control
	Manage stage
	Manage risk
No mapping	Controls
	Plans
	Stage

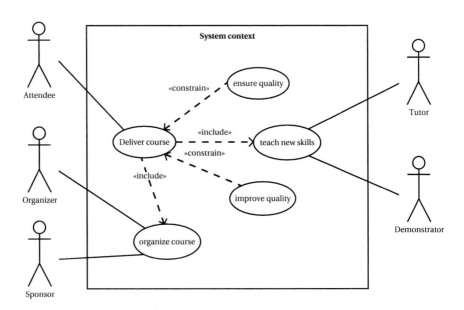

FIGURE 11.2 *A more populated requirements view*

Most of the components may be related to particular process groups, but several cannot. Hence the 'no mapping' entry in Table 11.1.

Of course, the mapping here is really only the first step in the exercise, as it is important to realize that something must be done about the inconsistencies that have been found.

4. Update the requirements view in Figure 6.16 to include more detailed relationships between the requirements.

The basic relationships need to be added to this diagram. The example answer in Figure 11.2 shows one possible solution.

It can be seen from Figure 11.2 that the two requirements 'ensure quality' and 'improve quality' have now been identified as constraints on the main requirement of 'Deliver course'. The other two requirements, 'organize course' and 'teach new skills', have been identified as inclusions in the main requirement 'Deliver course'.

5. Add the following roles to the stakeholder view: 'Sales person', 'Marketer' and 'Sales manager'. In which grouping will they appear?

In this example there are many possible permutations, depending on the exact definition of the roles. Two examples are shown in Figures 11.3 and 11.4.

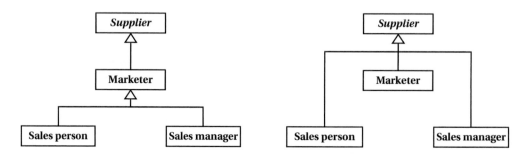

FIGURE 11.3   *Possible stakeholder view*   **FIGURE 11.4**   *Another possible stakeholder view*

In Figure 11.3 the roles of 'Sales person' and 'Sales manager' are considered to be types of 'Marketer'. In Figure 11.4 all three roles are defined as being types of 'Supplier' and are viewed at the same level of abstraction. Notice that 'Marketer' here is a role in its own right that will have instances, since it is not defined as an abstract class like 'Supplier' ('Marketer' is not in italics). It may be that in the example shown in Figure 11.3 the role of 'Marketer' has no instances; in this case it would be shown in italics.

6. Increase the number of artefacts in the information view in Figure 6.21.

Any artefact from any process may be added to this diagram.

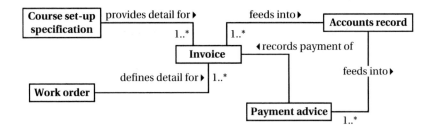

FIGURE 11.5 *Increased number of artefacts in an information view*

In Figure 11.5 a new artefact had been added, named 'Payment advice'. This would then need to be checked against the PCV to ensure consistency of the model.

Another option would be to provide more detail on the structure of a single artefact, as in Figure 11.6.

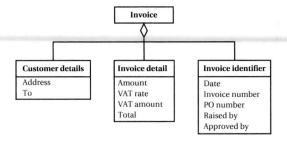

FIGURE 11.6 *A detailed breakdown of a single artefact*

In Figure 11.6 the 'Invoice' artefact had been broken down into more detail. Note that this must be consistent with the PCV, and, quite often, changes need to be effected based on a thorough breakdown of a single artefact.

7. Populate some of the existing processes in the process content views shown in Figures 6.3 to 6.10.

An existing process that has neither activities nor artefacts should be chosen, and the artefacts (represented as attributes) and activities (represented as operations) added.

Course delivery
Feedback form
Course setup specification
Comments form
Greet()
Deliver course()
Collect feedback()
Close course()
Gather comments()
Obtain follow-up details()

FIGURE 11.7 *A populated process shown as a class*

Figure 11.7 shows a populated process for 'Course delivery'. The artefacts here (shown as attributes) and the activities (shown as operations) have been abstracted from the associated process behaviour view (represented by an activity diagram) for this process (represented by the class).

8. Add some new processes to the process content view to reflect marketing-related processes.

Identify some new process names for processes related to marketing and add them to the process content view. In this case, it has been decided to include the processes as part of the 'Enterprise' process group.

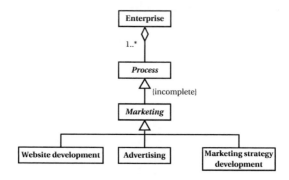

FIGURE 11.8 *Increased number of processes on a process content view*

The example in Figure 11.8 shows three new processes that have been identified. Note the use of the '{incomplete}' constraint to show that there may be more processes that do not appear on this diagram.

9. Add some new instances of stakeholders to the process information views in Figures 6.22 and 6.23. Ensure consistency with the original requirements view.

Any number of possibilities emerge here; the example in Figure 11.9 shows the addition of a single instance of the 'Project manager' stakeholder.

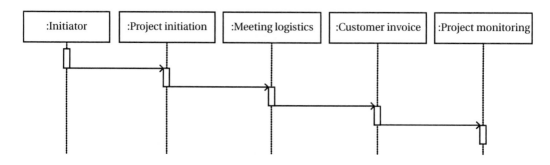

FIGURE 11.9 *A more populated process instance view*

Note that, in terms of consistency, the stakeholder instance that is added here should exist on the stakeholder view, and should also be related to the relevant use case on the requirements view.

Also, the interactions between the processes and the stakeholders, and between processes and other processes, could occur in almost any order. A simple linear execution is shown in this example.

10. Create a new process instance view diagram for any of the requirements in Figures 6.16 or 6.18.

Select a requirement and think of a single scenario that could possibly occur. This is then represented as a sequence of instances of processes in a process instance view.

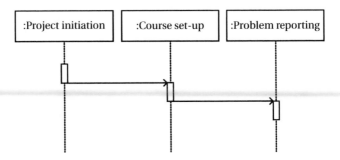

FIGURE 11.10   *A new scenario shown as a process instance view for a single requirement*

In the example shown in Figure 11.10, the 'cancel course' requirement was considered. It was decided that one possible scenario is the cancellation of the course during set-up, due to the customer reneging on the agreement. A 'Problem reporting' process is also included here to represent trying to learn lessons from what went wrong.

11. Modify the process realization view of the existing process meta-model to include instances of stakeholders under the process instance view.

The lower right-hand corner of the process meta-model realization view needs to be modified. Only the relevant section of the meta-model is shown in Figure 11.11.

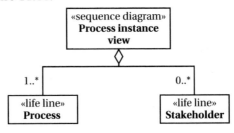

FIGURE 11.11   *Expansion to the process meta-model realization view*

In this example, a new element named 'Stakeholder' has been added, which is realized in UML using a '<<life line>>'. Note that the multiplicity is zero or more here, an indication that a stakeholder may or may not be present.

12. Create a process behaviour view for any of the processes in the process content views in Figures 6.3 to 6.10.

A populated process should be identified from the process content view, and then its behaviour defined using a process behaviour view (realized by an activity diagram in UML).

The example in Figure 11.12 shows the behaviour of the 'Course delivery' process.

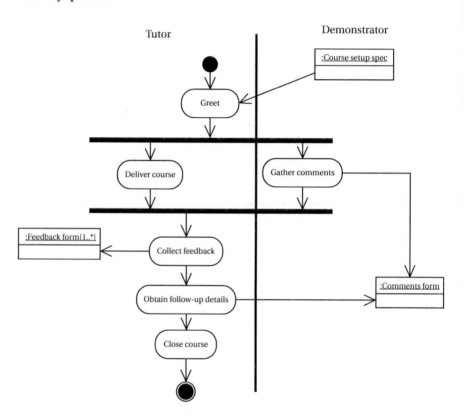

FIGURE 11.12   *Possible process behaviour view for a single process*

13. Define a process quagmire for the two process models introduced in Figures 6.28 and 6.29. Add some new source processes to the quagmire.

This quagmire will be a simple extension of the existing information view, with the addition of 'Prince II' as an artefact (class).

The example in Figure 11.13 shows the simple addition of 'Prince II'.

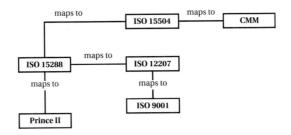

FIGURE 11.13   *Increased quagmire showing additional process models*

14. Consider the requirements view in Figure 6.17. What are the implications of moving the '<<extend>>' relationship, which currently exists between 'Cancel course' and 'Publicize', to between 'Cancel course' and 'Organize course'?

The relationship will now apply at a far higher level of abstraction and will apply to all the included use cases for 'Organize course'. Therefore, the 'Cancel course' use case will now apply to 'set up', 'publicize' and 'support' rather than just to 'publicize'. As a consequence of this, there will be far more possible scenarios that may be associated with 'Cancel course', and the complexity of this requirement increases dramatically.

A Summary of the Process Modelling Meta-model

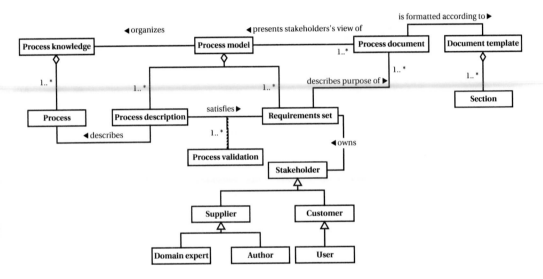

FIGURE A.1 *Process concept view*

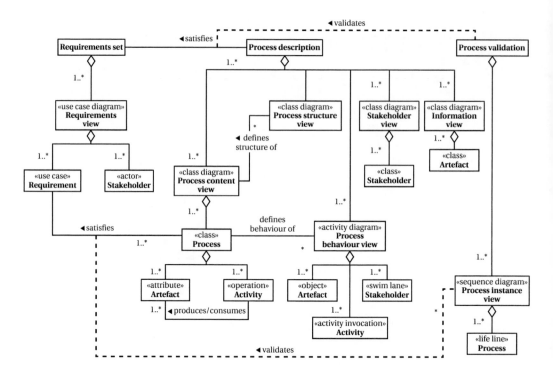

Figure A.2 *Process realization view*

B Summary of UML Notation

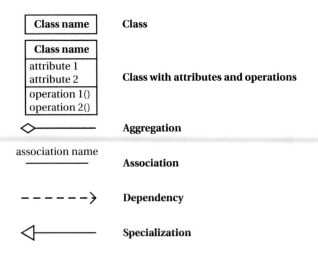

Class name	Class
Class name attribute 1 attribute 2 operation 1() operation 2()	Class with attributes and operations
◇———	Aggregation
association name ———	Association
– – – – –>	Dependency
◁———	Specialization

FIGURE B.1 *Graphical notation for class diagrams*

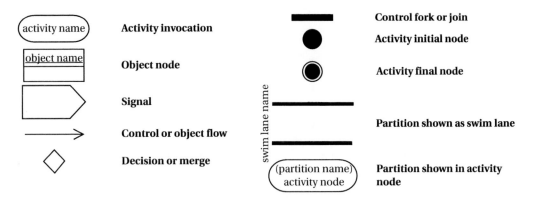

activity name	Activity invocation	▬▬	Control fork or join
object name	Object node	●	Activity initial node
	Signal	◉	Activity final node
——>	Control or object flow	swim lane name ———	Partition shown as swim lane
◇	Decision or merge	(partition name) activity node	Partition shown in activity node

FIGURE B.2 *Graphical notation for activity diagrams*

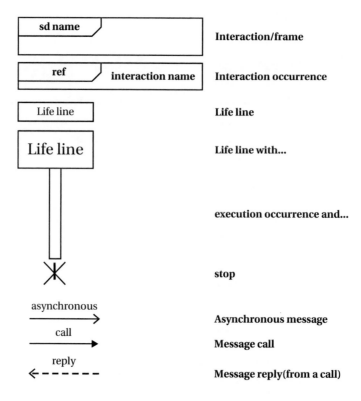

FIGURE B.3 *Graphical notation for sequence diagrams*

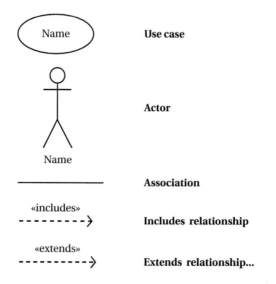

FIGURE B.4 *Graphical notation for use case diagrams*

References

Anderson, L., Krathwohl, D., Airasian, P., Cruikshank, K., Mayer, R., Pintrich, P., Raths, J., and Wittrock, M. (Eds.) (2001) *A Taxonomy for Learning, Teaching, and Assessing – A Revision of Bloom's Taxonomy of Educational Objectives*. Addison Wesley Longman, Inc.

Bentley, C. (2001) *PRINCE 2: A practical handbook. Computer Weekly Professional Series*. Butterman Heineman, Oxford.

Bloom, B. (Ed.) (1956) *Taxonomy of Educational Objectives: The Classification of Educational Goals*; Susan Fauer Company, Inc., 201–207.

BPMI (2002) *Business Process Modelling Language*. BPMI, California. Available from www.bpmi.org.

Brooks, Frederick P. Jr (1995) *The Mythical Man-Month: Essays on Software*. Addison-Wesley, Reading, MA.

Cabinet Office (2004) *eGIF: The electronic government interoperability framework*. UK Government, London. Available from www.govtalk. gov.uk.

Carnegie Mellon Software Engineering Institute (2002) *Capability maturity model integration, version 1.1*. Carnegie Mellon Software Engineering Institute, Pittsburgh, PA. Available from www.sei.cmu.edu/cmmi.

DoD (2007) *DoD architectural framework version 1.5*, http://jitc.fhu.disa.mil/jitc_dri/pdfs/dodaf_v1v1.pdf

Flowers, S. (1996) *Software Failure: Management Failure – Amazing stories and cautionary tales*. Wiley, Chichester.

Goldstine, H. (1972). *The Computer from Pascal to Von Neumann*. Princeton University Press, 266–267.

Holt, J. (2004) *UML for Systems Engineering: Watching the wheels*, 2nd edition. IEE Publishing, London.

Holt, J. (2007) The Brontosaurus of complexity. In *Proceedings of the 2007 IET Seminar on Model Based Systems*, http://www.theiet.org/

IEEE (2000) *IEEE Recommended Practice for Architectural Description of Software-Intensive Systems*. IEEE Computer Society.

International council on systems engineering (INCOSE) (2006) INCOSE competency framework, Issue 2.0. http://www.incoseonline.org.uk/

ISO 5807 (1985). *Information processing – Documentation symbols and conventions for data, program and system flowcharts, program network charts and system resources charts.* ISO, Geneva.

ISO 9001 (2000) *Model for quality assurance in design, development, production, installation and servicing.* ISO, Geneva.

ISO 12207 (2004) *Information technology: Software life cycle processes.* ISO, Geneva.

ISO 15288 (2002) *Systems engineering: System life cycle processes.* ISO, Geneva.

ISO 19501 (2005) *The unified modelling language.* ISO, Geneva.

ISO/IEC 15504 (2004) *Software process assessment.* ISO, Geneva.

Mazza, C., Fairclough, J., Melton, B., De Pablo, D., Scheffer, A. and Stevens, R. (1994) *Software Engineering Standards.* Prentice Hall, Hemel Hempstead.

MODAF (2008) *The MOD Architecture Framework Version 1.2.* http://www.modaf.org.uk/

Object Management Group (OMG) (2009), *Business Process Modeling Notation (BPMN) 1.2* http://www.omg.org/spec/BPMN/1.2.

Oxford English Dictionary (2002) ed. C. Soanes. Oxford University Press, Oxford.

Perry, S. (2006) When is a Process Model Not a Process Model – A Comparison between UML and BPMN. Presented at the IEE seminar on Process Modelling using UML, March. http://www.brass-bullet.co.uk/

Rumbaugh, J., Booch, G. and Jacobson, I. (2004) *The UML 2.0 Reference Manual.* Addison Wesley, Massachusetts.

TOGAF (2009) *The Open Group Architectural Framework.* http://www.opengroup.org/togaf/

Zachman, John A. (2008) The Zachman Framework™: The Official Concise Definition. http://www.zachmaninternational.com

Further Reading

ISO 90003 (2004) *Software engineering – Guidelines for the application of ISO 9001:2000 to computer software.* ISO, Geneva.

Slack, N., Chambers, S. and Johnston, R. (1998) *Operations Management.* London: FT Prentice Hall.

White, S. and Miers, D. (2008) *BPMN Modeling and Reference Guide: Understanding and Using BPMN.* Future Strategies Inc., Lighthouse Pt, FL.

Index

Notation: *Italics* denotes figures and **bold** denotes tables

abstraction factors 17
activities
    BPMN 163–164
    process content view 67–71
    process structure view 119, *120*
activity diagrams
    activity invocation 30–31, 71
    concepts 30–33
    control flows 31
    control forks and joins 31
    example 32, *32*
    graphical notation 30–33, *30, 203*
    object flows 31
    object nodes 31
    process behaviour view 71–73, *72*
    process modelling 33
    start and end states 32
    swim lanes 32, *32*, 71, *72*, 73
    UML diagrams 30–33
activity invocation 30–31, 71
activity ratio 102, *102–103*, 104, 112
actors in use case diagrams 36
aggregation
    overlapping 25, *26*
    relationship 25–26, *25–26*
agreement process group 120, *120*,
        129–130, *130*
animating processes 184, 189–190
ANSI/IEEE 1471-2000, 154
appendices 201–204
artefacts
    artefact ratio 102, *102–103*, 104,
        111–112
    BPMN 164–166
    definitions 4
    information view 147, 194–195, *195*
        case study 136–139, *138–139*
        relationship 73–74, *74*
    process content view 67–71
    process structure view 119, *120*
assessments
    process mapping 91, 92
    risk 7, 128
association
    BPMN 164
    direction 21–22, *21*
    graphical notation 21–22, *21–22*
    relationship 21–22, *21–22*,
        24–25, *24*
attributes, class 23–24
audits 80, 91–92
automation
    information view 73–74
    and tools 184, 189–190
awareness factors 11

balance ratio 71
BPMI *see* business process modelling
        initiative
BPMN *see* business process modelling
        notation

business analysis, process model
        interpretation 119
business considerations, tools
        188–189
business process management,
        definition 3
business process modelling,
        definition 3
business process modelling initiative
        (BPMI) 12–13
business process modelling notation
        (BPMN) 12–13, 161–167,
        162–163, 165–167
    background 162
    language 162–166
    populating 166–167, *167*
    process meta-model 162–167
business process re-engineering,
        definition 3

capabilities, tools 184–188
capability determination 90
case study 115–147
    approach used 117–118
    background 115–116
    information view 117, 136–139,
        138–139
    introduction 115
    ISO 15288 144–146, **144**, *145–146*
    Prince II 144–146, *144*, **144**, *146*
    process behaviour view 117,
        141–143, *142–143*
    process content view 117, 120–130,
        121–128, 130
    process groups 120–130
    process instance view 118, 139–141,
        140–141
    process mapping 143–146, *144–146*,
        144
    process meta-model 117–142, 147
    process model interpretation
        118–119
    process modelling 116–147
    process structure view 117,
        119–120, *120*
    requirements view 117–118,
        134–136, *135–137*
    stakeholder view 117, 130–134,
        131–134
    training 124–125, 134–139, *138–139*,
        141–142, *142*
choice of tools 188–189
class
    attributes 23–24
    definition 19–20
    graphical notation 19–20, *20*
    operations 24
    process concept view 54–55
    relationships 24–29, *25–27, 29*
    representing 20–29, *20*
    tailoring 49–50, *49*

class diagrams
    association relationships 21–22,
        21–22
    class representation 20–29, *20*
    concepts 19–20
    graphical notation 19–20, *20, 203*
    process content view 68
    process metal model 29
    process modelling 29
    process structure view 62
    relationships 24–29, *25–27, 29*
    stakeholder view 74
    UML 19–29
Common Object Request Broker
        Architecture (CORBA) 8
communication 55, 56
competency view 157–159, *157–158*
complexity
    process concept view 55
    process model interpretation
        118–119
    process structure view 65–66, *66*
    relationships 43–44, *44*
    requirements for process
        modelling 43–45, *44*
compliance, process mapping 91–92
consistency factors 41, 73, 77–79,
        89–90, 147, 192
<<constrain>> relationship 39–40, *40*
control
    case study 128
    flows 31
    forks and joins 31
    risk 6, 7
CORBA (Common Object Request
Broker Architecture) 8
coupling 44
course structures 177–179, *178*
coursework and projects 181–182, *182*

Department of Defence Architectural
        Framework (DoDAF) 154
dependency, example/uses/
        relationships 28–29, *29*
diagrams 161
    activity 30–33, 71–73, *203*
    class 19–29, 68, *203*
    consistency between 41
    sequence 33–35, 77
    UML 16–41
    use case 35–40
    see also graphical notation
direction in association 21–22, *21*
documentation factors 80, 81–82, *81*,
        185, 186–188
DoDAF (Department of Defence
        Architectural Framework) 154

element categories 163–166
elimination of risk 5
EN (European Normative) 8

end states 32
enterprise architecture 148–159
   competency view 157–159, *157–158*
   existing sources 153–154
   modelling 154–159
   ontology 150–151, *152*, 155–159, *156–158*
   process meta-model 149, *149*, 155, **155**
   process modelling 154–159, **155**, *156–158*
   requirements 151–153
   requirements view 151–152, *152*, 155, *158*, 159
   structure 150–151, *152*
   traceability 157
   views 150–152, *152*, 155, 157–159, *157–158*
enterprise process group 120–123, *120–123*
European Normative (EN) 8
evaluation of risk 7
events 163
execution paths 73
existing processes
   analysis 79–81, *81*
   process improvement 84–85, *84–85*
existing source factors 153–154
<<extend>> relationship 39, 147, 199
extending the process meta-model 86–90, *87–89*
extensible markup language (XML) 189

failure factors 11, 80
flowcharts 12, 161–162, 167–172, *168*, *170–171*
   background 167
   language modelling 167–169, *168*, *170*
   notation 161–162, 167–172, *168*, *170–171*
   process meta-model 169–171, *170–171*
   stereotypes 169–170, *171*

Gantt charts 87–88, *87*, 161
gateways 164
graphical notation
   activity diagrams 30–33, *30, 203*
   association relationships 21–22, *21–22*
   BPMN 163–167, *163, 165–167*
   class diagrams 19–20, *20, 203*
   classes 19–20, *20*
   sequence diagrams 33–35, *34–35, 204*
   text representation 161
   use case diagrams 36–40, *36, 38–40, 204*
guidelines, form of process 8–9

hazards
   definition 6
   identification 7
Health and Safety Executive (HSE) 7

IEC (International Electrotechnical Commission) 8
IEEE 1471 154

ignorance factors 83
<<include>> relationship 39
information, missing 42
information view 29, 73–74, *74*
   artefacts 147, 194–195, *195*
   automation 73–74
   case study 117, 136–139, *138–139*
   characteristics 73–74, *74*
   consistency 73
   extended 101–104, *101–103*
   process mapping 100–104, *100–103*
   stakeholders 147, 196, *196*, 197
inheritance in specialization 26–28, *27*
inter-relationships 73–74, *74*
interactions
   process modelling 43–45, *44*
   sequence diagrams 33–34
International Electrotechnical Commission (IEC) 8
International Standardization Organization (ISO) 8
   ISO 9001 105, *105*
   ISO 12207 105, *105*
   ISO 15288 105–111, *105–108*, **110**, 144–147, **144**, *145–146*, 193–194, *193*, **193**
   ISO 15504 105–111, *105–108*, **109–110**
   ISO 19501 14
invoicing 136–141, *137–139, 142*
ISO *see* International Standardization Organization

knowledge abstraction 82–84, *84*

lane elements 164
language
   BPMN 162–166
   flowcharts 167–169, *168, 170*
   processes 10–11
   UML 13, 19
leaf processes 66–67
life cycles
   concepts 64, *64*
   management 86–90, *87–89*
life lines 34, 35, *35*

maintenance, case study 125–127
management processes 127–128
mapping
   to different notations 161–172, *162–163, 165–168, 170–171*
   see also process mapping
marketing-related processes 147, 196, *196*
marking schedules 182–183
message flow 164
messages, sequence diagrams 34, 35, *35*
meta-model *see* process meta-model
metrics
   application 104–113
   interpreting the results 113–114
   and process mapping 91–93, 100–114
Ministry of Defence Architectural Framework (MoDAF) 154
misdirection factors 83

missing information 42
MoDAF (Ministry of Defence Architectural Framework) 154
model, definitions 5
modelling
   concepts 180
   enterprise architecture 154–159
   teaching guides 180–181
   tool capabilities 184, 185–186
   see also process modelling

notation 12–13
   comparisons 171–172
   issues in presentation 160–172
   mapping to different notations 161–172, *162–163, 165–168, 170–171*
   teaching guides 180–181
   see also graphical notation

object flows 31, 71
Object Management Group (OMG) 162
object nodes 31, 71
off-the-shelf process tailoring 48–49
OMG (Object Management Group) 162
ontology, enterprise architecture 150–151, *152*, 155–159, *156–158*
The Open Group Architectural Framework (TOGAF) 154
operations, class 24
operations management, definition 3
out of balance ratio 71
overlapping aggregations 25, *26*

perception factors 11
Pert charts 88
PGI *see* process group index
PGR *see* process group ratio
PI *see* process index
PM set-up 96, *96, 98*, 99, 107–108, *108*
PMI *see* process model index
pool elements 164
populating models/processes
   BPMN meta-model 166–167, 167
   process content view 147, 195–196, *195*
postgraduate courses 176–183, *178, 182*
PR *see* process ratio
presentation 160–172
   BPMN 161–167, *162–163, 165–167*, 171–172
   flowcharts 161–162, 167–172, *168, 170–171*
   introduction 160
   notation issues 160–172
   process modelling 160–172
Prince II 144–147, *144*, **144**, *146*, 193–194, *193*, **193**, 198–199, *199*
procedures, form of process 8–9
process 8–15
   compact definition 47, *47*
   evolution 47–48
   simple definition 46–47, *46*

process analysis
  process behaviour view 99–100, *99*
  process content view 96, *96*
  process mapping 96, *96*, 108–111,
    109–110
process behaviour view
  BPMN *165*, 166
  case study 117, 141–143, *142–143*
  characteristics 71–73, *72*
  consistency 147, 192
  execution paths 73
  flowcharts 167–168, *168*, 169, *170*
  Meeting Logistics process 72–73, *72*
  process content view 147, 198, *198*
  process mapping 97–100, *97–99*,
    102–103, *103*
process concept view
  characteristics 53–57, *54*, *57*
  extension *88*
  groupings *57*
  introduction 51–52, *51–52*
  summary 201–202, *201–202*
  teaching guides 180
process content view 29, 67–71, *68–69*
  case study 117, 120–130, *121–128*,
    130
  characteristics 67–71, *68–69*
  consistency 147, 192
  example 68, *68*
  existing process population 147,
    195–196, *195*
  extension 101, *101*
  marketing-related processes 147,
    196, *196*
  populating 147, 195–196, *195*
  process behaviour view 147,
    198, *198*
  process mapping 95–96, *96–97*, 101,
    101, 107–108, *108*
  warning signs 68–69, *69*
process document creation 81–82, *81*
process effectiveness 91
process group index (PGI) *103*, 104,
  112–113
process group ratio (PGR) *103*, 104, 111
process groups *103*, 104, 111–113,
  120–130
process identification
  process behaviour view 97, *98*, 99
  process content view 96, *96*
  process mapping 105–107, *105–107*
process implementation 91
process improvements 84–85, *85*
process index (PI) *103*, 104, 112,
  113–114
process instance view 77, *77*
  BPMN *166*, 166
  case study 118, 139–141, *140–141*
  process mapping 96–97, *97*
  requirements view 147, 197, *197*
  stakeholders 141, *141*, 147, 196–197,
    196–197
process iteration 43
process knowledge abstraction 82–84,
  84
process mapping
  case study 143–146, *144–146*, **144**
  definition 3

information view 100, *100*, 101–104,
  101–102, *103*
and metrics 91–93, 100–114
Prince II 144–146, *144*, **144**, *146*
problems 92–93
process behaviour view 97–100,
  97–98, *99*, 102–103, *103*
process content view 95–96, *96–97*,
  101, *101*, 107–108, *108*
process for 93–100
process instance view 96–97, *97*
process structure view 93, 101,
  106–107, *106–107*, 147, 193–194,
  193, **193**
requirements view 93–94, *94*
stakeholder view 94–95, *95*
process meta-model 79–86, *81–82*,
  84–85
  audits 80
  BPMN 162–167, *167*
  case study 117–142, 147
  class diagrams 29, 51, *51*
  consistency 78, **78**, 89–90
  enterprise architecture 149, *149*,
    155, **155**
  existing process analysis 79–81, *81*
  existing process improvements
    84–85, *84*, *85*
  extending 86–90, *87–89*
  flowchart inclusion 169–171,
    170–171
  information view 29, 73–74, *74*
    case study 117, 136–139, *138–139*
    process mapping 100–104,
      100–103
  introduction 53
  mappings to different notations
    161–172, *162–163*, *165–168*,
    170–171
  misdirection factors 83
  process behaviour view 71–73, *72*
    case study 117, 141–143, *142–143*
    process content view 147,
      198, *198*
    process mapping 97–100, *97–99*,
      102–103, *103*
  process concept view 51–57, *51–52*,
    54, *57*, 180
    extension *88*
    summary 201–202, *201–202*
  process content view 29, 67–71,
    68–69, 147, 195–196, *195–196*
    case study 117, 120–130, *121–128*,
      130
    process behaviour view 147,
      198, *198*
    process mapping 95–96, *96–97*,
      101, *101*, 107–108, *108*
  process document creation
    81–82, *81*
  process improvements 84–85, *85*
  process instance view 77, *77*
    case study 118, 139–141, *140–141*
    process mapping 96–97, *97*
    requirements view 147, 197, *197*
    stakeholders 141, *141*, 147,
      196–198, *196–197*
  process mapping 93–100

process realization view 51–53, *52*,
  57–59, *58*, 202, *202*
  extension 88–89, *89*
  stakeholders 147, 197–198, *197*
process structure view 62–67, *63–67*
  case study 117, 119–120, *120*
  extension 147, 191, *191*
  process mapping 93, 101,
    106–107, *106–107*, 147, 193–194,
    193, **193**
requirements for process modelling
  50–52, *51–52*
requirements view 59–62, *61*
  case study 117–118, 134–136,
    135–137
  process instance view 147,
    197, *197*
  process mapping 93–94, *94*
stakeholder view 29, 74–76, *75*
  case study 117, 130–134, *131–134*
  process mapping 94–95, *95*
  roles 74, 147, 194, *194*
  summary 201–202, *201–202*
tacit process knowledge abstraction
  82–84, *84*
teaching guides 179–180, 181–182,
  182
using 79–86, *81–82*, *84–85*
process model development 106–107,
  106–107
process model index (PMI) *103*,
  104, 113
process model interpretation 118–119
process modelling
  activity diagrams 33
  BPMN 12–13, 161–167, *162–163*,
    165–167
  case study 116–147
  class diagrams 29
  enterprise architecture 154–159,
    155, *156–158*
  flowcharts 12, 161–162, 167–172,
    168, *170–171*
  life cycle management 86–90,
    87–89
  mapping to different notations
    161–172, *162–163*, *165–168*,
    170–171
  notation 12–13
  presentation 160–172
  RACI matrix tables 12
  requirements 42–52
  sequence diagrams 35
  teaching guide 173–183, *174*,
    178, *182*
  techniques 12–13, 161–172,
    162–163, *165–168*, *170–171*
  UML diagrams 16–19
  use case diagrams 40
process partitioning 43
process quagmires 105–106, *105*, 147,
  198–199, *199*
process ratio (PR) *103*, 111
process re-alignment, definition 3
process realization view
  characteristics 53, 57–59, *58*
  extension 88–89, *89*
  introduction 51–52, *52*

process concept view 202, *202*
stakeholders 147, 197–198, *197*
process structure view 29, 62–67, *63–67*
  BPMN 162–163, *162*
  case study 117, 119–120, *120*
  complexity 65–66, *66*
  dangerous 65–67, *66–67*
  detailed 63–64, *63*
  extension 147, 191, *191*
  flowchart notation 167, *168*, 169
  leaf processes 66–67
  life cycle concepts 64, *64*
  potentially dangerous 65–67, *66*
  process mapping 93, 101, 106–107, *106–107*, 147, 193–194, *193*, **193**
  simple 62, *63*
  sub-processes 66–67
  Welsh National Curriculum 64–65, *65*
process validation 5, 59–62, 139
process verification 5, 59–62, 184–185
processes
  background 3–4
  characteristics 1–3, 8–9
  definitions 3–5
  language 10–11
  magic of 1–3
  manipulation 2
  problems with 9–11
  realism 10
  risk 5–8
  tailoring 47–50, *49–50*
product development 124, *125–126*
professional training *174*, 175–176
project process group 120–121, *120–121*, 127–129, *127–128*
projects and coursework 181–182, *182*

quagmire identities 105–106, *105*, 147, 198–199, *199*

RACI matrix tables 12
realism factors 10, 17, 42–43
recording findings, risk 7
relationships
  aggregation 25–26, *25–26*
  association 21–22, *21–22*, 24–25, *24*
  class diagrams 24–29, *25–27, 29*
  complexity 43–44, *44*
  <<constrain>> relationship 39–40, *40*
  dependency 28–29, *29*
  <<extend>> relationship 39, 147, 199
  <<include>> relationship 39
  process concept view 56–57
  representing 24–29
  requirements view 147, *193*, 194
  specialization 26–28, *26–27*
  within UML 38–41
  use case diagrams 37, 38–40, *38–39*
replacement of risk 5
requirements for enterprise architecture 151–153
requirements for process modelling 42–52
  complexity 43–45, *44*
  interactions 43–45, *44*

introduction 42
meeting through modelling 45–47, *46–47*
missing information 42
process iteration 43
process meta-model 50–52, *51–52*
process partitioning 43
realism 42–43
specific requirements 42–45
tailoring processes 47–50, *49–50*
traceability 45
UML modelling 45–47, *46–47*
requirements view 59–62, *61*
  case study 117–118, 134–136, *135–137*
  enterprise architecture 151–152, *152*, 155, *158*, 159
  <<extend>> relationship 147, 199
  process instance view 147, 197, *197*
  process mapping 93–94, *94*
  relationships 147, *193*, 194
responsibilities
  process structure view 147, 191, *191*
  stakeholder view 134, *134*
responsible, accountable, consulted and informed tables (RACI matrix tables) 12
reviews, risk 7
risk 5–8
  assessment 7, 128
  control 6, 7
  definition 6
  elimination 5
  evaluation 7
  hazards 6, 7
  recording findings 7
  replacement 5
  responsibilities 6–7
  reviews 7
  transfer 6
roles of stakeholders 74, 120, 147, *174*, 175–176, 194, *194*

sanity checks 119
schedule marking 182–183
sequence diagrams
  concepts 33–35
  graphical notation 33–35, *34–35, 204*
  interactions 33–34
  life lines 34, 35, *35*
  messages 34, 35, *35*
  process instance view 77
  process modelling 35
sequence flow 164
skills 90, 134, *134*, 147, 191, *191*
source process 91–92
source standards 91, 105–110
specialization
  relationship 26–28, *26–27*, 38–39
  tailoring processes 47–50, *49–50*
  use case diagrams 38–39
specific capabilities of tools 185–188
stakeholder view 29, 74–76, *75*
  case study 117, 130–134, *131–134*
  extension 133–134, *133–134*
  generic *75*
  names 75
  process mapping 94–95, *95*

process meta-models 74–76, *75*
robustness 75
roles 74, 147, 194, *194*
stakeholders
  definitions 4
  flowcharts 170
  information view 147, 196–197, *196*
  process instance view 141, *141*, 147, 196–198, *196–197*
  process realization view 147, 197–198, *197*
  requirements 28–29, *29*
  roles 74, 120, 147, *174*, 175–176, 194, *194*
standards 76, 80–81
  compliance 91
  form of process 8–9
  source standards 91, 105–110
  stakeholder view 131–132, *132*
  see also International Standardization Organization
start and end states 32
stereotypes 58, 88, 161, 169–170, *171*
structure of enterprise architecture 150–151, *152*
sub-processes 66–67
summary of process meta-model 201–202, *201–202*
summary of UML notation 203–204
support processes, case study 128–129
swim lanes 32, *32*, 71, *72*, 73, 164
symbols, flow charts 168–169, *168*
system, definitions 4
system boundary 37

tacit process knowledge abstraction 82–84, *84*
tailoring processes 47–50, *49–50*
target processes 91–92, 107–108
teaching guide 173–183, *174*, *178, 182*
  introduction 173–175, *174*
  marking schedules 182–183
  postgraduate courses 176–183, *178, 182*
  process meta-model 179–180, 181–182, *182*
  process modelling 173–183, *174*, *178, 182*
  undergraduate courses 176–183, *178, 182*
  university courses 176–183, *178, 182*
technical process group 120, *120*, 123–126, *123–126*
tender applications 90
text representation 161
  see also graphical notation
TOGAF (The Open Group Architectural Framework) 154
token flow 31
tools
  and automation 184, 189–190
  business considerations 188–189
  capabilities 184–188
  choice of 188–189
  general capabilities 184–185
traceability 45, 157

training
  case study 124–125, 134–139,
    138–139, 141–142, *142*
  teaching guide 173–183, *174,
    178, 182*
transferring risk 6

UML (Unified Modelling Language) 8
  advantages 14–15
  class tailoring 49–50, *49*
  consistency 78–79, *79*
  diagrams 16–41
    activity diagrams 30–33
    class diagrams 19–29
    consistency 41
    introduction 16
    modelling 16–19
    sequence diagrams 33–35
    use case diagrams 35–40
  government mandates 14
  introduction 13–15
  intuition 14
  ISO 19501, 14
  language 13, 19
  notation
    different formats 160–161,
      171–172
    summary 203–204
  process meta-model 50–52, *51–52*
  process realization view 57–58
  reasons for choosing 13–15
  relationships in 38–41
  requirements for process
    modelling 45–47, *46–47,
    50–52, 51–52*
  stereotypes 58
undergraduate courses 176–183, *178,
  182*
undocumented processes 80
university courses 176–183, *178, 182*
use case, definition 36
use case diagrams 35–40
  actors 36
  concepts 36–40
  <<constrain>> relationship
    39–40, *40*

decomposition of higher levels
  38–39, *39*
<<extend>> relationship 39
graphical notation 36–40, *36,
  38–40, 204*
<<include>> relationship 39
process modelling 40
process realization view 58
relationships 37, 38–40, *38–39*
specialization relationship 38–39
system boundary 37

validation 5, 59–62, 139
verification 5, 59–62, 184–185
views 17
  competency view 157–159,
    157–158
  consistency 77–79, **78, 79**
  enterprise architecture 150–152,
    152, 155, 157–159, *157–158*
  information view 29, 73–74, *74*
    artefacts 147, 194–195, *195*
    case study 117, 136–139, *138–139*
    process mapping 100–104,
      100–103
    stakeholders 147, 196–197, *196*
  process behaviour view
    BPMN *165*, 166
    case study 117, 141–143, *142–143*
    characteristics 71–73, *72*
    consistency 147, 192
    flowcharts 167–169, *168, 170*
    process content view 147,
      198, *198*
    process mapping 97–100, *97–99,
      102–103, 103*
  process concept view 51–57, *51–52,
    54, 57*
    extension *88*
    summary 201, *201*
    teaching guides 180
  process content view 29, 67–71,
    68–69
    case study 117, 120–130, *121–128,
      130*
    consistency 147, 192

marketing-related processes 147,
  196, *196*
populating 147, 195–196, *195*
process behaviour view 147,
  198, *198*
process mapping 95–96, *96–97,
  101, 101*, 107–108, *108*
process instance view 77, *77*
  BPMN 166, *166*
  case study 118, 139–141, *140–141*
  process mapping 96–97, *97*
  requirements view 147, 197, *197*
  stakeholders 141, *141*, 147, 196,
    196, 197–198, *197*
process realization view 51–53, *52,
  57–59, 58*
  extension 88–89, *89*
  process concept view 202, *202*
  stakeholders 147, 197–198, *197*
process structure view 29, 62–67,
  63–67, 93
  BPMN 162–163, *162*
  case study 117, 119–120, *120*
  extension 147, 191, *191*
  flowchart notation 167, *168*, 169
  process mapping 93, 101,
    106–107, *106–107*, 147, 193–194,
    193, **193**
requirements view 59–62, *61*
  case study 117–118, 134–136,
    135–137
  enterprise architecture 151–152,
    152, 155, *158*, 159
  <<extend>> relationship 147, 199
  process instance view 147,
    197, *197*
  process mapping 93–94, *94*
  relationships 147, *193*, 194
stakeholder view 29, 74–76, *75*
  case study 117, 130–134, *131–134*
  process mapping 94–95, *95*
  roles 74, 147, 194, *194*

XML (extensible markup language) 189

Zachman framework 153–154

Other products and services from the British Computer Society, which might be of interest to you include:

Publishing

BCS publications, including books, magazines, peer-review journals, and e-newsletters, provide readers with informed content on business, management, legal, and emerging technological issues, supporting the professional, academic and practical needs of the IT community. Subjects covered include business process management, IT law for managers and transition management. **www.bcs.org/publications**

BCS Professional Products and Services

BCS Membership. By joining BCS you will become a part of the UK's industry body for IT professionals, and the leading Chartered Engineering Institution for IT. Our aim is to be directly relevant to the priorities, needs and aspirations of our individual members at every stage of their career. **www.bcs.org/join**

BCS Group Membership Scheme. BCS offers a group membership scheme to organisations who wish to sign up their IT workforce as professional members. By encouraging their IT professionals to join BCS through our group scheme organisations are ensuring that they create a path to Chartered Status with the post nominals CITP (Chartered IT Professional). **www.bcs.org.uk/forms/group**

BCS promotes the use of the **SFIAplus™** IT skills, training and development standard in a range of professional development products and services for employers leading to accreditation. These include **BCS IT Job Describer**, **BCS Skills Manager** and **BCS Career Developer**. **www.bcs.org/products**

Qualifications

Information Systems Examination Board (ISEB) qualifications are the industry standard both here and abroad, and with over 100,000 practitioners now qualified, it is proof of their popularity. They ensure that IT professionals develop the skills, knowledge and confidence to perform to their full potential. There is a huge range on offer covering all major areas of IT. In essence, ISEB qualifications are for forward looking individuals and companies who want to stay ahead – who are serious about driving business forward. **www.iseb.org.uk**

BCS Professional Examinations are internationally recognised and essential qualifications for a career in computing and information technology. At their highest level, the examinations are examined to the academic level of a UK university honours degree and acknowledge practical experience and academic ability. **www.bcs.org/exams**

European Computer Driving Licence™ (ECDL) is the internationally recognised computer skills qualification which enables people to demonstrate their competence on computer skills. ECDL is managed in the UK by the BCS. ECDL Advanced has been introduced to take computer skills certification to the next level and teaches extensive knowledge of particular computing tools. **www.ecdl.co.uk**

Networking and Events

BCS's specialist groups and branches provide excellent professional networking opportunities by keeping members abreast of latest developments, discussing topical issues and making useful contacts. **www.bcs.org/groups**

The society's programme of social events, lectures, awards schemes, and competitions provides more opportunities to network. **www.bcs.org/events**

Further Information

This information was correct at the time of publication, but could change in the future. For the latest information, please contact:
BCS
First Floor, Block D
North Star House
North Star Avenue
Swindon
SN2 1FA, UK.
Telephone: 0845 300 4417 (UK only) or + 44 1793 417 424 (overseas)
www.bcs.org/contact

BUSINESS-FOCUSED IT & SERVICE EXCELLENCE 2nd Edition
DAVID MILLER

A revolutionary, new service excellence model that creates more accurate alignment between service providers and business customers, is central to this radical re-think on service delivery. IT remains crucial to the on-going success of most businesses, and David Miller's new model helps service providers gain a clear understanding of the businesses they seek to serve.

www.bcs.org/books/businessfocus Published: May 2008

Price: **£24.95** 208pp

ISBN: 978-1-902505-88-6

WORLD CLASS IT SERVICE DELIVERY
PETER WHEATCROFT

This practical manual helps you achieve and maintain new standards in service delivery. Written from a real-life business perspective, it supports the *ISEB Service Management Certificate* and is essential for IT managers, executives and consultants in the process of raising their service standards, considering offshoring or moving towards the ultimate goal of 24x7 service excellence. 'A mindset for how IT should engage with business' *(Information Age)*.

www.bcs.org/books/servicedelivery Published: Apr 2007

Price: **£24.95** 192pp

ISBN: 978-1-902505-82-4

GLOBAL SERVICES
MARK KOBAYASHI-HILLARY and DR RICHARD SYKES

Globalisation of the service industry can help transform your business and open up new opportunities for your industry. Outsourcing gurus Kobayshi-Hillary and Sykes deliver a groundbreaking assessment of the factors that can help shape this, through the creation of a new framework. 'A valuable, thought-provoking resource for any organisation working with an IT services budget - whether a provider or a consumer of those services' *(Information Age)*.

www.bcs.org/books/globalservices Published: Apr 2007

Price: **£30.95** 224pp

ISBN: 978-1-902505-83-1

IT PROCUREMENT HANDBOOK FOR SMEs

DAVID NICKSON

Large organisations can suffer badly when IT procurement goes wrong, but for Small-Medium Enterprises (SMEs), it can be fatal. David Nickson guides you through the entire procurement process. Whether you are identifying the changing IT requirements of your business, evaluating potential suppliers or managing them once appointed, this handbook means you can avoid the pitfalls which have led to the ruin of so many SMEs.

www.bcs.org/books/procurement Published: Feb 2008

Price: **£29.95** 208pp

ISBN: 978-1-902505-98-5

FINANCE FOR IT DECISION MAKERS 2nd Edition

MICHAEL BLACKSTAFF

A no-nonsense, step-by-step guide to the areas of finance as they relate to IT. Assuming no prior knowledge of finance, this guide teaches you how to construct a financial case for IT projects and covers other areas such as methods of financing, current legislation, cost/benefit analysis, budgeting, costing and pricing. It is designed both for business and non-commercial organisations, and is ideal for managers, practitioners, buyers, sellers and consultants.

www.bcs.org/books/finance Published: Jul 2006

Price: **£35.95** 344pp

ISBN: 978-1-902505-73-2

BUSINESS ANALYSIS

DEBRA PAUL and DONALD YEATES (Editors)

Improving the effectiveness of your IT through better alignment with the business is a precursor to increasing profitability. This practical, introductory guide provides you with the tools to achieve this. It teaches you about strategy analysis and how to model business systems and processes, and covers other topics including business case development, change management, and engineering/information resource management. The book also supports the *ISEB Diploma in Business Analysis*.

www.bcs.org/books/businessanalysis Published: Apr 2006

Price: **£30.95** 256pp

ISBN: 978-1-902505-70-1

EXPLOITING IT FOR BUSINESS BENEFIT

NEW

BOB HUGHES

IT is the driving force behind business, but often the technological agenda is set without reference to the commercial goals of the company. Bob Hughes' introduction to delivering competitive success through information technology gives IT and business practitioners the insight needed to make effective use of technology in the pursuit of those goals. Key areas covered include risk analysis, business-driven system design and Enterprise Resource Planning (ERP).

www.bcs.org/books/exploitingIT Published: Sep 2008

Price: **£24.95** 204pp

ISBN: 978-1-902505-92-3

Exploiting IT for Business Benefit

Bob Hughes — BCS

ELECTRONIC BUSINESS 2nd Edition

GEOFFREY SAMPSON

As technology continues to drive changes in the way we do business, more companies rely on electronic tools to carry out an increasing array of business functions. IT professionals have a greater role to play in the success of electronic businesses, and Geoffrey Sampson provides an overview of the main aspects, enabling you to have a better understanding of how IT and business interact.

www.bcs.org/books/electronicbusiness Published: May 2008

Price: **£24.95** 280pp

ISBN: 978-1-902505-89-3

IT-ENABLED BUSINESS CHANGE Successful Management

NEW

SHARM MANWANI

The high profile failure of major IT-related projects in both public and private sectors underlines the need for stringent change management. As businesses increasingly look to IT to enable that change, this book examines the types of business change processes that involve the use of IT, from the reasons organisations change the way they work, to how that change is managed and implemented.

www.bcs.org/books/businesschange Published: Sep 2008

Price: **£24.95** 176pp

ISBN: 978-1-902505-91-6

IT Enabled Business Change Successful Management

Sharm Manwani — BCS

BUSINESS PROCESS MANAGEMENT A Rigorous Approach

MARTYN A. OULD

Businesses adapt constantly to ensure they stay ahead of the game, but often they are held back by static IT systems dictating process and procedure. By learning how your organisation operates, and what activities and processes are carried out within it, you begin to understand the business more fully and can build better, more flexible IT systems to support improved efficiency and drive profitability.

www.bcs.org/books/bpm Published: Jan 2005

Price: **£35.95** 360pp

ISBN: 978-1-902505-60-2

A GUIDE TO GLOBAL SOURCING

ELIZABETH ANNE SPARROW

Commercial organisations are increasingly looking at outsourcing and offshoring to help manage costs and improve efficiencies. Elizabeth Sparrow offers a detailed examination of the opportunities and obstacles you are likely to face when considering outsourcing, and includes a country-by-country assessment of offshore services. Other global delivery models are also considered, including setting up joint ventures or shared service centres and acquiring overseas companies.

www.bcs.org/books/globalsourcing Published: Nov 2004

Price: **£35.95** 192pp

ISBN: 978-1-902505-61-9

INVISIBLE ARCHITECTURE

JENNY URE and GUDRUN JAEGERSBERG

Designing and building new IT systems, means you are likely to face specific challenges. Quite often the biggest of these are not the technical but the 'socio-technical', especially when implementing across national borders. Through the use of real life examples, *Invisible Architecture* shows how you can actually harness these 'soft' factors to give you that competitive advantage. The potential consequences of ignoring these problems are also exposed.

www.bcs.org/books/invisiblearchitecture Published: Mar 2005

Price: **£35.95** 100pp

ISBN: 978-1-902505-59-6

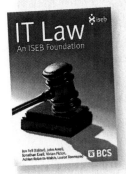

PROJECT MANAGEMENT IN THE REAL WORLD

ELIZABETH HARRIN

Project Management in the Real World

Elizabeth Harrin

Fast forward to professional project management, with this ultimate short-cut. It summarises over 250 years of expertise from experienced project managers and offers hints and tips on all aspects of project management including how to manage budgets, manage teams and manage yourself. These are backed up with theory and references alongside case studies from the UK, USA, France, Holland and Australia. 'Good common sense stuff' (*Health Informatics Now*).

www.bcs.org/books/realworldPM Published: Nov 2006

Price: **£25.95** 232pp

ISBN: 978-1-902505-81-7

PROJECT MANAGEMENT FOR IT-RELATED PROJECTS

BOB HUGHES (Editor)

Covers subjects ranging from project planning, monitoring and control to change management, risk management and communication between project stakeholders. Each chapter includes an overview of learning objectives, details of syllabus content, activities and multiple choice questions, so you can carry out self-assessment exercises and measure your own performance. Covers the entire syllabus of the *ISEB Foundation Certificate in IS Project Management*.

www.bcs.org/books/projectmanagement Published: Aug 2004

Price: **£25.95** 144pp

ISBN: 978-1-902505-58-9

PROFESSIONAL ISSUES IN INFORMATION TECHNOLOGY

FRANK BOTT

Professional Issues in Information Technology

This book explores the relationship between technological change, society and the law, and the powerful role that computers and computer professionals play in a technological society. Designed to accompany the BCS Professional Examination Core Diploma Module: *Professional Issues in Information Systems Practice*. The author is former head of computer science at the University of Wales, and has previously lectured at the University of Missouri.

www.bcs.org/books/professionalissues Published: May 2005

Price: **£24.95** 264pp

ISBN: 978-1-902505-65-7

PRINCIPLES OF DATA MANAGEMENT

KEITH GORDON

Organisations increasingly view data as a valuable corporate asset and its effective management can be vital to your organisation's success. This professional reference guide covers all the key areas including database development, data quality and corporate data modelling. It is not based on a particular proprietary system, so is business focused, providing the knowledge and techniques required for you to successfully implement the data management function.

www.bcs.org/books/datamanagement Published: Aug 2007

Price: **£30.95** 272pp

ISBN: 978-1-902505-84-8

Principles of Data Management
Facilitating Information Sharing

Keith Gordon

PRACTICAL DATA MIGRATION

JOHN MORRIS

Practical Data Migration

John Morris

Ensuring the success of your data migration projects is crucial, especially if you are looking to achieve maximum return on your investment. By following the best practice model devised by author John Morris, this guide will help you ensure a smooth and problem-free migration. The guide contains techniques and strategies, blended with real-life examples and clear definitions of the most commonly used terminology.

www.bcs.org/books/datamigration Published: Apr 2006

Price: **£30.95** 224pp

ISBN: 978-1-902505-71-8

BCS GLOSSARY OF COMPUTING AND ICT - 12th Edition

BRITISH COMPUTER SOCIETY

The international bestselling guide to computer terms is now in its 12th edition. Containing over 3,000 terms arranged by theme and defined in context, The Glossary is fully indexed and cross-referenced throughout. It supports the National Curriculum and National Qualifications Framework and is an ideal study aid and reference tool for those studying ICT or taking courses where computers are used, including GCSE, A-level and ECDL.

www.bcs.org/books/bcsglossary Published: Sep 2008

Price: **£19.95** 476pp

ISBN: 978-1-906124-00-7